Retail
Communities
Customer-Driven Retailing

Retail
Communities
Customer-Driven Retailing

Don E. Schultz, Ph.D.
Martin P. Block, Ph.D.
& BIGresearch

PROSPER

Retail Communities: Customer-Driven Retailing
by Don E. Schultz, Ph.D., Martin P. Block, Ph.D. & BIGresearch

ISBN 978-0-9819415-4-7

Library of Congress Control Number 2009911779

Printed in the United States of America

10 9 8 7 6 5 4 3 2 1

Published by Prosper Publishing
Web site: www.goprosper.com

Prosper Publishing books are available at special quantity discounts to use for sales promotions, employee premiums, or educational purposes. To order or for more information, please call 614-846-0146 or write to Prosper Publishing, 450 West Wilson Bridge Road, Suite 370, Worthington, OH, 43085.

Cover and Interior Book Design by Sun Editing & Book Design (www.suneditwrite.com)

Dedication

"Change will lead to insight far more often than insight will lead to change."
　　　　　　　　　　　　　—Milton Erickson

A few years ago the marketing model was declared broken by one of the world's largest marketers. The recognition that the old model died ushered in an era of change for marketers—change that has left no one unscathed in the marketing battle for the hearts and minds of customers. "The customer is boss" is more than a slogan in today's world. The customer is in control, and this new reality has marketers scrambling to understand how they behave, what they want, why they want it and when. The problem is there are many different types of customer communities and media options. It's almost impossible to apply the old broken model.

This book is dedicated to those marketing professionals who recognize that the customer really is boss, all customers aren't the same and the retailers who know their customers best will win.

　　　　　　　　　　　　　—G.W.D

Contents

Preface

This has been a difficult book for us to write. Not because of a lack of data — eight years of consumer feedback data provided plenty of that. Not for lack of framework. While different, the structure used in the text makes eminently good sense: start with the customer-centered, not vendor-centered, view of retailing and understand the communities that retailers and customers build for each other and themselves. Thus, the name we've given this work. And not because there were no clearly defined text objectives. Those will become apparent as you read.

Instead, what was challenging was the rapidly changing economy and the resulting impact on social structures (communities) and exchange processes around the world. The entire field of commerce, particularly retailing, is undergoing radical change. That's what created the difficulty.

Our thought processes would be heading in one direction and another economic bombshell would explode. Or, another topic would emerge. Or, we'd discover new insights from our research. It's hard to keep focused in the mélange of toxic assets, bail-outs, derivative bundling, social networks and demise of revered business organizations that have assaulted everyone over the past year or so. Each has had an impact on the economy and, as a result, retailing.

Simply put, the consumer's level of confidence in the economy, rising unemployment and a host of other issues have been reflected in what has happened, or will happen, to retailing. All of which has been influenced by how the marketplace is behaving: melting one instant, crashing the next and, surprisingly, sometimes showing glimmers of hope for recovery — wholly depending on the day and who was pontificating at the time.

We are living in a time of discontinuous change, as Figure 1 illustrates.

FIGURE 1: THE DISCONTINUITY MARKETPLACE

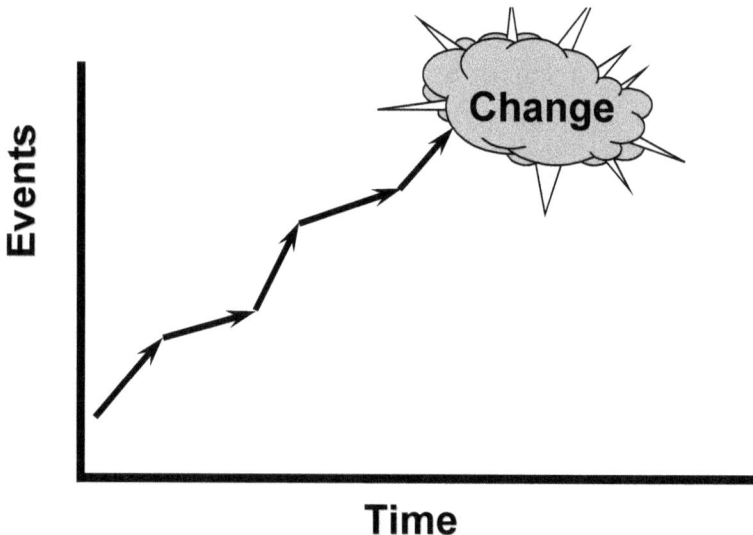

Source: Agora, Inc.

We've seen major dislocations in many of the things we've always held dear: loss of respect and value for some of our cultural icons; declining trust in all types of institutions that have traditionally been the bulwarks of society. The result has been a discontinuity of how business is conducted, particularly at the retail level: changed consumer shopping habits brought on by job losses; overstretched retailers disappearing or liquidating; malls and mall owners in bankruptcy; and new retail formats flourishing and then folding. In short, a change in the assumed fundamentals of business as they are or should be conducted — especially in retailing.

The major problem is when recovery comes, it will most likely be in a radically different form and format from anything we've ever witnessed before. We're living through a transformational period in which what we've always known, expected and believed will probably no longer be relevant and, in fact, may be wrong.

In this transformational time, this book and the approach it takes are designed to provide insights into how retailing works in the twenty-first century. The wheel of retailing is turning again, as it has done for centuries. But, this time, it may be impossible to predict where it will stop and where the various retail formats we see today may succeed or fail.

The reason for this change? Consumers. Consumers are now in control of the marketplace. This has always been so, but it is truer today than ever before. Consumers tell us what works and what doesn't. They tell us that with their behaviors, their shopping patterns and their responses to marketing efforts. The consumer is the key to understanding the marketplace and how it is evolving.

The behavior of consumers, which is now so much more measurable, has much greater predictive power for the future than a time-specific sampling of their attitudes and/or feelings. They vote with their pocketbooks, and that's hard to ignore. While specific predictions about retail formats, and the marketing communications used to support them, may change, the basic concepts are already becoming apparent. Based on BIGresearch's Simultaneous Media Usage™ (SIMM®), Consumer Intentions and Actions™ (CIA™) and Shopper Mindset™ data, fairly accurate estimates of how customers and consumers are likely to respond to retail initiatives are becoming possible.

One of the most important consumer insights regards the formation of communities, that is, how consumers and retailers create communities for themselves and others. These communities of interest are groups of people who band together, often with little planning or foresight, to find solutions to their problems, answers to their questions and locate information, from both internal and external sources, they can use now and in the future. In the past, we've suspected these communities of interests have existed, but now technology is enabling us to identify them and grasp how they identify each other. The world is connected — more connected than we'd ever thought possible.

This book begins and ends not with retail formats or merchandising approaches, or even logistical systems, but with what drives all retail: customers and consumers. The people with money in their pockets who initially pick and choose a retail facility — be that bricks and mortar, online or something in between — and then decide whether to return to it. It is the customer's reactions to the retailer's efforts that matter. And, that's what fills this book: what customers do; how retailers can identify customer signals; and how they should respond.

This idea of response is what sets this retailing approach apart from all the others. We argue that the ability of the retailer to respond, adapt and change to fit the flow of the consumer marketplace is what will separate success from failure in the twenty-first century. The retailer no longer leads the consumer, the consumer leads the retailer, and that means radically different management approaches are needed. In *Retail Communities*, we outline what some of these approaches might be. This is a book about how retailers can respond to customer demands. We believe that retailers must know as much about customers and potential consumers as they have traditionally known about the products they stocked in their stores and the margins they tried to achieve on their sales. We advocate moving from an inside-out approach — how do we sell what we've bought and stocked — to an outside-in approach where everything is focused on consumers: what they want; how they want it; how they want to learn about the retail facility and the stock; what influences them; and a host of other factors that determine whether a retailer will succeed or fail in the new transformational marketplace.

All the information in this book comes from customers, from what they have told us through our research studies over the past seven years. The data has been continuously gathered directly from the customer (in online panels) in sufficiently large numbers that the results are clear and compelling. All the tables, charts, illustrations and examples have been constructed from consumer-reported data. You'll find little in the way of theory. It's all about consumer behaviors and the insights derived from those behaviors. In essence, this is a compendium of what consumers have shared with BIGresearch over the past several years — condensed into one short text.

We make reference to three principal sources of information:

- Consumer Intentions and Actions Survey (CIA): This survey monitors the reactions of over 8,000 consumers per month to determine their purchasing activities and intentions for the future. It delivers fresh, demand-based information on where the retail consumer is shopping and their changing behavior. CIA is conducted monthly (since October 2001).

- Simultaneous Media Usage Study (SIMM): This study provides a tool for understanding the inter-relationships of consumer multiple media usage activities—such as time spent per medium, media usage combinations and most influential media forms—all of which impact marketing effectiveness and the Return on Investment (ROI) of marketer communication expenditures. SIMM data is available for specific retailers or targeted consumer groups through such differentiators as age, gender, income, lifestyle and geography. SIMM is conducted twice yearly (since 2001).

- Shopper Mindset : This survey covers nine key types of shopping trips (e.g. stock up trip, one bag trip, leisure time trip, etc.), and includes multiple channels of trade including home improvement and leisure. It covers trip motivations, average spend level per trip and what's in the bag. It also monitors the impact of behaviors before and during the trip, promotion tactics and media influence. The Shopper Mindset survey provides actionable solutions to specific category opportunities for retailers. The Shopper Mindset was conducted in February 2007 and included 5,392 respondents.

All these studies have been vetted in both the academic and professional fields. They've been tested in the marketplace. Some of the largest and most successful retail and CPG organizations in the country use this data to make their management decisions. So, we know it works. And, increasingly, we know how retailers can use this sort of data to improve their operations and their returns.

The book is divided into four parts, beginning with "How Retailing Works from a Customer View." The second part, "How Customers Shop," covers how people visit stores and how they shop online. The third part, "Customer Insights," addresses how information and knowledge about how future customer behavior can be estimated in advance. The final part, "How Consumers Behave in a Down Market," was purposefully kept until last, since, we believe, it is this type of data that will provide the basis for the transformational marketplace we see developing in the future.

Chapter

1

A Holistic Model of Retail Marketing and Communications

Retailing is a complex system that brings manufacturers, middlemen, the manufacturer's sales force, retailers themselves and consumers together in a holistic, networked structure that, to be successful, must provide benefits for all parties. The complexity of the system comes from the multiple interactions among and between the various parties. Think of it as a network of interacting parts and parties, any one of which impacts and influences any or all the others. The various players in the retailing system create a form of networked community with common interests, who are interdependent with each other. If they function together, they create greater value for each other and the whole than if they were working alone.

This networked, interdependent concept is difficult for many Western managers and researchers to understand. The traditional,

Western cultural tendency has been to investigate and examine each of the system's parts separately, individually and independently. Thus, historically, we have studied the "consumer," the "manufacturers," the "retailer," the "logistical system" and on and on. The difficulty has been in putting all the pieces and parts together. While we have some understanding of the flow of supply chains, logistics and the like, few methodologies have tried to put everything together. Yet, it is this inter-connectedness that explains and illustrates the retailing system, that is, the interactions that occur and the communities that are formed. Figure 2 depicts a limited number of those interactions.

FIGURE 2: MARKETPLACE COMMUNICATION SYSTEMS

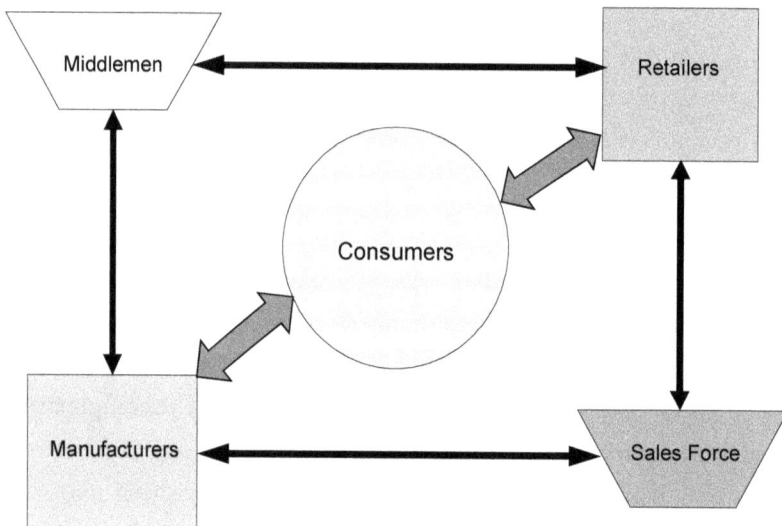

Source: Agora, Inc.

No matter what interactions occur, in retailing, the consumer is, or should be, at the center. Without the consumer or end user, none of the other parties or players can create, share or harvest value. If the consumer does not react and respond to the various offers and efforts of the retailing system's players, nothing happens. Thus, consumers are the hub of the entire retailing structure since their actions drive and influence all the other elements.

For discussion in this text, the manufacturer and its sales force(s) have been identified separately from the middleman and the retailer. It's not that they are genuinely separated but our research has shown that the actions of the manufacturer and selling elements typically impact consumers before they enter the retail store. Thus, we view their actions as being external to the retail location itself.

Conversely, the retailer and accompanying middlemen—brokers, distributors, wholesalers and the like—through their actions and activities, generally influence consumers inside the store. Even in the case of online retailing, this differential identification seems to hold.

As a general rule, only the retailer has direct interactions with the consumer inside the store. There are some instances where various forms of commerce between the manufacturer and consumer or end user can occur, for example, when manufacturers are also direct sellers, such as catalogs firms, direct selling systems and the like. However, for our purposes, we will limit our discussion to the traditional retailing formats.

Surrounding the entire system is the general marketplace. This consists of a multitude of marketing and communication interfaces between and among all the participants, as well as a host of other factors. In today's unstable economic climate, these other factors include the actions of government and its agencies, financial institutions, including credit card organizations, and media, all of which have a major impact on the retail marketplace. Therefore, when we talk of retailers and retailing, we must recognize that what goes on inside the retail store is often the culmination of a host of other external forms of marketing, communication and societal influences, which come together at the point of sale (POS).

In this text, we take a somewhat different view of the entire field of retail. As with a more traditional analysis, we also see retailing as a system that culminates in a consumer purchase. But consumer purchases should reward all system players. No consumer sales means no rewards for anyone. Thus, for us, the consumer is the keystone in any retailing system. And that's where we start.

Starting with Consumers

Since consumers drive the system, any understanding of retail must start with them—who they are, what is their shopping purpose, what experience and background do they bring to the retail location, what they do once there, how they react to retail promotion, and so on. The challenge is, unless the retailer and manufacturer know, understand and are motivated to serve retail consumers better, simply knowing their in-store behaviors (typically the output of most POS scanner systems) provides few insights on how to motivate them to action.

The key to retailing is learning from every consumer interaction and then adjusting or adapting the retail facility to either maintain the present purchase interactions or change the system to improve and enhance potential consumer responses in the future.

The purchase event is the result of a multitude of factors. Trying to untangle those factors simply by looking at what the retailer or manufacturer or channel partners or media or all the other players in the system did is a useless task. There are simply too many elements and activities that might have influenced the consumer and generated the observed result. Thus, in retailing, everything must start with consumers for only they know what motivated them to make their purchase actions, the records of which dominate current point of sale-based analyses.

Understanding Retail Theater

To understand the consumer purchase response, we start our analysis with another model, one that identifies the elements that influence and impact the consumer. We call it "retail theater," for each element must play a part for the overall success of the system.

FIGURE 3: BUILDING RETAIL THEATRE

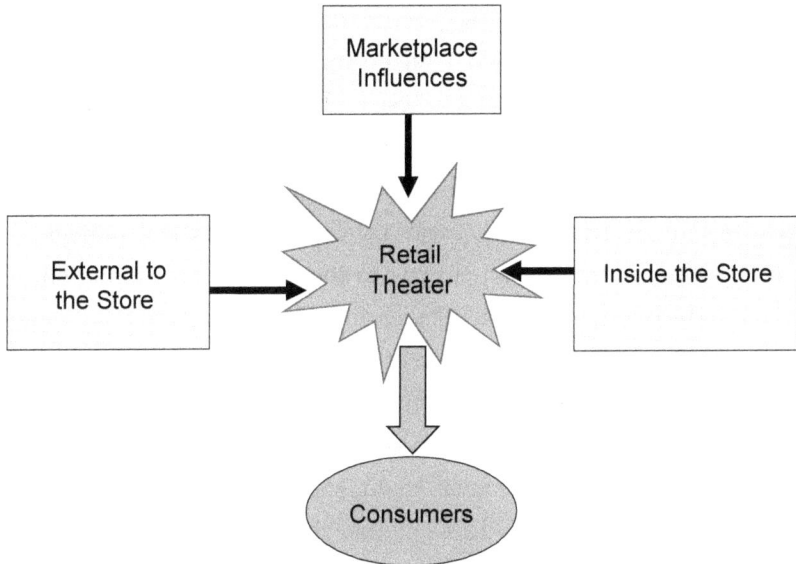

Source: Agora, Inc.

As shown, retail theater is the centerpiece of the consumer's retail experience. It is where all the factors and elements mentioned above come together—the external to the store activities, the marketplace influences and the retail promotional activities inside the store. If the theater is right, sales usually occur. While our graphic illustration is quite simple, it is truly a complex process. For example, consumers generally come into the retail store, or any other purchase situation, with some type of background and experience in the product category, the retail system through which it is offered and the values they believe they will receive from the purchase of the product. Often, consumers have some prior experience purchasing in the product category, in some instances, from a specific retailer. That often sets the tone for the retail theater, but there are other factors, too.

As shown above, the manufacturer and the retailer interact, the consumer and his or her personal influences interact and then the entire system interacts. And, most importantly, all these interactions are driven by the customer or consumer. That's what's unique about this view of retailing. It focuses on the buyer, not just the seller. You'll see this view illustrated time and again throughout this book.

In spite of the complexity of these multiple interactions, actual and hypothetical models of how these interactions occur can be developed. To create a more transparent and understandable approach, we'll limit the discussion in this text to three major factors: (a) what the manufacturer does to influence the consumer prior to the time that consumer enters the retail theater; (b) what the retailer does inside the store to influence that same consumer at the point-of-purchase; and (c) what external marketplace factors occur that influence the consumer over which the manufacturer and retailer have no control. While these can be major factors—the tightening of retail credit, employment displacements or social issues such as pandemics—neither the retailer nor manufacturer has control over them. They must, however, be recognized, for they do have an impact on the activities, events and outcomes that occur in the retail theater.

Further, we recognize that many of the latest promotional tools being delivered through new and unique media systems—such as the emerging social networks of Facebook, MySpace and even Twitter—along with word of mouth from other consumers, also may have a major impact on the consumer's final purchase decisions. Unfortunately, in most cases, the retailer and the manufacturer have little or no influence on those factors, and, more importantly, have limited ways to influence how they are generated, delivered or even their impact on consumers. So, we acknowledge these new interactive consumer influence systems but do not deal directly with them in the following discussions. Our models are limited to thirty-one standard digital and analog activities in their online and offline formats and the twenty-three in-store promotional variables, which the retailer can employ. Together, however, they provide a fairly good view of the majority of actions and activities retailers and manufacturers might consider.

With these caveats, we can now move forward to a discussion of retailing in the United States today, and how, with new knowledge and background, it can be improved.

The balance of this chapter is devoted to a basic, but somewhat unique, discussion of how we believe retailing works for the manufacturer and retailer in today's rapidly changing marketplace. That will set the stage for the various analyses that follow.

Marketing

Marketing, whether at the manufacturer or retailer level, is defined as the management process responsible for identifying, anticipating and satisfying customer requirements profitably through various channels. In order to understand marketing, one must view it as a management process that defines how the various systems in the institutional categories intersect and interact.

The modern term "marketing" evolved from the original meaning of its root, "market," which was a central location where sellers brought wares that would attract interested buyers. In many of the early markets, the retailer and manufacturer were one and the same. But as the marketplace evolved and specialization occurred, those two functional groups separated. Yet, even today, retailers and manufacturers are interdependent and must rely on each other for their success.

That success is often aided by retailers and manufacturers sharing a fundamental customer orientation, the development of an integrated organizational effort focused on achieving customer satisfaction and a common view of generating a financial profit for themselves and others in the system. It is this interdependency that drives much retailing today.

Customer Focus and Reciprocity

With the consumer as the driving force for the entire retailing system, it is he or she who determines overall success or failure. Thus, for all parties to profit, the consumer must feel the system benefits him or her. Unless it does, no one in the system is successful. We use the concept of reciprocity here to indicate a situation where all parties mutually benefit.

One would think that these common goals and rewards would promote considerable cooperation between all the institutional categories. Unfortunately, that's not always the case. As we will see in some of the analyses that follow, an adversarial relationship between retailers and manufacturers can exist. This works to the detriment of all parties.

Retailers and Retailing

A retailer is defined as an institution that sells directly to the ultimate consumer, usually in small quantities. It is necessary, for the purposes of this book, to distinguish between consumer markets, commonly referred to as B-to-C, and business markets, called B-to-B. This text will focus primarily on the business to consumer retail system because that is the basis of the data captured by BIGresearch in its various data gathering initiatives.

We must also acknowledge the middlemen in the system—the wholesalers, brokers, agents and others that commonly facilitate the interchange of products and services between the manufacturer and retailer. These middlemen normally comprise the logistical chains that exist between the supplier and the retailer. These middlemen have little direct contact with consumers, so, while we recognize they have an important role, we have not included a discussion of them in this text.

Retailer and Manufacturer Interactions

The typical retailer seeks to obtain goods from a manufacturer (using some type of logistical chain) at a price lower than they hope they can then re-sell them to consumers. The difference between the price paid and the price sold is the retail margin.

Since the retailer is concerned primarily about margin and the manufacturer is generally driven by economies of scale in manufacturing or volume, the retailer is encouraged to purchase and inventory goods the manufacturer has made, which can then, it is hoped, be sold sometime in the future. Thus, the manufacturer is always trying to "load" the retailer with more product to improve his production and economies of scale, while the retailer, in turn, is trying to drive the manufacturer's price down to generate improved margin on the products inventoried. This often results in the retailer's greatest expense being the cost of the inventory acquired, which is used to stock and merchandise the store. While it is true that today there are a multitude of methods by which manufacturers and retailers manage this inventory and store stocking, for this text, we assume the manufacturer transfers title of the products to the retailer who in turn transfers the title to the ultimate consumer at the final sale.

The retailer's road to profitability is determined by margin and inventory turnover, that is, how fast he or she can recoup the investment made in the stock-keeping units (SKUs). Goods in inventory tie up working capital and, as a result, represent a cost to the retailer. Therefore, the movement of existing stock or flow through the store is extremely important to the retailer.

Meanwhile, manufacturers commit to production facilities that require volume in order to achieve profitability through economies of scale. Holding of manufactured products in inventory is also a cost to them and must be managed carefully. The differences in cost structures and holding costs between the retailer and manufacturer often create radically different objectives for the two parties. That often creates substantial friction in the retailing systems.

Who Knows Consumers Best?

Retailers, because they have direct access and control over the final transaction with the ultimate consumer, often have the advantage of knowing the consumer better than the manufacturer. For example, many retailers are able to gather consumer purchase data and create consumer databases, which give them valuable insights into the purchasing habits of consumers. That data is often not available to the manufacturers.

Manufacturers, on the other hand, often have the advantage of product knowledge and, sometimes, larger marketing budgets. Add to this, the well developed negotiation capabilities manufacturers have developed in pricing at various channel levels, as well as the impact and influence of the middlemen, and it is easy to understand why the goals of the retailers and that of the manufacturers can be at odds. Both retailers and manufacturers, however, need to understand retail strategy, or what encourages consumers to make purchases, no matter what brand or selling approach either is using.

This book is about what has been learned about retail strategy based upon the consumer data collected by BIGresearch over the past eight years in the U.S. Those databases form the basis for this book.

Retail Strategy

A retail strategy requires at least two components. First, the identification of a target market, that is, the group or groups of consumers to whom the retailer wishes to appeal. Commonly, those target markets are determined by surrogate systems such as location of the retail store, type of products stocked, type of merchandising approach used, and so on. If the retailer is a brick and mortar facility, the retail foot traffic commonly determines the type of consumers exposed to the retail operation, and, therefore, the people likely to shop at the store. That is the basis of the retail mantra "Location, Location, Location."

Other retailers define their audiences more specifically. For example, food retailers commonly locate in areas where large numbers of families live or work since those are commonly the largest grocery volume buyers. These target markets, therefore, have been defined on the basis of geography. However, other factors may be used to determine locations such as demographic variables, attitudinal or lifestyle characteristics, or previous purchase behaviors by the consumers. All are important in developing a successful retail operation.

The second component is the marketing mix, that is, the controllable variables that the retailer can use to satisfy the target group of consumers. These variables include the traditional "four Ps," that is, product, price, place and promotion (McCarthy, 1964). These are felt to be the basic elements of the marketing mix.

The promotion variable includes the advertising and promotional materials made available to consumers, such as in-store activities and various independent media and merchandising channels. Measuring the impact of these promotional activities has been a special focus of the BIGresearch studies.

Promotional Response

Promotion response and results have a long history in both academic, (Schultz, 1998), (Blattberg and Neslin, 1995), (Totten and Block, 1994), and professional, (Bogart, 1984), (Sass, 2007), research, analysis and evaluation. With the availability of retailer scanner (point-of-sale) data showing what products were purchased, by whom, in what quantities and at what times—which began in the United States in the middle 1970s (Schultz and Barnes, 1995)—both marketers and retailers began to connect consumer promotional exposure and the consumer's resulting behaviors. From that, a wide variety of books, articles and research reports have emerged, all attempting to explain and illustrate why and how media and in-store promotion "work" (Moreau, Krishna and Harlam, 2001), (Kumar and Leone, 1988), (Guadagni and Little, 1983), (Leeflang, Wittink, Wedel and Naert, 2000).

Published studies have been ongoing and wide ranging, from the longitudinal work of brand analysis and purchases prior to the store visit by Uncles and Ehrenberg (1988) to the consumer perception studies of promotion conducted by Friestadand and Wright (1994) and the persuasion knowledge work of Dickson (1986), Krishna (1991) and Raghubir (1999). Almost all these studies have focused on trying to determine how consumers respond or responded to the various pre-store and in-store promotional activities employed by marketers.

Further, much of this work has been devoted to understanding how these factors may have altered consumer shopping behaviors in specific retail locations. Unfortunately, many of these studies are uni-dimensional, that is, they attempt to identify consumer response to manufacturer's efforts or to isolate what happened in the store, ignoring what went on before the consumer arrived at the retail location.

In this text, we treat manufacturer and retailer efforts as a combined effort. Since both influence and impact consumer behaviors, we believe, they should be considered together. And, if we start with consumer reactions to these promotional activities, it becomes clear that we are dealing with a holistic system, not just the pieces and the parts employed by either party.

A Consumer View

Our view of retail marketing response and influence is based entirely on a consumer perspective, namely, what consumers believe influence their purchase behaviors, both (a) prior to their store visit, as a precursor to the shopping trip, and (b) which in-store activities they say are most influential once they are in the shopping environment. Since the BIGresearch data has been captured in the same format with the same variables since the early part of the twenty-first century it enables longitudinal analyses to be conducted. Thus, trends can be identified in addition to point-in-time responses. This eight or so year history of marketing, media and promotional influence, using the same methodologies, is unique in the industry. Thus, it is possible to identify the changes in the importance and influence of pre-store media exposure and in-store promotional activities. Equally, we can look for trends in impact or effect and what might precede the next changes.

When the media exposure prior to the in-store visit is factored in to the in-store response equation, radically different views of why consumers behave as they do in retail stores emerge. Additionally, because the studies are focused on consumer views of pre-store media exposure and in-store promotional activities together, predictive models of what might be the most effective pre-store visit media activities and in-store promotional programs are possible. Thus, rather than simply reporting on what has occurred in the past, predictive models of what might be the best, forward-looking marketing, media and promotional investments can and have been developed and will be discussed in the following chapters.

Pre-Store Visit Media Consumption

Beginning in 2002, Pilotta and Schultz, later joined by Block, generated a stream of research based on media consumption, covering what media forms consumers use, how much time they spent with each and which ones they stated had the most influence on them and their purchase decisions (Pilotta, Schultz, Drenik and Rist, 2004). The general model was later presented at the ESOMAR/ARF World Audience Measurement and M3 conferences in 2004, 2005 and 2006 (Schultz and Pilotta, 2004), (Schultz, Pilotta and Block, 2005), (Schultz, Pilotta and Block, 2006).

Over time, the model has been populated with data from the SIMM studies, which are discussed in the next chapter.

We define media influence prior to the store visit as the brand messages consumers have received through various media-delivered systems prior to their entry into the retail location. This would include influences such as brand television commercials, newspaper advertising and Web sites. Promotions external to the store visit are the events and activities, generally in the form of various incentives, marketers employ and distribute to consumers prior to their store visit. This is done in an attempt to influence consumer behavior while they are shopping in the store. Examples of these types of influences include direct mail delivered coupons, contests, sweepstakes and special events.

Note: Appendix A provides a list of the thirty-one pre-store visit media and promotional variables on which consumers report in the SIMM studies.

In-Store Promotional Activities

Once the consumer enters the retail store, they are commonly exposed to a wide range of in-store promotional activities developed by the retailer, the manufacturer or the two working in tandem. The SIMM studies include twenty-three in-store promotional activities, ranging from in-store coupons to suggestions by store staff to parking lot events. (See Appendix B for a list of these variables.)

In-store promotional influences are defined as the activities and promotional elements the retailer develops, or perhaps creates in combination with the manufacturer, that are located in the retail store and are designed to influence the shopper's behavior on that specific shopping trip.

Word-of-Mouth Influences

Word of mouth (WOM) involves activities and events that normally occur outside the purview of either the retailer or marketer. They commonly occur between and among consumers themselves. For the purposes of this book, we will not attempt to include WOM in our analysis or discussion, although information is in the data set. We limit our analysis to those factors that the retailer or manufacturer can manipulate in an effort to influence consumer behaviors. Since it is not practically possible to try to manage or manipulate WOM, we leave that for another day.

Product Categories and Classes of Trade

There are dramatic differences between specific product categories and classes of trade that have been captured in the BIGresearch data. Discussions of some of these differences follow in later chapters. We also comment on some of the key generalizations about what drives retail promotional and media response as a result of the product category and where the shopping for those product categories occurred. (We call this class of trade in the following pages.) Both will help in the understanding of what drives retail success in today's marketplace.

The consumer reported information in the SIMM database includes eight basic product categories sold at retail. These are electronics, apparel and clothing, groceries, home improvement, medicines and eating out. Two additional categories, car and truck, and telecommunication services, are included in the data set, but, because they are unique to those categories, they will be not analyzed or reported here.

There are fifteen classes of retail trade in the data set as well. These include convenience stores, department stores, discount stores, dollar stores, drugstores, grocery stores, organic or natural grocery stores, consumer electronics stores, office supply stores, home improvement stores, membership warehouses, online retail operations, dining restaurants, quick service restaurants and specialty stores.

With this brief background on retail and retailing, along with the structure of the text, we can move to a discussion of the influence of Pre-Store Visit Media on consumers and how that impacts how they shop in the retail store.

Appendix A: 31 Media Forms

- Web site
- Word of mouth
- Television
- Cable
- Retail channel shopped
- Radio
- Article about product in media
- In-store promotion
- Newspapers
- Newspaper inserts
- Direct mail
- Magazine
- Internet advertising
- Outdoor billboards
- Picture phone
- Instant messenger
- Internet service provider (ISP)
- Broadband
- IPTV
- Search engine use
- E-mail advertising
- Yellow pages
- Satellite radio
- Text message
- MP3 player
- Web radio
- Video games
- Personal digital assistant (PDA)
- Cell phone
- Blogging
- TiVo

Appendix B: 23 In-Store Promotional Activities

- Used a list
- Up and down the aisles
- Coupons
- In-store specials
- Brands
- Sample
- Prices from the web
- Products information from the web
- Pharmacist
- Online research

- Inserts
- Read labels
- Point of sale
- Displays
- Shelf coupons
- Store staff
- Register tape coupons

- In-store events
- Parking lot
- Social cause offer
- In-store TV
- In-store radio
- Other

References

Blattberg, Robert C. and Scott A. Neslin. *Sales Promotion: Concepts, Methods, and Strategies*. Prentice Hall, Upper Saddle River, NJ, 1995.

Bogart, Leo. *Strategy in Advertising: Matching Media and Messages to Markets and Motivations*, 2nd ed. Crain Books, Chicago, 1984. 222–225.

Dickson, Peter R. and Alan G. Sawyer. *Point-of-Purchase Behavior and Price Perceptions of Supermarket Shoppers*. Marketing Science Institute, Cambridge, MA, 1986.

Friestadand, Marian and Peter Wright. "The Persuasion Knowledge Model: How People Cope with Persuasion Attempts." *Journal of Consumer Research* 21 (June 1994).

Guadagni, Peter M. and John D.C. Little. "A Logit Model of Brand Choice Calibrated on Scanner Data." *Marketing Science* 2 (Summer 1983) 203–238.

Krishna, Aradhna, Imran S. Currim and Robert W. Shoemaker. "Consumer Perceptions of Promotional Activity." *Journal of Marketing* 55 (April 1991) 4–16.

Kumar, V. and Robert P Leone. "Measuring the Effect of Retail Store Promotions on Brand and Store Substitution." *Journal of Marketing Research* 25 (1988) 161–169.

Leeflang, Peter S.H., Dick R. Wittink, Michel Wedel and Philippe A. Naert. *Building Models for Marketing Decisions.* Springer, New York, 2000.

McCarthy, E.Jerome. *Basic Marketing, a Managerial Approach.* Richard D. Irwin, Inc., Homewood, IL, 1964.

Moreau, Page, Aradhna Krishna and Bari Harlam. "The Manufacturer-Retailer-Consumer Triad: Differing Perceptions Regarding Price Promotions." *Journal of Retailing* 77 (April 2001) 547–569.

Pilotta, Joseph J., Don E. Schultz, Gary Drenik and Phil Rist. "Simultaneous Media Usage: A Critical Consumer Orientation to Media Planning." *Journal of Consumer Behavior* 3 (2004) 285–292.

Raghubir, Priya and Kim Corfman. "When Do Price Promotions Affect Pretrial Brand Evaluations." *Journal of Marketing Research* 2 (May 1999) 211–222.

Sass, Eric "Nielsen Rolls Out In-Store Measurement." Media Daily News (May 8, 2007)

Schultz, Don E. *Sales Promotion Essentials: The 10 Basic Sales Techniques… and How to Use Them*, 3rd ed. Mcgraw-Hill, New York, 1998.

Schultz, Don E. and Beth E. Barnes. *Strategic Advertising Campaigns*, 4th ed. NTC Business Books, Lincolnwood, IL, 1995. 208.

Schultz, Don E. and Joseph J. Pilotta. "Developing the Foundation for a New Approach to Understanding How Media Advertising Works." 3rd ESOMAR/ARF World Audience Measurement Conference, Geneva: June 13–18, 2004, Geneva.

Schultz, Don E., Joseph J. Pilotta and Martin P. Block. "Implementing a Media Consumption Model." 4th ESOMAR/ARF World Audience Measurement Conference, June 22–25, 2005, Montreal.

Schultz, Don E., Joseph J. Pilotta and Martin P. Block. "Media Consumption and Consumer Purchasing." ESOMAR WM3 Conference, June 4–7, 2006, Shanghai.

Totten, John C. and Martin P. Block. *Analyzing Sales Promotion: Text and Cases*, 2nd ed. Dartnell Corporation, Chicago, 1994.

Uncles, Mark D. and Andrew S.C. Ehrenberg. "Patterns of Store-Choice: New Evidence from the USA." In: Wrigley, Neil, ed. *Store Choice, Store Locations, and Market Analysis*. Routledge, London, 1988.

Chapter

2

Understanding Retail Consumers

All consumers are not alike. They differ in many ways, particularly in their shopping habits. These are, of course, most important to retailers. In this chapter, the retail shopping habits of consumers, as they have reported them through the BIGresearch Shopper Mindset studies, are examined and analyzed. These shopping habits provide the basis for one of the methods of identifying consumer communities used in this book.

It should be noted that the BIGresearch approach, in the methodologies developed from the SIMM, Shopper Mindset and Consumer Intentions and Actions (CIA) data, is to focus on reported consumer behaviors. While consumer attitudes and feelings about products, services and shopping are doubtless helpful in understanding the entire marketplace, consumer retail behaviors are what are most important in managing retail organizations. The reason? Retailers are primarily interested in buyers—the people who actually come into the retail facility and spend money—not in potential or hoped for consumers whom they may never see.

The categories that have been tracked—groceries, apparel/clothing, electronics, medicine, eating out, telecommunications, car/truck purchases and home improvements—were chosen because they include a large majority of all retail sales. So, while we do not claim to discuss all retailing situations in this text, the categories analyzed will provide general direction that all retailers can use.

With these points in mind, we begin our discussion centering an analysis of the basic consumer shopping behaviors.

Basic Consumer Shopping Activities

As noted earlier, all the following information has been derived from the Shopper Mindset database (SIMM 11, 2007).

A. Average Monthly Shopping Trips

Nearly everyone shops at some time or another, but some consumers shop more than others. It is the heavy shoppers who drive sales for most retailers. Commonly, these shoppers can be described by the Pareto principle, that is, a small portion of the total retail shoppers make up a major portion of all retail purchasing. Often this is called the 80/20 rule because 20% of a retailer's customers can often be responsible for 80% of the firm's total sales or more. Thus, we often see a very skewed shopper distribution both for products purchased and retail stores shopped.

In spite of the skewed nature of the shopper behaviors, the best way to understand the overall marketplace is to first analyze the behavior of all shoppers. We can then drill down into specific customer groups, retail formats and product categories to better understand specific retailing opportunities.

In the Shopper Mindset data, the average person reports making 16.1 shopping trips during a four-week period, or just over four trips per week.

By dividing all Mindset respondents into quintiles (groups of 20), as shown in Figure 4, it is clear that shopping trip frequency varies considerably (a form of the Pareto principle at work). For example, the top quintile reports 33.6 shopping trips every month (Note: Four weeks is used as a "month," which is common in retail analysis. That equates to 13 equal shopping periods per year), or an average of just over one trip per day. The lowest quintile reports just 5 trips in a month, or just over one trip per week.

FIGURE 4: AVERAGE MONTHLY SHOPPING TRIPS QUINTILES

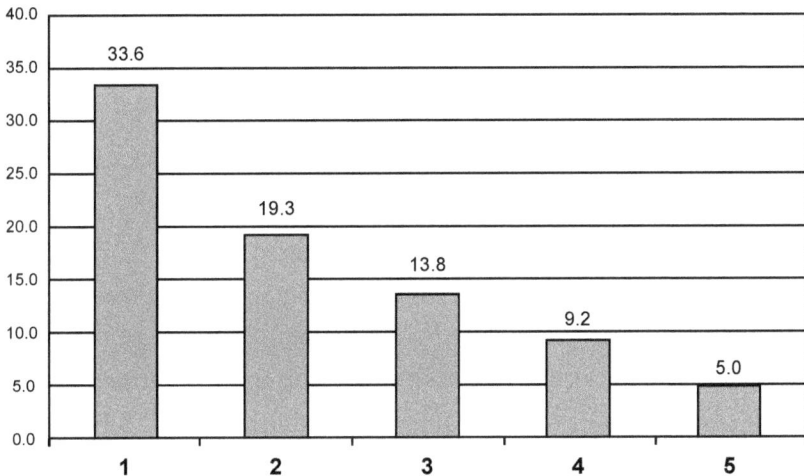

Source: BIGresearch

The two most frequent types of shopping trips reported were ones consisting of "one bag," that is, acquiring fewer than 12 items. The eating out trip (that includes all fast food and other types of restaurants reported) is shown separately. That data is shown in Figure 5.

Stock up trips and special purpose trips, namely, looking for a specific item, are less frequent but still important shopping occasions. The leisure time trip, identified as "shopping for entertainment and fun," occur, on average, at a rate of just under once every two weeks.

FIGURE 5: Monthly Shopping Frequency by Types of Trip

	Average	Percent
Stock up trip (a lot at one store)	2.3	14.2
"One bag" trip (fewer than 12 items)	5.1	31.4
Leisure time trip (shop for fun)	1.8	11.2
Special purpose trip (specific item)	2.5	15.8
Eating out trip (fast food and eat-in)	4.4	27.4
Total trips	16.1	100.0

Source: BIGresearch

The Shopper Mindset data also provides data that enables estimates of the average dollar value of each type of trip. While the data is self-reported, the averages are based upon the reports of thousands of individual consumers, thus, the law of large numbers adds confidence that the data is relatively accurate.

As shown in Figure 6, the average consumer spends $122.88 on a stock up trip. This is about four times the $36.58 spend on an average one bag trip. It's worth noting that the spend on a leisure trip is an average of $81.94, second only to the stock up trip. An eating out trip, which again includes all types of eating establishments, is $49.58. So, as can be seen, the purpose and value of shopping trips varies widely.

FIGURE 6: Average Spending by Type of Trip

	Average Per Trip Spend
Stock up trip	122.88
"One bag" trip	36.58
Leisure time trip	81.94
Special purpose trip	69.65
Eating out trip	49.58

Source: BIGresearch

Combining the average shopping trip frequency and purchasing amounts enables an estimation of the total shopping purchase amounts. (Note: Again, this is based on the "retail month," of four equal seven-day periods, resulting in conservative estimates as calendar months are comprised of around four and a third weeks).

The average total shopping amount per retail month is $1,009. Figure 7 shows the quintile breakdowns for these purchases. There are substantial differences across consumers when grouped in this way. The highest quintile (20% of the sample) reports an average $2,079 per month, compared with $336 for the lowest quintile. The second quintile is approximately half of the top quintile.

FIGURE 7: AVERAGE MONTHLY SHOPPING PURCHASE AMOUNT QUINTILES

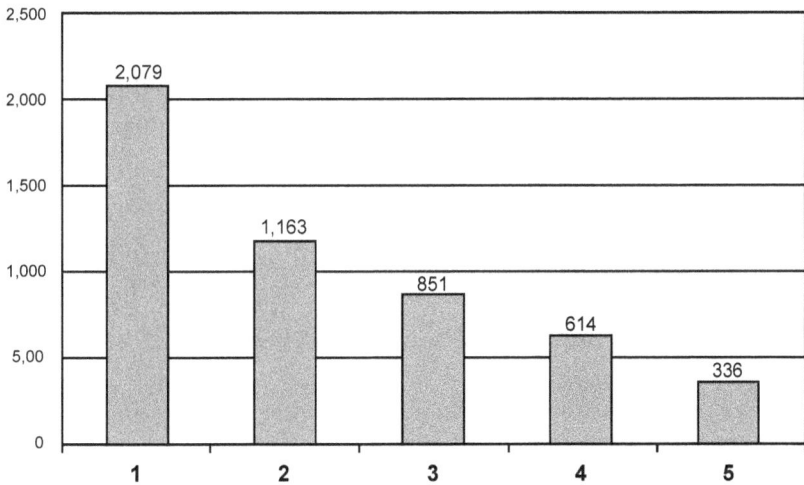

Source: BIGresearch

The average purchase amount by customer group provides an excellent criterion measure from which to derive some retail market communities. Obviously, customers who spend more have more value to both the retailer and the manufacturer. Although the amount spent is not a perfect derivative of actual profitability for either retailer or manufacturer, it does provide a reasonable proxy for management decisions. It is certainly better than some of the more qualitative retail segmentation methodologies currently being used by both retailers and consultants.

Additionally, there is considerable variation in consumer shopping spending. That makes it a good variable to illustrate differences in value among the various shopping communities.

B. Key Predictive Variables

The challenge in determining which consumer groups are, or might be, the most valuable for individual retailers and their manufacturing partners, is to identify the key predictor variables most related to overall consumer shopping spending. A statistical examination of the Shopper Mindset data reveals that age, number of persons in the household and income are the most important differentiators, that is, they are most associated with the average consumer purchase amount.

Figure 8 shows, for example, monthly average spending by age category. As can be seen, the spending level declines with age. The highest spending consumer group is the 18–24 year old category. That group spends nearly 40% more compared with the overall average spend of all groups — $1,402 per month compared with $1,009.

While some of the other age categories show a decrease in spending, those changes are relatively minor. For example, the difference in spending between the 25–34 age group, at $1,085, and the over-65 group, at $894, is only $191.

FIGURE 8: AVERAGE MONTHLY SPENDING BY AGE CATEGORY

	Monthly Average
18–24	1,402
25–34	1,085
35–44	1,038
45–54	990
55–64	928
65+	894
Total	1,009

Source: BIGresearch

Income is another solid indicator of shopping spend found in the Shopper Mindset data. Figure 9 shows the relationship between reported annual income and the average monthly shopping spend. In general, the amount spent on shopping increases with income, from a low of $919 for those making less than $15,000 to a high of $1,255 for those making more than $150,000. The middle-income categories, between $25,000 and $75,000, report spending nearly the same amount on average (within $19 per month). Interestingly, the average monthly retail spend increases at a much slower rate than does consumer income itself. The highest income category spends only about a third more than the lowest income category, yet has at least ten times the reported income. Thus, it would appear there is a certain level that consumers have found is needed for their ongoing sustenance and that amount does not vary much, regardless of income. While there may be discretionary dollars available, they apparently are being used for other consumer wants and needs rather than retail shopping in the eight product categories studied.

FIGURE 9: AVERAGE MONTHLY SPENDING BY INCOME CATEGORY

	Monthly Average
Less than $15,000	919
$15,000 to $24,999	978
$25,000 to $34,999	1,009
$35,000 to $49,999	990
$50,000 to $74,999	993
$75,000 to $99,999	1,045
$100,000 to $149,999	1,075
$150,000 or more	1,255
Total	1,009

Source: BIGresearch

The last variable that sheds some light on consumer spending differences is the size of the household. Many commonly used retail market segmentation approaches are based on the household size in terms of the number of children aged 17 and under in the group. Shopper Mindset data suggests that the total number of persons in the household is a better predictor. This, no doubt, reflects contemporary lifestyles where adult children and parents become part of the same household, as well as the traditional dependent children under the age of 17.

Figure 10 shows a consistent increase in the average monthly shopping spend as the size of the household increases, for example, from $877 per month for a single person household to $1,125 for a household of five or more. The biggest change appears to occur as the single person household expands to two persons. Thus, the old adage that two can live as cheaply as one is probably not as accurate as one that said, four people can live as cheaply as three.

FIGURE 10: AVERAGE MONTHLY SPENDING BY NUMBER IN HOUSEHOLD

	Monthly Average
1	877
2	989
3	1,060
4	1,076
5 or more	1,125
Total	1,009

Source: BIGresearch

C. Retail Communities

By bringing all the variables found in the Shopper Mindset data together, it is possible to clearly identify some specific retail market communities based on the three variables of age, number of persons in the household and income, and then relating those to reported consumer shopping behaviors.

We should note that the purpose here is to develop unique retail communities, or groups, that will facilitate the general discussion of retailing and how retail strategy might be developed. While there may be other market segmentation schemes for particular retailers or manufacturer product categories or even proprietary approaches for particular retailers, the behavioral communities discussed in the following sections seem to provide a managerially relevant approach to developing an effective retail strategy.

D. A Different Analytic Tool

A statistical tool that includes the analysis of the combinations of the previously discussed predictor variables and helps explain the differences in the average monthly shopping purchase amount is CHAID (Chi-Square Automatic Interaction Detection). CHAID is a statistical technique that proceeds in a sequential analytical fashion, identifying the binary split that explains the greatest criterion variable. In the following retail examples, purchase amount is used as that criterion measure.

Each binary split creates what are called "child groups." Each child group is then subsequently split into additional child groups. The process creates a "CHAID tree," which ultimately stops branching when variables or cases are exhausted or no more statistically significant differences can be identified.

Figure 11 shows a "pruned" (the output of the CHAID analysis is so detailed, we have chosen to "prune" the trees for better managerial understanding) CHAID tree using purchase amount as the criterion variable and age, income and family size as potential predictor variables. The process starts with 100% of the sample, that is, all shoppers reporting spending an average of $1,009 per month. The first split is for those who are under 28 years of age and who report spending an average of $1,334 per month. We have labeled that group the "Twenties" segment in the chart below. Those consumers 28 and over were then split. That division occurred between the ages of 28 and 57, and the other group 57 and older. Thus, in terms of age, we have identified three groups. The under-28 group could not be split further, that is, no statistically significant difference could be observed by either household size or income. Thus, that is the end of the CHAID sequence for that group.

As shown, the 28–57 age group yielded three household size groups, which were labeled "Families" (three or more persons), two people, termed "Pairs," and individuals, which were called "Singles."

The first CHAID split also yielded three groups in the age 58 and over category. The CHAID analysis further split that group into three income-based groups: incomes of $20,000 or less, which we have termed the "Bronze" group; incomes of $20,001–50,000, a group called the "Silvers"; and those with a household income of $50,001 or more, the "Gold" group.

FIGURE 11: RETAIL SEGMENTS BASED ON MONTHLY
SHOPPING SPENDING — CHAID TREE

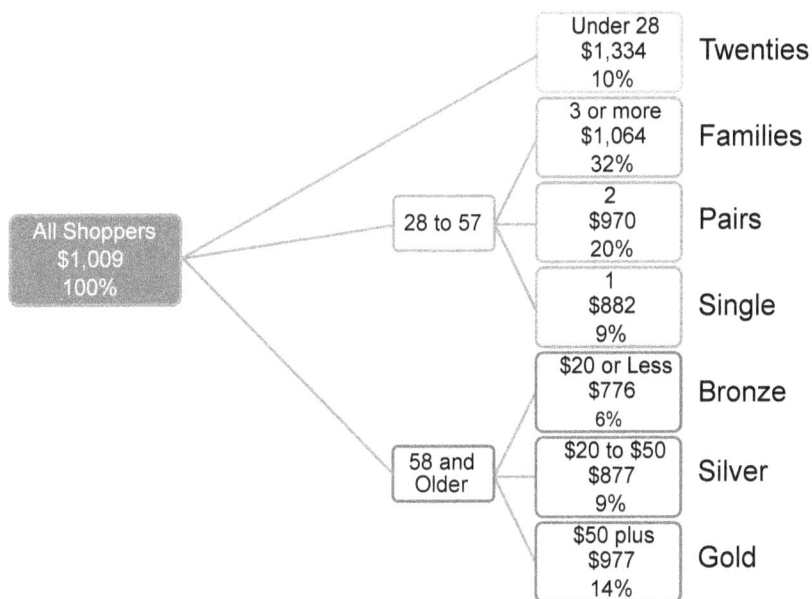

Source: Agora, Inc.

Thus, the full CHAID analytical process has yielded seven retail market communities. The first group, the Twenties, represent 10% of the total, but have the highest spending, again at $1,334 per month. Household size and income do not differentiate any further in this group. In the middle age category, it is household size that most clearly shows a difference, and not income. Those that spend the most are those in households with three or more people, spending on average $1,064. Those are labeled as Families (32% of the market). Pairs, two member households, report spending $970 per month (20% of the market). Singles spend $882, but only represent 9% of the market.

Among those over 58, the key predictor variable is income. Arranging this segment into three income groups—$20,000 and less, $20,001 to $50,000, and $50,001 and more—provides the best statistical splits.

The income groups have been further divided into levels. The lowest income group, Bronze, spends only $776 per month and is 6% of the market. The middle-income group, Silver, spends $877 per month and makes up 9% of the market. The highest income group, Gold, spends $977 per month and represents 14% of the market.

E. Retail Community Profiles

When aggregated in this way, that is, into like behaving communities, the retail groups show some interesting demographic differences. Figure 12 shows that the Twenties and Gold groups, the highest segments in terms of shopping spend, both have more males than females. Families, as might be expected, have the highest proportion of children by far. Nearly three out of four of these groups report having children 17 and under in the household.

There are some key differences in the various groups, too. Some of the highlights include: Singles and Twenties, as might be expected, are less likely to be married; Families and the older segments are much more likely to own their own homes; Singles and Twenties are more likely to rent; and Twenties are more likely to report living with their parents.

FIGURE 12: DEMOGRAPHIC CHARACTERISTICS OF RETAIL COMMUNITIES

	Twenties	Families	Singles	Pairs	Bronze	Silver	Gold	Total
Female (%)	43.3	72.7	56.9	72.8	72.8	63.2	49.7	64.2
Income ($000)	49.0	64.8	41.3	60.7	18.1	39.5	88.3	57.5
Age	23.2	44.1	46.9	47.4	64.5	65.0	63.9	48.9
Kids (%)	44.5	72.9	0.6	7.9	7.7	5.6	13.3	32.0
Married (%)	25.3	69.4	0.8	62.0	24.9	60.8	72.3	54.1
Own (%)	28.1	68.1	49.5	69.0	62.6	83.7	86.7	66.3
Rent (%)	43.5	21.4	48.7	26.8	34.5	14.3	5.5	25.1
Parents (%)	26.6	3.8	1.6	3.8	2.2	0.8	0.4	5.0

Source: BIGresearch

In terms of ethnicity, as shown in Figure 13, Hispanics are more likely to belong in the Twenties and Families community groups. Blacks are found among Twenties and Families, but are the highest among Singles. Asians are concentrated in the Twenties. Whites are concentrated in the older segments, but are the majority in all segments.

FIGURE 13: ETHNIC CHARACTERISTICS OF RETAIL COMMUNITIES

	Twenties	Families	Singles	Pairs	Bronze	Silver	Gold	Total
Hispanic	16.7	12.3	6.6	6.5	1.9	2.6	3.4	8.3
Black	10.9	11.1	16.5	8.9	5.8	5.8	3.8	9.3
Asian	7.5	1.0	1.2	1.0	0.6	0.2	0.4	1.5
White	67.7	73.5	74.8	84.4	90.7	91.3	86.6	79.7

Source: BIGresearch

Population density shows some differences as well. Figure 14 shows the top 25 Metropolitan Statistical Areas (MSA) as defined by the U.S. Census Bureau. Other MSAs are smaller areas, but large enough to have an MSA designation (populations above 50,000). Figure 14 shows Singles and Golds are more likely to live in a larger metropolitan area. Silver and Bronze segments are more likely located in a rural area or in a small town. Singles are less likely to live in a rural area.

FIGURE 14: POPULATION DENSITY OF RETAIL COMMUNITIES

	Twenties	Families	Singles	Pairs	Bronze	Silver	Gold	Total
Top 25 MSA	34.3	34.5	37.7	30.3	25.2	28.4	36.0	33.1
Other MSA	46.7	44.3	47.2	47.0	42.8	45.7	47.3	45.8
Rural	18.9	21.3	15.1	22.7	31.9	26.0	16.7	21.2

Source: BIGresearch

Figure 15 shows a summary of the retail communities by their purchasing and income characteristics. Twenties make by far the most shopping trips in a month. They make a trip almost every day and spend the highest amount per trip, which explains the most spending per month. Twenties spend, on average, about 52% of their income on shopping.

Families and Pairs are similar in that they each spend about 28% of their income on shopping. Families make slightly more trips and spend more per trip. The Gold community spends the least amount of their monthly income shopping, even though they make as many trips and spend about the same as the overall average. The Bronze community spends about the same proportion of their income as the Twenties, but spend considerably less and make the fewest shopping trips.

FIGURE 15: SHOPPING TRIPS AND SPENDING BY RETAIL COMMUNITIES

	Total Trips	Purchase Amount	Total Shop	Monthly Income	Shop % of Income
Twenties	20.6	87	1,334	3,930	52.0
Families	17.0	86	1,064	4,909	28.0
Singles	14.3	63	882	3,352	36.9
Pairs	15.8	74	970	4,911	28.8
Bronze	12.0	60	776	1,504	52.3
Silver	13.9	65	877	3,292	28.1
Gold	15.6	74	977	6,041	14.8
Total	16.1	76	1,009	4,479	31.4

Source: BIGresearch

The identification of these consumer-created communities and some basic knowledge of their spending levels form one of the retailer communication planning approaches used in this text. We will use these self-created communities as a method of identifying the influences various marketing communications activities by retailers and manufacturers have, or can have, on these groups. We begin that process in the next chapter.

Chapter

3

Understanding Consumer Behaviors

R etailing is a complex activity involving the interactions of a number of buyers, sellers and intermediaries. Yet, the most critical factor is the shopper, the person who has the resources and incentives to purchase products and services. In Chapter 2, we reported on retailing in the form of aggregated consumer behaviors, in other words, the retailing communities that consumers create for and among themselves. That was based primarily on combined consumer behaviors—how many shopping trips were taken, how much was spent, and so on, all factors that are critically important to retailers. We also identified some retail consumer communities. In this chapter, we look primarily at the single shopping event, which means individual views of shoppers' behaviors. That, we believe, helps explain how retail communities are created and provides considerable insights into what drives actual results through consumer behaviors in the retail facility.

I. Focusing on the Last Shopping Trip

The last shopping trip provides the best focus for understanding how consumers view the shopping experience. It is the easiest for respondents to remember and report on and, therefore, we believe, the most relevant way to understand consumer shopping behavior.

A. Shopping Trip Circumstances

The majority of shopping trips are taken alone, as shown in Figure 16. So, while we like to think of consumers as gregarious and our television commercials show happy groups of shoppers patrolling the entire store, for the most part, no matter what the occasion, the individual shopper is alone. For example, 70.2% of all one bag shopping trips were done alone by the shopper. Shopping trips that are most likely to include a companion are eating out and leisure time trips.

FIGURE 16: PRESENCE OF COMPANIONS BY LAST TRIP TYPE

	Stock Up	One Bag	Leisure	Special	Eating Out	Total
I was alone	50.8	70.2	37.4	57.4	41.9	56.0
Spouse	29.0	14.7	23.9	22.0	29.2	23.1
Kids	12.9	8.7	11.7	10.7	11.7	11.0
Female friend(s)	3.9	2.8	13.5	3.0	8.1	4.5
Male friend(s)	2.4	1.0	4.9	2.1	6.7	2.6
Relative(s)	7.1	4.3	14.1	6.9	10.8	7.1
Business associate	0.1	0.3	0.6	0.2	1.6	0.4
Other	1.9	1.0	3.7	2.7	1.9	1.9

Source: BIGresearch

The importance of this "shopping alone" is critical. It illustrates that while consumers do create communities through their shopping behaviors, often, these are not specifically recognized by others. Thus, the so-called herd mentality, where shoppers mimic or copy other shoppers, while an interesting concept, doesn't seem to find proof in the Shopper Mindset data.

In Chapter 1, we suggested that understanding consumer in-store shopping behaviors must include both prior-to-the-store promotional exposures as well as those that occur within the retail facility, or in-store. That becomes obvious when we look at where shopping trips originate. Figure 17 shows that over two out of three shopping trips originate from the consumer's home. And, that is where most external-to-the-store promotional contacts occur. Thus, understanding the promotional context of both prior-to-the-store and in-store promotional activities are necessary to understand how consumers' final in-store behaviors can be influenced. Starting from work or being "out doing other things," which leads to the shopping trip, are the next most frequent categories. Children's school or activity are relatively rare points of origin for shopping trips.

FIGURE 17: PLACE OF ORIGIN BY LAST TRIP TYPE

	Stock Up	One Bag	Leisure	Special	Eating Out	Total
Home	78.6	61.1	68.4	68.6	68.1	69.7
Work	8.0	19.5	8.6	12.2	13.5	12.9
Children's school	0.8	1.3	0.9	0.7	0.6	0.9
Children's activity	0.4	0.7	0.9	0.4	0.6	0.6
Out doing other things	7.8	12.5	14.1	11.5	11.0	10.6

Source: BIGresearch

Figure 18 shows Thursday as the overall peak shopping day for most individuals. The least preferred shopping days are Sunday and Monday. The leading eating out days are slightly different, with Thursday and Friday, as might be expected, the primary occasions.

FIGURE 18: DAY OF WEEK OF LAST SHOPPING TRIP BY TRIP TYPE

	Stock Up	One Bag	Leisure	Special	Eating Out	Total
Monday	8.6	8.7	8.3	7.7	8.3	8.4
Tuesday	12.9	12.3	8.3	10.2	11.1	11.8
Wednesday	16.6	20.0	16.0	16.9	17.1	17.7
Thursday	19.8	23.8	18.7	24.2	20.6	21.8
Friday	16.9	16.8	17.2	19.3	20.3	17.7
Saturday	16.0	10.5	23.3	15.6	15.6	14.6
Sunday	9.0	7.4	7.1	5.6	6.0	7.5

Source: BIGresearch

Figure 19 shows that early afternoon — noon until 4:30 p.m. — is the leading time of day for shopping trips. Late morning and early evening are the next most frequent times. It is interesting that four out of five shopping trips occur between 10 a.m. and 7:30 p.m., raising some questions about the move to retail stores being open 24 hours.

FIGURE 19: TIME OF DAY OF LAST SHOPPING TRIP BY TRIP TYPE

	Stock Up	One Bag	Leisure	Special	Eating Out	Total
6 a.m.–10 a.m.	9.6	8.0	4.6	6.4	7.3	8.0
10 a.m.–noon	26.0	17.1	20.6	22.0	17.5	21.3
Noon–4:30 p.m.	37.1	36.7	45.1	40.5	31.4	37.4
4:30 p.m.–7:30 p.m.	19.4	26.9	17.8	23.3	30.0	23.5
7:30 p.m.–11 p.m.	6.3	9.9	7.7	6.5	10.3	8.0
11 p.m.–1 a.m.	1.1	1.0	1.5	0.4	1.6	1.0
1 a.m.–6 a.m.	0.2	0.2	0.9	0.3	1.1	0.4

Source: BIGresearch

II. Preparation for the Shopping Trip

As might be expected, the most frequent reason for making shopping trips is to replenish needs, a clear indication of the consumable nature of the U.S. market. As Figure 20 shows, "to replenish needs" accounts for as many as 93% of stock up trips down to only 22% for leisure shopping, and, on average, for about 60% of all shopping trips. The next most given reason for the shopping trip is to find something. Reasons that relate to amusement or entertainment—such as to relax, spend time with a friend or to enjoy an experience—are given for about one third of shopping trips. The purpose of the trip is also strongly related to the type of trip. Stock up and one bag trips are dominated by replenishment, while special trips are to find something. Leisure trips are dominated by the purpose of relaxation.

FIGURE 20: PURPOSE OF LAST SHOPPING TRIP BY TRIP TYPE

	Stock Up	One Bag	Leisure	Special	Eating Out	Total
To replenish needs	93.4	60.2	22.1	32.6	24.0	60.7
To find something	27.9	52.2	33.4	78.3	20.5	43.2
To prepare a meal	17.4	22.6	7.7	12.8	5.6	16.3
To relax	9.9	9.6	55.2	9.4	34.0	15.3
I was hungry	7.3	9.9	10.1	3.8	57.9	13.6
Time with a friend	5.6	4.8	36.8	7.4	28.6	10.2
Family asked me	8.9	11.0	12.9	10.7	6.7	9.8
Something I want	6.3	6.7	29.4	9.8	9.2	8.7
Purchase a gift	3.2	3.8	9.8	9.0	6.0	5.1
Enjoy an experience	2.7	1.4	17.8	2.6	3.0	3.2
Research a purchase	2.4	1.8	6.4	4.7	2.1	2.8
To learn	2.0	1.7	4.9	3.8	1.7	2.4

Source: BIGresearch

Nearly half of all shoppers say they prepare a list before making the shopping trip (see Figure 21). That becomes a key factor when one is trying to understand how in-store promotion works. If the list is made up in advance, the importance of promotional exposure prior to entering the retail environment increases in importance and must be considered along with any in-store promotion. About one third of respondents say they use coupons or read ads at home before making the shopping trip. As shown, all these planning activities are considerably higher for when making a stock up trip. For example, nearly two out of three shoppers say they prepare a list for the stock up trip.

Interestingly, just over one out of five shoppers say they use a frequent purchaser card. This in spite of the great amount of publicity these cards have gotten. As might be expected, the use of frequent purchase card is highest for the stock up trip, and lower for most other types of trips.

The most surprising data revealed in Figure 21 is the very low percentages of consumers doing research online prior to the shopping trip. In many research reports from other sources, consumers say they are doing more and more online comparisons prior to purchase. The Shopper Mindset data simply does not bear that out.

FIGURE 21: PREPARATION FOR LAST SHOPPING TRIP BY TRIP TYPE

	Stock Up	One Bag	Leisure	Special	Eating Out	Total
Prepare a list	68.5	41.9	20.2	33.7	21.9	46.2
Use any coupons	48.2	22.3	23.6	16.9	19.5	30.2
Read any ads at home	41.9	24.7	22.4	20.8	15.2	28.8
Use a frequent purchaser card	27.7	24.7	12.0	15.0	11.6	21.8
Read labels	30.0	14.3	7.4	8.8	8.6	17.8
Ask store personnel	10.7	8.5	14.7	19.5	10.8	11.7
Read ads at the store	14.6	9.8	9.2	6.7	5.7	10.5
Watch in-store advertising	15.3	8.3	8.9	7.5	6.0	10.4
Taste anything	10.2	4.9	7.1	2.2	16.7	7.8
Visit any store displays	5.3	3.8	12.3	4.9	4.8	5.2
Do research online prior	3.3	1.5	4.6	7.4	2.9	3.4
See product demonstrations	3.9	1.6	3.1	1.5	1.9	2.5

Source: BIGresearch

Where shopping occurs is also a critical variable in understanding how consumers operate in the retail marketplace. Stock up trips are most frequently made to discount stores, followed by grocery stores and then membership warehouses (see Figure 22). One bag trips are most frequently made to grocery stores, which represents a slight shift from the stock up trip. Special trips are no doubt guided by the particular item sought, with the discount store being the leading class of trade. A leisure trip is also dominated by the discount store, followed by the department store and the specialty store.

FIGURE 22: CLASS OF TRADE OF LAST SHOPPING TRIP BY TRIP TYPE

	Stock Up	One Bag	Leisure	Special	Eating Out	Total
Convenience store	0.5	1.4	0.5	0.6	3.4	1.0
Department store	3.2	3.4	15.9	14.3	9.0	7.4
Discount store	32.3	23.7	26.5	19.4	17.9	25.9
Dollar store	3.5	4.2	3.2	1.9	0.7	3.1
Drugstore	4.2	6.8	4.2	5.7	3.4	5.0
Grocery store	29.3	28.5	5.8	13.0	18.6	22.2
Natural grocery store	1.3	2.0	0.5	0.6	0.7	1.2
Electronics/office	1.7	2.3	4.2	6.3	2.8	3.1
Home improvement	1.7	2.0	1.6	5.1	4.1	2.6
Membership warehouse	7.5	2.8	2.1	2.9	3.4	4.6
Dining restaurants		0.3	0.5	0.3	2.1	0.4
Quick service rests		0.6			6.1	0.7
Specialty store	3.8	5.1	14.3	11.4	4.1	6.9
Other	10.4	15.8	18.5	17.1	21.4	14.9

Source: BIGresearch

III. Shopping Mood

In the shopper's own words, about one out of two say they were "good" or "happy" when they started their last shopping trip (see Figure 23).

This rate is consistent across all types of shopping trips. Thus, shopping is not necessarily the chore or task that it has often been portrayed as in other reports. People apparently look forward to shopping. Therefore, it is the retailer's job to make the shopping trip live up to expectations. Equally important, the starting moods do not seem to vary much by type of shopping trip made.

FIGURE 23: MOOD STARTING LAST SHOPPING TRIP BY TRIP TYPE

	Stock Up	One Bag	Leisure	Special	Eating Out	Total
Calm	7.6	6.1	9.5	7.7	5.7	7.0
Good	35.0	34.2	35.6	33.7	34.0	34.5
Great	3.2	2.8	5.2	3.1	3.5	3.2
Happy	15.0	15.3	23.0	16.2	16.7	16.0
Hungry	1.0	1.9	0.3	0.6	6.7	1.8
Hurried	3.4	5.7	0.9	6.3	1.7	4.2
OK	11.7	9.2	5.8	8.9	7.6	9.6
Tired	6.6	7.5	1.5	5.2	7.5	6.4

Source: BIGresearch

IV. What Was Purchased

The most frequently purchased items tend to be food and food re-lated—fresh foods products, packaged foods and beverages—all of which were purchased on over half the shopping trips (see Figure 24). Health and beauty aids and household supplies are purchased in about one out of four trips. Other items, including apparel, entertainment, home improvement and office supplies, are all purchased in fewer than one out of ten trips. Overwhelmingly, in the Shopper Mindset data, shopping trips are dominated by items sold through grocery and discount stores, which accounts for why "to replenish needs" was the main reason given for shopping—as was discussed in relation to Figure 20.

Figure 24 below shows the top-ranked product in the various categories tracked in the Shopper Mindset data.

FIGURE 24: ITEMS PURCHASED DURING LAST SHOPPING TRIP

	Percent
Apparel	10.2
Women's apparel	5.2
Beverages	46.3
Milk	25.5
Fresh foods	57.8
Bread	33.7
Candy	3.3
Packaged foods (box, can, or frozen)	54.1
Entertainment/leisure items/electronics	6.5
DVD/VHS movies/series	2.9
Health & beauty care items	23.8
Toilet paper	10.0
Home improvement	3.8
Small hardware for home projects	1.3
Household supplies (non-food)	28.7
Cleaning supplies	15.7
Natural/organic products	6.9
Fruit/produce or herbs/spices	3.5
Office or business supplies	4.7
Paper, pens, notebooks, etc.	3.3
Other	15.5
Gas	3.0

Source: BIGresearch

V. Retail Theater—What Influences Purchases?

There are a wide variety of things shoppers say influenced them during their last shopping trip. One of the first observations to note is that shoppers generally report going to only a few departments within the store they visited (see Figure 25). This selective approach is approximately three times as popular as visiting every department within the store. Thus, we can see the individual nature of the shopping experience. While retailers would like shoppers to visit the entire store, apparently few do. But, shopping needs vary. Those on a leisure trip report they are much more likely to go to every department within the store. There is, then, an opportunity to attract shoppers to other departments within the store, but how to do this must be carefully thought out based on the communities that consumers create and in which they operate.

FIGURE 25: STORE MOVEMENT DURING LAST SHOPPING TRIP BY TRIP TYPE

	Stock Up	One Bag	Leisure	Special	Eating Out	Total
Go to just a few departments	36.2	48.1	40.5	43.8	24.9	40.0
Go to every department	5.8	7.4	18.1	6.7	7.5	14.4
Go just to the perimeter	1.9	4.6	1.8	4.6	4.4	3.5

Source: BIGresearch

The most important single influence during the last shopping trip was the store location (see Figure 26). The importance of location is clearly higher for the stock up and one bag trip. Following location is ease in getting in and out of the retail facility. Interestingly, "lowest prices," "store being clean," and "carrying the brands I want to buy" all have less sway than location and ease of entry/exit design. Store layout, liking the in-store atmosphere and having wide aisles influence only about one in five shoppers, in spite of the major emphasis retailers have put on store redesign in the past few years. Characteristics relating to store personnel, such as good customer service and knowledgeable sales people appear to be even less important. Frequent shopper programs, special promotions and double coupons are also less important than have often been reported in other studies.

FIGURE 26: INFLUENCES DURING LAST SHOPPING TRIP BY TRIP TYPE

	Stock Up	One Bag	Leisure	Special	Eating Out	Total
Convenient location	68.2	74.3	46.9	53.1	58.6	65.2
Easy to get in and out	47.3	44.0	29.4	33.3	38.3	41.8
It has the lowest prices	53.0	35.8	34.7	36.3	27.3	40.8
Store is clean	49.4	37.8	29.4	29.0	33.7	39.4
Carries brands I want to buy	51.7	33.7	27.0	32.3	26.0	38.5
Product selection overall	41.2	28.2	26.4	30.9	23.3	32.5
Quality merchandise	34.4	24.9	27.3	26.7	23.7	28.5
Good customer service	30.1	24.5	21.8	23.1	25.7	26.2
Fresh foods selection	34.5	22.0	10.1	11.6	22.1	23.9
Store layout	30.7	21.3	19.9	17.9	17.9	23.5
Like the in-store atmosphere	24.2	18.3	19.9	14.4	17.8	19.8
Wide aisles	28.4	16.3	12.6	13.6	15.4	19.7
Frequent shopper card	24.4	22.2	10.1	12.5	11.1	19.4
Open 24 hours	21.0	17.1	12.9	11.5	13.7	16.9
On way to another destination	10.6	18.2	17.2	16.6	13.0	14.6
A special promotion offer	9.4	7.7	15.6	14.0	8.7	9.9
Double coupons	15.0	10.3	4.9	3.8	4.8	9.9
Knowledgeable sales people	6.9	5.3	5.8	7.3	6.0	6.3
Natural/organic products	6.2	5.3	2.1	2.7	3.0	4.7
Kid-friendly atmosphere	3.5	2.2	1.5	2.0	3.5	2.7
Store decision made by others	2.1	1.9	5.5	1.9	5.4	2.6
Fashion ideas	1.0	0.9	7.4	3.7	1.7	1.9

Source: BIGresearch

With this background on what we know about consumers and their shopping beliefs, preferences and behaviors, we can now move to identifying how they group themselves together into consumer and retail communities.

Chapter

4

Retail Communities and Communication Influences

O ver the past few years, much has been said and written about "consumer communities." This is a very natural transition as marketers increasingly realize that "market" is a term they have created, while "communities" are what their consumers and customers have and are creating for themselves on an ongoing basis. With the customer focus of this text, our emphasis from here on will be more on communities and how consumers organize and create them, and how marketers might recognize and interact with them, than on the traditional marketing segmentation methodologies of the past.

I. Consumer Created Communities

This idea of consumer communities is particularly important in today's interactive marketplace. Consumers create these communities, interact in and within them, merge them, drop out and move on. That's something marketers have great difficulty identifying with traditional marketing tools. It is further evidence that consumers have gained control of the marketplace. Therefore, the primary goal of today's marketer must be to understand and operate within the confines the consumers have established, not the historical systems and methodologies marketing organizations have created.

Marketers like to think of "markets" as being clearly identifiable and definable, with measures and structures that can be influenced and managed over time. For example, marketers talk about the automobile market, the Asian market, the diamond market and even the clearly designated SMA (Statistical Market Area) determined by the U.S. Census Bureau. Consumers and their communities are much less specific in their definitions, but much more practical in their application. That's because consumers belong to multiple communities: geographic communities, such as the town or city in which they live; religious communities; sports communities; hobby communities, and so on. So, while it's easy for marketers to structure markets to fit their production needs, it becomes much more difficult for retailers to identify the multiple communities customers and other consumers have created for themselves. Yet, one of the key ingredients in successful retailing in the months and years ahead will the ability to identify, interact with and, in some cases, even help consumers and customers create communities for themselves, communities that are beneficial for both the consumers themselves and the retailer.

One of the key reasons for increased focus on consumer communities is the increasing realization by marketers that they do not create all the value in their products and services. In most instances, the real value is co-created; simply meaning that value is created by some combination of the marketer and the consumer coming together, sharing knowledge and background and, together, creating value for both. Value is not created only by the marketer. Consumers must be involved and make some input. Together, the marketer and the consumer provide the real value of the product or service. This is an area we will return to several times in the following chapters.

In the analysis of the SIMM, Shopper Mindset and CIA data sets, it becomes clear that there are many, perhaps innumerable, consumer communities, and not all of them are the same for each retailer. So, for purposes of this text, we'll define a community as a set or group of people who think, act and behave in similar ways or who have similar values that drive them to similar marketplace behaviors.

II. Behavior Is the Key Element

As before, it is consumer behaviors that define the retail communities—not only the physical manifestations such as age, sex, income level, geographic location or other typical marketer-focused segmentation variables. While some of the existing segmentation methodologies and values may be useful, we have found behaviors much more valuable and useful in developing retail strategies and executions.

The challenge is that, from a retailing perspective, each one of these consumer-created communities is unique. Thus, the Shopper Mindset data, discussed in Chapter 2, is composed of sets of consumer communities based on their shopping behaviors, which can be identified by various aggregation approaches. If the retailer knows something about each of the communities, which can be derived from the consumer responses to the Shopper Mindset questions, it becomes much easier to develop retail programs, either in-store, online or in other ways that would appeal to them. The same is true for the identifiable consumer communities in the SIMM and CIA data. When we approach retailing from a consumer view identifiable consumer communities abound, all with common needs and requirements or with common identifiers or elements that the retailer can use to plan his or her marketing and communications strategies. Therefore, we argue, the true skill needed in retailing today is an understanding of the complex nature of the various communities and networks consumers have created for themselves, so that relevant and meaningful retail marketing and communication programs and activities can be developed and implemented.

Due to the nature of the U.S. marketplace, there will be some overlaps in terms of the Shopper Mindset, SIMM and CIA consumer communities. Those will be pointed out when and where applicable. The key element in the analysis that follows, however, is that consumers are complex, interconnected, networked groups of individuals. Yet, they do have enough similarities so that the retailer can, by identifying the innate communities, use that information to create more effective, short-term and long-term, ongoing relationships with them.

Today's consumer groups are not the same as those of a few years ago or even last year. Vast changes have occurred in the consumer's situation. The Beaver Cleaver family types of the 1970s, while they still exist in some markets and in some areas (generally in new or emerging markets), are not the preponderance of today's U. S. retail communities. Unfortunately, in too many cases, it seems this family type is still being used to develop retail marketing segmentation schemes. By the same token, all consumer groups are not the postmodern neo-positivists that others propose, to whom, it is suggested, marketing is not only irrelevant, it may well be anathema. Indeed, there are all types of consumer communities and, sadly, many of them don't seem to fit neatly into the identifiable groups marketers and retailers have created.

Quite simply, today, consumers develop in self-organizing groups that come together, interact, revise themselves to fit their own needs and then re-form again in dynamic ways that are continuously changing. So, the key element to success in today and tomorrow's retail marketplace is understanding the change and dynamism of that marketplace.

III. Three Forms of Communication

In this text, consumer communities have been identified in three ways:

1. Communities that can be identified based on what consumers experience external to entering the retail shopping situation. Typically, these experiences come from the marketing and communication programs manufacturers and retailers use to try to influence in-store behaviors. In other words, these programs might be seen as precursors, or priming effects of advertising and promotion, designed to influence later consumer in-store retail behaviors. These prior-to-the-store experiences are generally identifiable through the SIMM studies of consumer media consumption, which is how these communities have been aggregated into consumer audiences in this text.

2. Identifiable communities that are created during the retail shopping experience. These come about as a result of the consumer's exposure to the marketing and promotional materials retailers and their manufacturer partners employ in the retail store, online or in some other form of consumer retailing experience. Common examples of these in-store, or retail, activities are shelf-talkers, bin displays and in-store digital signage. These are also identified in the SIMM studies, but differ from the traditional out-of-store media exposures.

3. The third group comprises communities created by non-retailer groups and activities found in the general marketplace. These external influences from other sources may occur either outside the shopping experience or external to the store, the key factor being they are developed and controlled by other people or organizations, for the most part, non-product organizations. These include influential non-governmental organizations (NGOs),

such as those of the Green movement, non-profit organizations such as the Cancer Society promoting proper eating habits or even the rapidly emerging online blogger groups and social networks, such as Facebook or YouTube, or new technologies such as Twitter. All of these have created identifiable consumer communities and have an influence on consumers and their shopping habits. They are, however, generally outside the control of the manufacturer or retailer. Thus, they are difficult to manage or even influence, but they must be recognized in any retailing situation for they do have marketplace impact.

In this text, we focus primarily on the first two influences: those developed primarily by the manufacturer on behalf of that firm's brands that are sold at retail; and those developed and delivered primarily by retail organizations to generate in-store purchasing of existing stock-keeping units (SKUs). We do not discount the other external influences, but, since they generally cannot be controlled by either the retailer or the manufacturer, they are beyond the scope of our current research, investigation and planning.

In the next chapter, we focus on the marketing and communication activities generated and controlled by manufacturers in support of their brands. These efforts may include assistance or implementation from the retailer. Generally, however, they are designed to encourage shoppers to select the advertised brand when shopping at retail. These programs and activities are commonly promoted through various forms of general media in the broad marketplace prior to the consumer's retail store visit. Thus, we term them external to the store.

Chapter

5

External Influences on In-Store Shopping

ollowing the structure outlined in Chapter 3, we start first with the various types of marketing communication activities manufacturers and retailers use to influence consumer's product and brand choices prior to the time they enter the actual retail environment. Since marketing communication has changed so dramatically in the past few years, a review of the current marketing communications marketplace is useful.

I. The Changing Marketing Communications Marketplace

The types and forms of marketing communication available to manufacturers and retailers have changed over recent times. Where once print (newspapers and magazines) and broadcast (radio and television) made up the bulk of marketers distribution alternatives, today, there are almost overwhelming choices. In the SIMM (Simultaneous Media Use) studies, 31 different media forms are tracked, including the broad general category of in-store promotion. While those provide brand sellers with many alternatives, they also create an often bewildering number of promotional choices. Therefore, today, the critical choice of which media form or forms is the most effective is more important than ever.

A. Traditional Push Marketing Communication

The marketing communication challenge today is (see Figure 27) in what has been termed the "push and pull" marketplace. The illustration shows the complexity of the alternatives available to marketers and retailers as they attempt to influence consumers and their behaviors once they are in the retail situation.

FIGURE 27: Push and Pull Marketplace

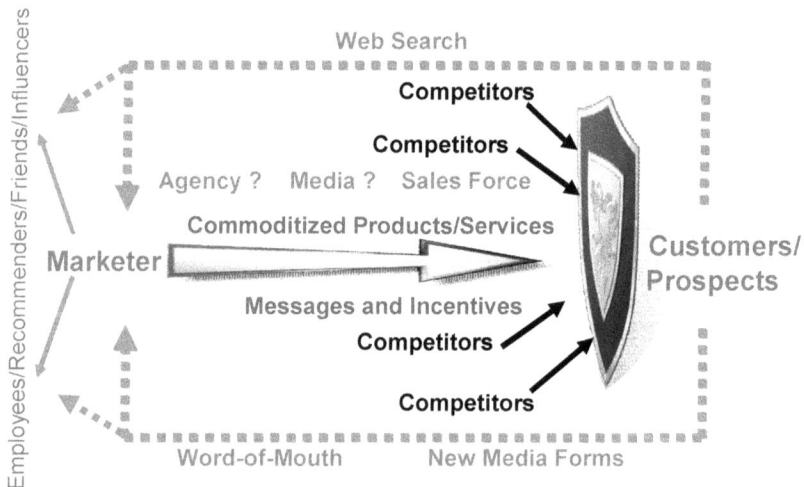

Source: Agora, Inc.

As illustrated, today's marketing communication system has two basic parts. The first is the traditional outbound system in which manufacturers and retailers, using various media forms, "push" communication out toward consumers (shown in the center of the model). This system is the one that most manufacturers and retailers have always used. In the push system, the manufacturer or retailer controls the communication program. They decide what products or offers to promote, when to promote them, through what media forms, the level or amount of communication to be distributed, and so on. The consumer is commonly viewed simply as a receiver of the marketing communication and promotional programs the manufacturer or retailer is distributing. Marketers define the groups of consumers to whom they want to direct their promotional messages through the forms of media used for distribution. This is the traditional approach to marketing communication. As shown, however, consumers now have developed methods of blocking or avoiding this onslaught of seller-generated marketing communication, thus, they are no longer the simple "target markets" assumed by both manufacturers and retailers. The various forms of information technology have shifted much of the marketplace power to the consumers.

B. New Media Pull Forms

We identify these new media systems as being outside the traditional outbound marketing communication methodologies. They are commonly referred to as "pull" communication, that is, they are approaches controlled by the consumer that allow them to gather marketing information as needed or required, not as dictated by the marketing organization. Today, the consumer has access and control of communication systems such as the Web and Internet, mobile telephony and social networks such as YouTube, Facebook and now Twitter (identified above as forms of word of mouth). All are consumer controlled. Thus, in this pull system, the consumer creates his or her own communities, as described in the previous chapter, by accessing the various new media forms. These consumer created communities may or may not match the segments manufacturer and retailers have developed. It is this continuous consumer media exposure that challenge both the manufacturer and retailers today.

C. Where Do Retail Experiences Occur?

The primary issue in the push and pull marketplace is who creates the consumer retail exposure and experience. Traditionally, the experience was controlled by the marketer through various communication channels. Today, however, in pull communication systems, the consumer's brand experiences may come from communication with the firm's customer service or tech support groups, distributors, intermediaries, bloggers, influencers and even with other consumers. Thus, both manufacturers and retailers must take a much wider view of marketing communication than the traditional media-dominated systems of the past.

It is this push and pull communication system that retailers must understand going forward. While both manufacturers and retailers will continue to push promotional messages and incentives out to consumers, consumers today have increasing information-gaining alternatives. Consumers can, if they desire, pull various forms of information from the marketing organization, or other sources, or combine that with other consumers to create entirely new retail communities. That's what makes today's marketplace so unique — one marketers, particularly retailers, have never experienced before. And, it is one that many are still struggling to understand and manage, often with out-of-date tools and methodologies. This push and pull communication system has created some new challenges for all marketers, one of which is simultaneous media consumption.

II. The Importance of Simultaneous Media Usage

At the same time as these new media alternatives have been developing, consumers have been changing their media habits, too. Where once the family gathered in the lounge around the television set to watch *Leave It to Beaver* or *The Ed Sullivan Show*, today, each person has his or her own personal communication system—ranging from an iPod to bedroom television to on-the-move Blackberries. With the growth of these new forms of communication has come a new phenomenon: consumers multitasking with media, creating simultaneous media usage.

Today, consumers are often using two or more communication tools at the same time—online, monitoring television, flipping through a magazine and chatting on a cell phone, simultaneously. This consumer multitasking has created major challenges for media firms and their external research suppliers in measuring media audiences, since audience size has traditionally been used by these organizations to price their media vehicles to advertisers. If a person is online, chatting on a cell phone and flipping through a magazine, in what media audience should he or she be counted?

A. Media Consumption Becomes Key

With the rise of the number of media forms available to the consumer, the incidence of media multitasking and rapidly fragmenting media audiences, BIGresearch, in 2002, began to develop the SIMM (Simultaneous Media Usage) studies to measure these differing individual media patterns. The basic premise is that only consumers know which media forms they use and in what combinations. Thus, a series of ongoing online questionnaires was developed. Using a double opt-in consumer research methodology, large and deep enough to provide a twice-yearly representative sample of the entire U.S. population, the SIMM studies now provide one of the most comprehensive views of media consumption and usage available. The most current SIMM wave is Number 14, June 2009, which means there is now sufficient data so that longitudinal media consumption studies can be conducted.

Each SIMM wave is quite exhaustive. For example, consumers are asked to provide information on their media habits, media usage, the influence of media on their purchasing decisions, favorite retailer, planned purchases and a host of other product consumption issues. The sidebar describes the SIMM research studies in more detail and describes some of the basic information found in those studies.

The SIMM Database

The analyses, findings and methodologies used here are based on the SIMM database, which has been collected twice each year since October 2001 in the U.S. The SIMM data is developed and administered by BIGresearch, Columbus, Ohio. There are now over 200,000 individual responses stored in the database. This allows researchers to develop trend analyses and compare various media forms over time.

All responses held in the database have been generated online using a double opt-in e-mail consumer response methodology. The samples have been drawn using accepted online survey methods. The same approaches and methodologies have been used over the entire eight-year period. The surveys that make up the SIMM responses are anonymous and self-administered.

The questions asked are based on several basic categories: demographics; leisure time; media influence on spending; frequency of purchases; Web site most often shopped; planned purchases in the next thirty days; media behaviors; census region; and other factors. The questionnaires are designed to be completed and returned very quickly.

BIGresearch data respondents are not paid for their participation. Rather, they participate in a quarterly contest for modest prizes. The questionnaire takes approximately ten to fifteen minutes to complete.

BIGresearch uses proprietary software that weights and balances all participants on the fourteen age and sex cells used in the U.S. Census. This assures a nationally representative sample in each wave.

Figure 28 shows the history of the fourteen waves of SIMM studies. The number of completed interviews is shown by survey. Over 22,000 responses are included in the most recent wave. The number of variables collected has also increased dramatically over the history of the surveys. The first wave had just over 100, while the most recent wave had over 1,000 variables.

FIGURE 28: SIMM History Completed Interviews and Variables Measured

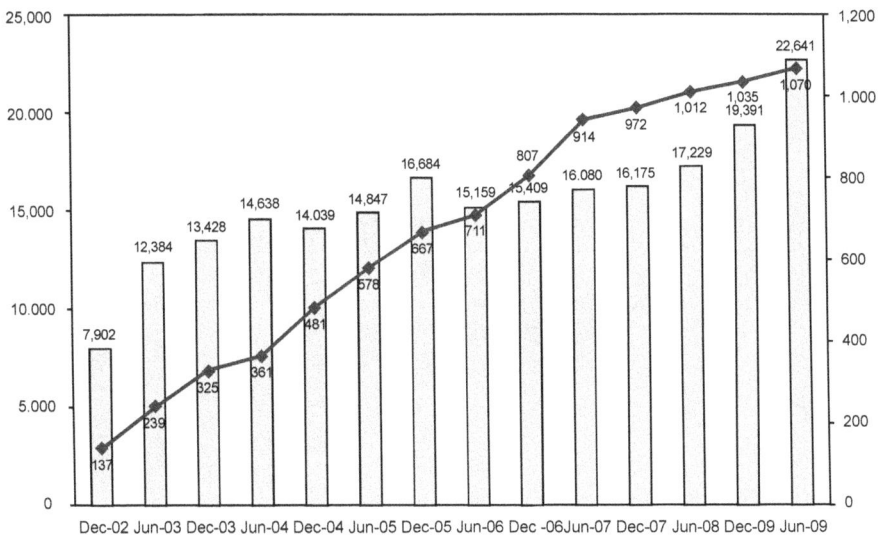

Source: BIGresearch

Of particular interest to media planners, buyers and researchers is the fact that each SIMM study is representative of the entire U.S. population. As Figure 29 illustrates, the most recent SIMM survey shows demographic characteristics that are very close to U.S. Census estimates, thus, confirming the representativeness of the SIMM data.

FIGURE 29: Selected Demographic Characteristics of SIMM (June 2009)

	Percent		Percent
Male	48.4	White	66.4
Female	51.6	Hispanic	12.9
Married	53.7	African-American	10.2
Children in household	31.8	Other	6.5
		Multiracial	3.0

Source: BIGresearch

Figure 30 shows the distributions by reported age and household income for the SIMM wave conducted in June 2009. The average age is just under 48 years, and the average household income is about $70,000.

FIGURE 30: Age and Income of SIMM (June 2009)

Ages	Percent	Income (000)	Percent
18–24	9.5	Less than $15	6.2
25–34	14.6	15 to 25	6.8
35–44	19.6	25 to 35	10.0
45–54	26.0	35 to 50	15.6
55–64	20.2	50 to 75	23.7
65 and over	10.1	75 to 100	17.2
		100 to 150	14.5
		150 and over	6.1
Average	47.8	$70,574	

Source: BIGresearch

SIMM Media Consumption Characteristics

The SIMM database includes thirty-one media forms, ranging from over-the-air television to in-store signage to Web radio. This usage data is collected in each SIMM study, thus, making time series analyses of changes in media usage over various periods possible and practical.

In addition to the media forms used, three unique media consumption and usage characteristics are tracked in each SIMM study:

- Experiential time — the individual consumption of media by person by dayparts. There are seven dayparts: 6–10 a.m., 10–noon, noon–4.30 p.m., 4.30–7.30 p.m., 7.30–11 p.m., 11 p.m.–1 a.m., and 1–6 a.m. This allows SIMM data to be compared and contrasted with traditional individual media measures.

- Simultaneity — the multitasking/overlapping of media consumption by consumer, that is, how media forms are consumed and in what combination at the same time. This enables the researcher and media planner to identify the potential synergy that might be possible through the purchase of various media combinations during certain time periods. It also helps identify more accurately the actual media audience by medium. In comparison, traditional media measures are conducted on one media form at a time, such as television only or radio only.

- Media engagement influence — consumers report the influence each individual media form has on their product decisions in each of the measured product categories. In addition, since respondents also report their preferred retailers by product category, it enables the marketer to connect his or her media expenditures to channel and usage by consumers. This is a true, consumer-reported engagement measure, which identifies the value of the medium to the consumer in terms of the impact and effect it has on their purchase decisions. Thus, it moves beyond media engagement to media impact.

In addition to the media questions, many traditional demographic and leisure time questions are asked. Thus, the questionnaire is quite comprehensive. For example, there are thirteen standard demographic and thirty-five leisure time questions in the survey instrument. These range from questions about individual and team sports to antique collecting to gambling.

A substantial amount of information on products and services is also obtained. Information regarding thirteen major product categories, consisting of thirty-seven specific products, is gathered in each survey. These are related to over 266 specific retailer choices (that is, favorite retailer for the various product categories), along with thirty-nine automotive brands, more than fifty cable television channels, fifteen television formats, five newspaper categories, over fifty magazine titles, twelve search engine alternatives, thirty-five specific Web sites, ten video game platforms, twelve questions regarding disease states and twenty-three spending and purchasing questions. In short, the SIMM data provides one of the most comprehensive views of U.S. consumers, their media usage and media consumption available.

Purchasing and SIMM Reported Data

There are other key elements in the SIMM database that relate specifically to individual purchase behavior. These expand the view of how consumers act and react in a multi-channel media world, such as:

- Competitive shopping and customer loyalty trends
- Six-month purchase outlook and intent to purchase for soft goods by product category. In addition, frequency of product purchases is also gathered
- Consumer merchandise—purchased or planned
- Shopping trends
- Cross shopping behavior
- Search behavior and purchasing
- Fast food frequency

All of these are cross-tabulated with media consumption to provide a better view of customers and prospects and the impact media has on their purchasing habits.

Of critical importance to the development of the media consumption study are the questions that relate consumer choice of media use which indicate the media forms that most influence purchase decisions. These questions form the basis for the media influence questions. There are nine merchandise categories to which these questions are applied:

- Groceries
- Apparel/clothing
- Electronics
- Medicine
- Eating out
- Telecommunications
- Car/truck purchases
- Home improvements
- Financial Services

And there are thirty-one media alternatives used in the questionnaire:

- Web site
- Word of mouth
- Television
- Cable
- Retail channel shopped
- Radio
- Article about product in media
- In-store promotion
- Newspapers
- Newspaper inserts
- Direct mail
- Magazine
- Internet advertising
- Outdoor billboards
- Picture phone
- Instant messenger
- Internet service provider (ISP)
- Broadband
- IPTV
- Search engine use
- E-mail advertising
- Yellow pages
- Satellite radio
- Text message
- MP3 player
- Web radio
- Video games
- Personal digital assistant (PDA)
- Cell phone
- Blogging
- TiVo

With this broad range of media forms used and their value to the consumer, plus, the ability to connect that data to past and planned purchases, the media planner and buyer have new views of consumers that have never before been possible.

With consumers now controlling their own media and communication access, the critical questions for marketers move from what messages and information they distribute to what consumers access, take in and use. Today, it is not nearly as important to identify the media forms where retailers and manufacturers spend their promotional funds—the traditional approaches of total spend and share of voice (SOV)—as the common method of judging and evaluating media, as it is to know what media forms consumers access and use. That information forms the heart of the SIMM studies.

B. Media Consumption Is Critical Variable

In recognition of the need for better measures of consumer media consumption, not just marketer distribution, Schultz and Pilotta began, in 2004, to develop a media consumption model, using the SIMM data. That is illustrated in Figure 31.

Their approach was to first identify where consumers are spending their media time, that is, the media forms they are consuming. Their basic premise was that the media form or forms the consumers use likely indicate their importance to them. Further, by knowing consumer media consumption, more effective media plans could be developed. For example, there is clear evidence today from the SIMM studies that consumers who patronize Walmart have different media consumption patterns from those whose primary retailer is Target or Kmart. Thus, the first media consumption measure is what media forms are being used by which consumers. That is then enhanced by the amount of time they spend with that media form.

FIGURE 31: MEDIA CONSUMPTION MODEL

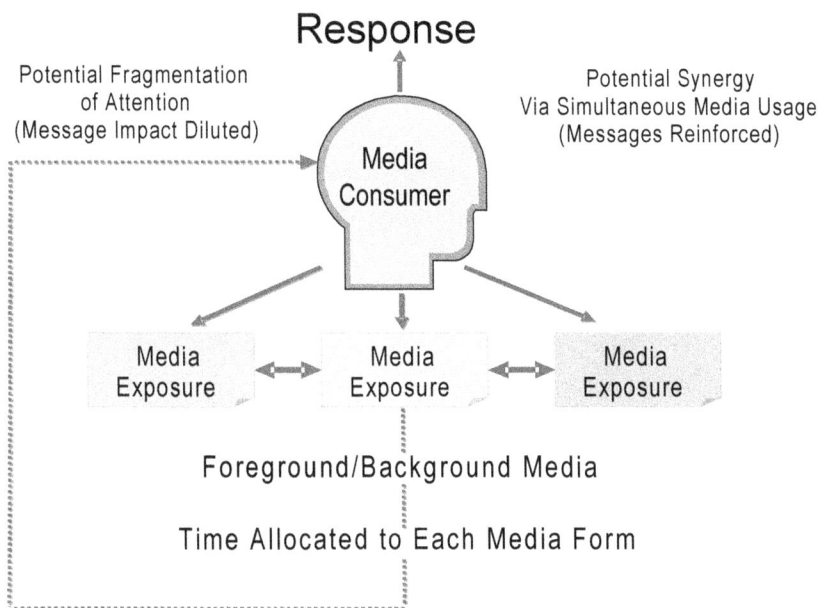

Response

Potential Fragmentation
of Attention
(Message Impact Diluted)

Potential Synergy
Via Simultaneous Media Usage
(Messages Reinforced)

Media
Consumer

Media
Exposure

Media
Exposure

Media
Exposure

Foreground/Background Media

Time Allocated to Each Media Form

Source: Agora, Inc.

In addition to these basic measures, additional questions are asked about which media forms are used together and which are used simultaneously. Thus, the SIMM studies provide a relevant view of U.S. consumers' media consumption on an ongoing basis. The fact that the SIMM studies have been conducted using the same format, in the same way, using essentially the same questions consistently over the past eight years, make them an incredibly reliable source for consumer analysis.

C. Foreground and Background Media

One of the important media concepts emerging from the SIMM data is the understanding that consumers now create what are called "foreground" and "background" media forms for themselves. That simply means the consumer is able to manage multiple media forms by focusing on one, or perhaps two, to which they are giving full attention—the "foreground" media. At the same time, they may be monitoring several other media forms with partial attention. Those are, therefore, called "background" media. This consumer ability to create foreground and background media forms for themselves gives them the ability to continuously monitor a substantial amount of media information.

This tendency when applied to the consumers' habit of continuously switching back and forth among and between media forms, gives marketers, particularly media planners, many problems when trying to construct traditional media plans. Thus, we argue, consumer media consumption is the only relevant media measure marketers can use today for allocating their promotional resources.

This media consumption understanding becomes even more important when one realizes that almost all traditional media measures are based on intra-media usage, that is, what specific media delivery vehicle is being consumed by what media audience. For example, current TV ratings only identify which television shows generate the largest audience but say nothing about simultaneous usage or what other media forms are being consumed at the same time. The same is true of radio, which measures only radio audiences, magazine audiences measure only what titles are used, and so on. Few, if any, media measures attempt to identify inter-media usage, that is, what broad media forms are being used together such as television and magazines or coupons and in-store or outdoor and mobile. The question is, then, what are the media usage communities consumers have created for themselves through their choice of media forms. This is one of the primary challenges of marketing communication planning today: media synergy created by consumer media multitasking.

Further, since the SIMM studies provide a nationally projectable sample of the U.S. population in each wave, it is also possible to drill down into the data to look specifically at products, retailers, media forms and a host of other variables. We will illustrate the various uses of SIMM data in understanding consumers and their retail proclivities throughout this text.

III. The Critical Elements of Media Consumption

In the analyses that follow, four critically important media consumption measures are used to identify retail shopping communities: (a) which media forms are consumed by each consumer in the sample, (b) the amount of time spent with each of the media forms, (c) the media forms used together, that is, in what media combinations and which are used simultaneously, and (d) the influence each media form consumed has on the consumer's purchase decision by product category. It is the understanding of these combinations that enables retailers to identify which media forms are most important to consumers. Therefore, those are the ones that should be considered in developing marketing communication programs that can be more effective in impacting consumer behaviors once they enter the retail environment.

The second element in media consumption is how the media is consumed by various consumer segments. Using the Shopper Mindset data, we have been able to identify seven consumer communities based on their media consumption. Those groups were identified in Chapter 2: Twenties, Families, Pairs, Singles, Bronze, Silver and Gold. Their media consumption is described in the following paragraphs.

A. Media Usage by the Shopper Mindset Communities

While not all consumers are the same, by the same token, they are not all totally different. The nuances of these consumer differences, gained through consumer insights, are what enable retailers and their manufacturer partners to develop effective marketing programs.

In Figure 32, media usage in minutes per day for each of the seven segments is shown. Here, we show only the top twelve of the thirty-one media forms gathered through the SIMM studies. (The data that follows comes from the SIMM 14 Study, June 2009.)

FIGURE 32: MEDIA USAGE (MINUTES PER DAY) (JUNE 2009)

	Twenties	Families	Singles	Pairs	Bronze	Silver	Gold	Total
Email	105.2	139.6	153.7	138.2	122.0	119.6	128.1	126.8
TV	94.9	121.7	137.3	127.5	155.9	143.7	124.3	118.3
Internet	120.6	126.4	147.3	127.7	115.9	107.9	109.5	117.7
Radio	53.5	80.0	80.3	76.6	47.5	61.0	69.1	69.4
Direct mail	36.3	55.8	56.9	55.9	48.8	55.6	57.0	51.3
Magazine	31.3	49.2	49.7	49.3	39.2	45.3	55.6	45.6
Newspaper	23.2	40.8	38.3	40.2	39.5	47.4	51.9	39.3
IM	55.9	37.6	49.0	32.6	21.9	17.8	19.2	33.6
Games	54.2	32.3	30.1	28.7	23.4	24.5	16.8	29.6
Satellite radio	12.6	20.7	22.7	21.1	9.3	12.3	25.5	19.5
Web radio	17.2	14.5	16.2	13.6	4.1	4.7	9.1	12.5
Blog	16.8	9.0	9.4	7.3	4.5	3.4	4.1	8.1

Source: BIGresearch

A quick glance at the SIMM data confirms what has often been reported, consumers spend huge amounts of time each day with various media forms. That knowledge, in and of itself, is somewhat mind-numbing. For example, people in the Singles category report spending a total of 672 minutes daily with the twelve media forms shown. When one considers the day is composed of only 1,440 minutes (24 hours x 60 minutes per hour = 1,440) that means single people, as reported in SIMM, are spending 58% of their time with these top twelve media forms. If the other twenty-one media forms were included, the total and percentage would be even higher. This may seem inconceivable, considering that each person must be devoting some time to sleeping, eating and other necessary activities, but the answer, of course, is multitasking or simultaneous media usage. In other words, single people today have been able to stretch the twenty-four-hour day into more than twenty-four hours by multitasking and using various forms of media simultaneously.

Of greater interest are the differences in media usage by the various retail media forms. As might be expected, instant messaging, video games and blogs skew very heavily to the younger groups, for example, the Twenties. Television and newspaper are more heavily consumed by the Bronze and Silver groups, while magazines are more prevalent with the Golds. Interestingly, direct mail, often considered junk media, is the fifth-ranked media form in terms of consumption. Most likely that has something to do with the consumer's involvement with catalogs and other long-form direct mail techniques.

As suggested earlier, while time is an important variable in media consumption, the influence of the media form on retail purchases is even more important. Figure 33 shows the media influence of the top twenty media forms from the SIMM data. In that chart, all product categories have been aggregated to illustrate the differing value consumers place on each of the media forms. Also of interest, SIMM data can be disaggregated if a marketer wants to review specific products or brands.

FIGURE 33: AVERAGE PRODUCT MEDIA INFLUENCE (PERCENT) (JUNE 2009)

	Twenties	Families	Singles	Pairs	Bronze	Silver	Gold	Total
Word of Mouth	28.2	38.5	36.7	36.5	27.2	32.4	34.1	34.2
Coupons	23.3	31.9	28.0	30.9	21.1	26.8	27.2	28.4
Inserts	10.8	23.3	20.6	23.0	22.1	24.4	24.2	21.1
TV	17.5	23.1	23.2	23.2	18.6	18.5	19.6	20.6
In-store	15.7	21.3	18.7	20.5	15.3	18.5	18.8	18.9
Newspaper	9.9	18.6	17.1	18.7	19.0	23.4	24.9	18.6
Direct mail	13.6	20.5	17.6	19.2	16.2	17.5	18.9	18.2
Read article	12.6	19.4	18.1	19.4	14.5	18.0	21.1	17.9
Magazine	13.1	16.3	15.3	15.0	11.1	12.3	15.7	14.7
Email	11.0	13.7	13.1	12.9	9.5	10.1	12.5	12.2
Cable	13.5	13.8	13.5	13.1	8.9	8.2	10.8	12.2
Radio	10.9	13.7	11.8	12.3	7.7	9.7	10.7	11.7
Internet	12.1	11.4	11.5	10.5	8.8	9.4	9.7	10.6
Product place	7.5	6.9	6.5	6.5	6.1	6.0	5.2	6.3
Yellow pages	4.4	5.3	5.6	5.1	6.9	7.0	5.9	5.3
Outdoor	7.0	5.8	5.2	5.0	4.6	4.0	3.8	5.1
Satellite	3.0	2.3	2.3	2.0	1.3	1.3	1.7	2.1
Blogs	4.6	2.2	2.5	1.9	1.4	1.0	0.9	2.1
IM	3.0	1.6	1.9	1.3	1.6	1.4	1.0	1.6
Web radio	2.8	1.6	1.7	1.2	1.6	1.1	0.8	1.5
Text	3.2	1.5	1.4	1.1	1.1	1.0	0.7	1.5
Video games	3.1	1.4	1.3	1.1	1.3	1.1	0.6	1.4

Source: BIGresearch

As can be seen in the chart on the previous page, various media forms have more or less influence on what consumers purchase. For example, word of mouth (WOM) is the top ranked media form among all consumer groups. Consumers are therefore saying that having recommendations or suggestions from other people is the most influential media form when they are considering a retail purchase. WOM is followed in this example by coupons and inserts (Sunday newspapers) and then television among the Twenties community. The same four media forms occur among the age segments (although not in the same order). They begin to vary considerably, however, when earning power is considered. The Gold group is more heavily influenced by newspapers and "read article" (public relations) than are other groups. The differences in media influence have, then, something to do with the development of new media, but not to the extent that one might expect.

The one key thing, which seems to flow across all consumer communities, is the heavy emphasis in the U.S. market of what might be considered promotional media—coupons, inserts, direct mail and the like. SIMM-type studies in China show much more influence coming from traditional media in those communities—television, newspapers, radio and the like. It seems the U.S. market is heavily price-driven and, thus, the influence of the promotional media forms.

A substantial amount of information can be gleaned from this type of analysis, with the new segmentation approach and the SIMM media consumption data.

We move next to the impact and effect of inside-the-store or internal marketing and communication activities.

Chapter

6

In-Store Influences on In-Store Shopping

n the previous chapter, the proposition was made that to understand retail promotion, one must look at the information
consumers have captured and stored away in their minds prior to
entering the retail shopping situation. That must, then, be connected
to the consumers' in-store experiences. Data was presented from
the Shopper Mindset studies that illustrated the media consumption consumers had prior to their store visits and how that might
impact their behaviors once they enter the retail location. When
the two, that is external and internal exposures, are combined, a true

understanding of how marketing and communication works in the retail environment begins to emerge.

This issue is important since most historical retail promotional analysis has been focused on either what happened prior to the retail experience or what occurred only in the store. There appear to be few studies, or even research approaches, that attempt to combine the two. The Shopper Mindset data clearly shows that the two are not only related, they are intertwined.

In this chapter, we add the consumer views of in-store promotion to the external-to-the-store data from Chapter 5. That makes it possible to create a holistic view of how consumers see the entire spectrum of retail promotion. As has been argued throughout this text, it is the consumer's perspective that is important, not what the retailer has done in the past or wants to do in the future.

In the second part of this chapter, consumer views of the two elements, in-store and external-to-the-store, are combined, based on the seven Shopper Mindset consumer communities introduced in Chapter 2. When this consumer influence data is aggregated, some rather revolutionary views of consumer retail influence and promotional response are possible.

I. Aggregated Influence of In-Store Promotional Activities

Figure 34 on the next page illustrates the percentage of consumer respondents who rated each of the twenty in-store promotional activities as being "influential" or "very influential" on their in-store purchasing behaviors. These are the views of the Shopper Mindset respondents on the aggregated eight product categories reported in the June 2007 study.

FIGURE 34: INFLUENCE OF IN-STORE PROMOTIONAL
ACTIVITY ON PURCHASE BEHAVIORS (PERCENT "VERY
INFLUENTIAL" OR "INFLUENTIAL")

	Total		Total
Samples in-store	53.1	In-store signage	28.0
Samples to home	47.6	Ads on shelves	25.2
Reading labels	46.3	Parking lot events	20.0
Shelf coupons	45.6	In-store television	13.8
Store loyalty card	43.5	In-store radio	12.7
In-store flyers	42.5	Information kiosks	11.6
Special displays	42.5	Checkout lane ads	10.2
Samples ordered online	31.8	Floor graphics	9.1
In-store events	31.4	TV at gas pumps	8.8
Coupons on register tape	30.2	Ads on shopping carts	7.1

Source: BIGresearch

As can be seen, "samples in-store" is the most cited promotional activity in terms of what influences consumer behaviors. That is followed by "samples to home" (samples sent previously to the respondent's residence), then "reading labels" and, fourth, "shelf coupons." About half of the promotional activities identified were reported to have an impact by more than 30% of the respondent group. In spite of the results found in other promotional studies, Shopper Mindset respondents did not identify any single promotional element that can assure retailer sales results. Thus, there does not seem to be a "silver bullet" of retailer promotion just waiting to be applied. Additionally, Shopper Mindset consumer response does not seem to line up very well with how retailers are investing their in-store promotional resources. For example, in-store television and in-store radio rank well down on the consumer list of most influential retail promotional activities, while, based on trade reports, retailers appear to be investing substantial sums in developing them. Even the old stand-by ads on shelves is not very highly ranked by a large percentage of the Shopper Mindset consumers.

How consumers rate each of the retail promotional activities, that is, which they believe is the most important, provides a somewhat different picture. Figure 35 below illustrates how consumers ranked each of the in-store promotional activities on a five-point scale (five being the highest). Shelf coupons is the second-ranked activity when viewed this way, and samples ordered online falls in the rankings. This illustrates that while large numbers of consumers may say various in-store promotional activities are influential, it is the importance of those activities that should matter to retailers when planning their in-store promotional activities.

FIGURE 35: INFLUENCE OF IN-STORE PROMOTIONAL ACTIVITY (MEAN OF FIVE-POINT SCALE)

	Total		Total
Samples in-store	3.35	Ads on shelves	2.60
Shelf coupons	3.14	Samples ordered online	2.56
Reading labels	3.13	Parking lot events	2.28
Samples to home	3.12	In-store television	2.01
In-store flyers	3.07	Information kiosks	1.99
Special displays	3.05	In-store radio	1.96
Store loyalty cards	3.00	Checkout lane ads	1.91
In-store events	2.70	Floor graphics	1.82
Coupons on register tape	2.70	Ads on shopping carts	1.68
In-store signage	2.61	TV at gas pumps	1.65

Source: BIGresearch

II. Influence of In-Store Promotional Activities by Shopper Mindset Retail Communities

While aggregated figures are helpful in understanding the broad range of potential consumer in-store promotional possibilities, when those summary numbers are disaggregated into the seven consumer communities developed from the Shopper Mindset data (described in Chapter 5) it is possible to see the differences between them. While some of the activities are important to all of the consumer communities, that is, the ones where consumers say the promotional activity is "influential" or "very influential" in their purchase decisions, others have less or not so strong appeal. For example, in-store samples are still the top-rated activity for all groups except the Silvers and Golds. Others, however, change rather dramatically in terms of their value to the specific consumer communities, for example, special displays are important to the Twenties, Family and Single communities but less so to the Bronze, Silver and Gold groups. It is this understanding of the promotional value to the individual groups that can determine the retailer's overall success in developing effective in-store promotional activities.

When we dig down into the data, it becomes clear that each retail consumer community has its own set of in-store preferences. Perhaps the most striking differences are those between the Twenties and the Gold groups. The Twenties appear to be much more attuned to in-store media (in-store television and in-store radio) than the Golds, while the Golds prefer the more traditional activities such as reading labels, shelf coupons and store loyalty cards. Again, understanding the impact and effect of in-store promotion from the consumer's view sheds a whole new light on promotional development.

We see similar differences when influence of in-store promotional activity is based on consumer ratings using a five-point scale (see Figure 37).

FIGURE 36: INFLUENCE OF IN-STORE PROMOTIONAL
ACTIVITY ON PURCHASE BEHAVIORS (PERCENT "VERY
INFLUENTIAL" OR "INFLUENTIAL")

	Twenties	Families	Singles	Pairs	Bronze	Silver	Gold	Total
Samples in-store	53.9	56.8	47.9	54.3	48.3	49.3	43.9	53.1
Samples to home	44.5	52.7	46.6	50.2	40.9	44.3	37.8	47.6
Reading labels	39.6	46.0	50.9	51.4	46.4	53.4	50.7	46.3
Shelf coupons	42.6	49.1	45.9	49.1	39.3	46.8	36.9	45.6
Store loyalty cards	38.5	47.3	46.1	46.3	33.4	43.0	40.7	43.5
In-store flyers	39.8	45.9	38.7	45.8	42.2	40.3	36.7	42.5
Special displays	42.7	46.2	41.0	42.7	37.7	37.7	34.4	42.5
Samples ordered online	33.2	34.3	31.2	33.4	23.8	28.8	21.7	31.8
In-store events	36.4	34.1	27.5	30.6	27.7	25.8	19.7	31.4
Coupons on register	32.2	31.6	28.4	29.3	29.5	31.1	24.1	30.2
In-store signage	27.6	31.3	29.3	29.7	16.5	19.8	21.8	28.0
Ads on shelves	25.9	27.6	26.8	25.5	19.4	20.6	17.8	25.2
Parking lot events	26.0	22.0	17.9	17.9	14.3	12.5	9.7	20.0
In-store television	21.7	13.6	12.0	10.8	8.4	8.5	6.2	13.8
In-store radio	19.9	12.5	10.3	10.0	8.2	6.8	5.7	12.7
Information kiosks	15.4	12.1	9.7	10.0	8.4	8.3	7.2	11.6
Checkout lane ads	16.0	10.3	8.8	7.6	9.7	6.9	3.7	10.2
Floor graphics	13.6	8.6	6.9	7.7	8.1	7.2	5.4	9.1
TV at gas pumps	15.8	8.2	6.5	5.7	7.0	5.0	2.4	8.8
Ads on shopping carts	11.3	7.3	5.8	4.8	7.0	3.5	2.5	7.1

Source: BIGresearch

FIGURE 37: INFLUENCE OF IN-STORE PROMOTIONAL
ACTIVITY (MEAN OF FIVE-POINT SCALE)

	Twenties	Families	Singles	Pairs	Bronze	Silver	Gold	Total
Samples in-store	3.34	3.47	3.18	3.42	3.10	3.27	3.14	3.35
Shelf coupons	3.05	3.27	3.12	3.27	2.77	3.10	2.92	3.14
Reading labels	2.92	3.14	3.22	3.32	2.96	3.27	3.31	3.13
Product samples to home	3.02	3.30	3.09	3.26	2.77	2.93	2.80	3.12
In-store flyers	2.96	3.21	2.94	3.17	2.94	3.04	2.88	3.07
Special displays	3.02	3.17	3.02	3.13	2.79	2.87	2.85	3.05
Store loyalty cards	2.89	3.13	3.02	3.11	2.42	2.90	2.87	3.00
In-store events	2.86	2.79	2.57	2.71	2.46	2.46	2.30	2.70
Coupons on register	2.71	2.76	2.64	2.73	2.56	2.76	2.49	2.70
In-store signage	2.56	2.73	2.62	2.72	2.06	2.25	2.46	2.61
Ads on shelves	2.54	2.71	2.63	2.67	2.31	2.50	2.41	2.60
Samples ordered online	2.67	2.68	2.54	2.66	2.07	2.31	2.12	2.56
Parking lot events	2.49	2.39	2.17	2.26	1.91	1.94	1.86	2.28
In-store television	2.34	2.06	1.92	1.91	1.59	1.66	1.63	2.01
Information kiosks	2.11	2.03	1.96	1.99	1.63	1.83	1.83	1.99
In-store radio	2.27	2.02	1.86	1.85	1.59	1.57	1.53	1.96
Checkout lane ads	2.15	1.94	1.84	1.83	1.69	1.72	1.58	1.91
Floor graphics	2.01	1.82	1.74	1.77	1.57	1.71	1.66	1.82
Ads on shopping carts	1.89	1.71	1.62	1.61	1.59	1.48	1.41	1.68
TV at gas pumps	2.00	1.67	1.54	1.52	1.34	1.31	1.29	1.65

Source: BIGresearch

Consumer ratings are perhaps a stronger measure of the in-store promotional alternatives. They seem to indicate which activities could and should be used and which probably should be avoided. In Figure 37, we have separated the in-store activities into promotional buckets by consumer community.

Another way of comparing the importance of potential in-store activities is to group them into categories. That has been done in the figures that follow. Four categories of in-store promotional activities have been created, namely:

1. Value promotions — these would include product samples in-store, product samples delivered to the home, shelf coupons, product samples ordered online and coupons on register tapes

2. Displays — these consist of reading product labels, special displays, in-store events/contests and parking lot/sidewalk events

3. Store loyalty cards

4. Advertising—which would include in-store flyers, in-store signage, ads on shelves, in-store television, in-store radio, information kiosks, checkout lane ads, floor graphics, TV at gas pumps and ads on shopping carts.

When the promotional activities are grouped in this way, more strategic views of in-store activities can be considered. For example, the retailer can understand which of the broad categories of in-store promotional alternatives have the most impact on the various consumer created communities and, from that, start to develop more specific in-store promotional activities by product lines.

FIGURE 38: INFLUENCE OF IN-STORE PROMOTIONAL
ACTIVITY CATEGORIES (PERCENT "VERY INFLUENTIAL" OR
"INFLUENTIAL")

	Twenties	Families	Singles	Pairs	Bronze	Silver	Gold	Total
Value promotions	41.3	44.9	40.0	43.3	36.4	40.0	32.9	41.7
Displays	36.2	37.1	34.3	35.6	31.5	32.3	28.6	35.1
Store loyalty cards	38.5	47.3	46.1	46.3	33.4	43.0	40.7	43.5
Advertising	20.7	17.8	15.5	15.7	13.5	12.7	11.0	16.9

Source: BIGresearch

From Figure 38, it is clear that store loyalty cards have the greatest impact on the greatest number of consumer communities. More importantly, however, when viewed this way, various forms of advertising have substantially less influence on consumer behaviors.

FIGURE 39: INFLUENCE OF IN-STORE PROMOTIONAL
ACTIVITY CATEGORIES (INDICES BASED ON FIGURE 38)

	Twenties	Families	Singles	Pairs	Bronze	Silver	Gold	Total
Value promotions	99.1	107.8	96.0	103.8	87.3	96.1	78.9	100.0
Displays	103.3	105.7	97.9	101.7	90.0	92.2	81.7	100.0
Store loyalty cards	88.4	108.8	105.8	106.4	76.8	98.7	93.4	100.0
Advertising	122.4	105.0	91.5	93.0	79.7	75.0	64.7	100.0

Source: BIGresearch

When the various categories are viewed on the rating scale, we see how the different categories appeal to the different communities. In this chart, advertising has high ratings from the Twenties group and very low ratings from the Golds. Probably the most interesting finding is the low ratings given to all categories by the Golds.

With this understanding of how consumers and consumer communities view in-store promotional activities, we move to the development of a more holistic view of the entire area of retail promotional planning. By combining the Shopper Mindset and SIMM data—the external-to-the-store promotional exposures and in-store consumer promotional influencers—we gain a better understanding of how retail promotion works across the consumer spectrum.

III. Understanding the Combination of External-to-the-Store and In-Store Promotional Influences on Consumers

The Shopper Mindset and SIMM data confirm what retailers and their manufacturer partners have always suspected, it is the combination of their promotional activities prior to the retail visit and the impact of the in-store promotion that follows that drive retail sales. However, few published studies have looked at promotional impact in this way.

Factor analysis has been used in the examination that follows to provide insights into how the external and internal activities interact. Figure 40 shows the results of the factor analysis of the internal or in-store factors previously described. The factor analysis identifies three basic promotional activity groups, which we have labeled "digital signs," "in-store and display" and "free samples." These three factors explain 59.5% of the variance in the model, a fairly strong result.

FIGURE 40: INTERNAL INFLUENCE FACTORS EXPLAIN 59.5%

	Digital Signs	In-store & Display	Free Samples
Ads on Shopping Carts	0.76		
In-store Television	0.75		
In-store Radio	0.74		
Check-Out Lane Ads	0.73		
Floor Graphics	0.73		
TV at Gas Pumps	0.72		
Information Kiosks	0.63		
Parking Lot/Sidewalk Events	0.56		
Shelf Coupons		0.74	
Special Displays		0.69	
In-store Flyers		0.67	
Ads on Shelves		0.66	
Reading Product Labels		0.59	
In-store Signage	0.42	0.58	
Store Loyalty Cards		0.58	
Product Samples In-store		0.54	0.53
Coupons on Register Tape		0.53	
In-store Events/Contests	0.44	0.46	
Product Samples Delivered To Home			0.78
Product Samples Ordered Online			0.78

Source: BIGresearch

In Figure 41, the results of the same type of factor analysis of the external-to-the-store activities are shown. (These are the promotional variables that were discussed in Chapter 5.) Those three factors have been labeled "digital media," "value offers" and "mass media."

FIGURE 41: EXTERNAL INFLUENCE FACTORS EXPLAIN 53.8%

	Digital Media	Value Offers	Mass Media
Text	0.83		
Video Games	0.81		
IM	0.81		
Web Radio	0.74		
Blogs	0.70		
Satellite Radio	0.59		
Outdoor	0.46	0.42	
Yellow Pages	0.42		
Coupons		0.71	
Direct Mail		0.70	
Inserts		0.66	
Email		0.60	
Newspapers		0.60	
Magazines		0.51	0.44
Internet		0.45	
Cable			0.82
Broadcast TV			0.81
Radio			0.57

Source: BIGresearch

In this analysis, 53.8% of the variance is explained. Not quite as strong as the in-store model, but still a very strong statistical result.

The real value of this information, however, comes when we combine the two factor analyses and compare them side by side.

IV. Combining Internal and External-to-the-Store Shopper/Consumer Influences

In the next seven charts, we illustrate what occurs when the external-to-the-store and internal consumer influences are combined and compared. The charts show the combination of the two forms of retail promotional activities. The charts also show the factor scores (as calculated in the factor analysis from Figures 40 and 41), which have been standardized and rescaled so they represent percentages.

A separate chart has been developed for each of the seven consumer communities identified in the Shopper Mindset data. Figure 42 illustrates the influences for the Singles community.

FIGURE 42: INTERNAL AND EXTERNAL-TO-THE-STORE SHOPPER INFLUENCES — SINGLES

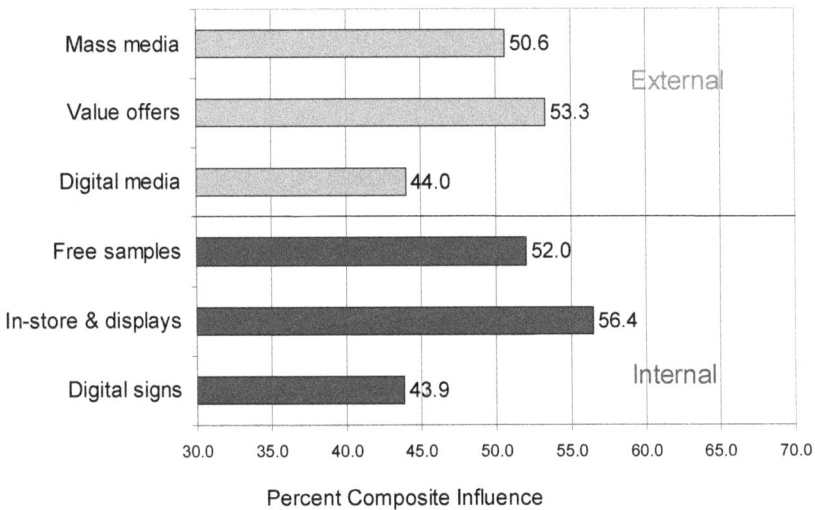

Percent Composite Influence

Source: BIGresearch

As shown above, the two most important influences for the Singles group in the aggregated eight product categories are "in-store and displays" and "value offers." The least important factors are "digital media" and "digital signs." This data is directional only, but it does identify which promotional activities consumers report as having the most impact on their purchase decisions. Interestingly, one of the most important promotional activities is external-to-the-store, that is, value offers, and the other is internal, or in-store, namely, in-store and displays. From this, the retailer can begin to understand what combination of external and internal activities might make the best combination to influence this community. Perhaps of equal importance is the knowledge that digital media (external) and digital signs (internal) have the least impact on this consumer group.

Figures 43–48 illustrate the same analysis for each of the other six segments from the combined Shopper Mindset and SIMM data. Each of the segments has its promotional preferences, which are evident in the factor scores. We comment briefly on each of the segments below, and then summarize the findings at the end of this section.

The Twenties group, unlike the Singles, is highly influenced by both digital media (external) and digital signs (internal). In fact, this community shows the greatest preference for the digital forms of retail promotion of any of the seven communities.

FIGURE 43: INTERNAL AND EXTERNAL-TO-THE-STORE SHOPPER INFLUENCES — TWENTIES

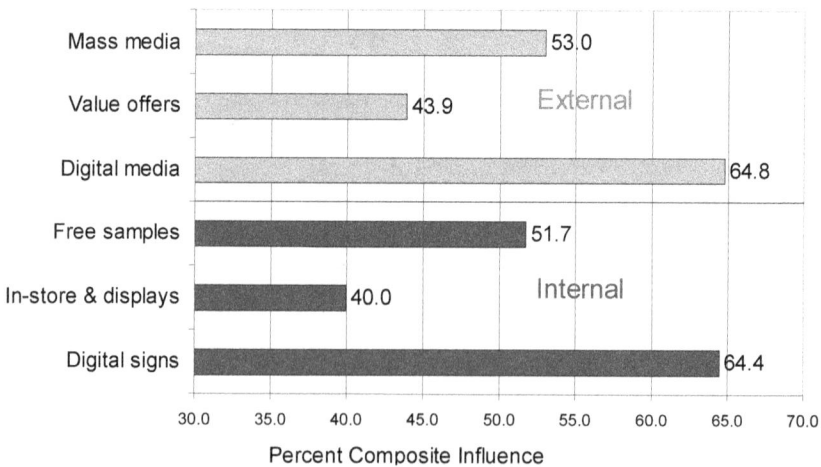

Source: BIGresearch

Interestingly, however, the Twenties show little preference for value offers and in-store & displays.

The Pairs community is the most evenly split between the external and internal activities. There is little difference in the six factors in terms of their reported influence. One could read this information as "good news," in that, the community prefers all forms of retail promotional activities, or "bad news," since there is little difference between any of the six promotional categories and, thus, this group may be more resistant to any form of retail promotion. These findings demand a more detailed analysis, likely by individual product category, for promotional planning.

FIGURE 44: INTERNAL AND EXTERNAL-TO-THE-STORE SHOPPER INFLUENCES — PAIRS

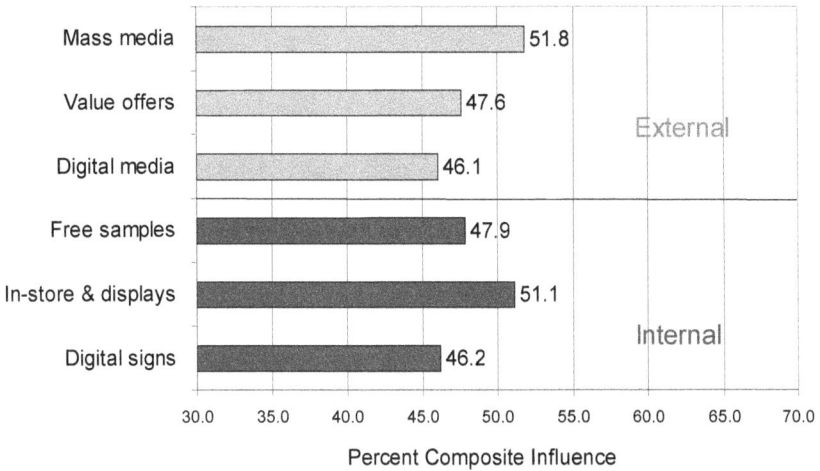

Source: BIGresearch

Figure 45 shows the influence of the promotional factors for the Family group.

FIGURE 45: INTERNAL AND EXTERNAL-TO-THE-STORE
SHOPPER INFLUENCES — FAMILIES

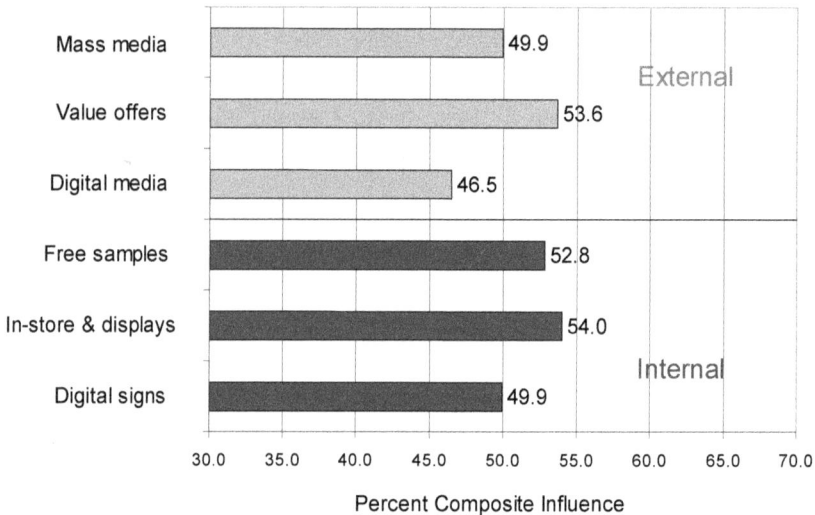

Percent Composite Influence

Source: BIGresearch

Families seem to show more preference for the value-based promotional alternatives, preferring value offers (external) and samples and in-store and displays (internal). That would be expected as the respondents from this community are likely providing for a larger number of people than those in the other three groups previously discussed (Singles, Twenties and Pairs). What is also interesting is the impact of all media forms, mass media, digital signs and digital media on the Family consumer community preferences. We can conclude that to influence this community, a combination of external and internal will be needed.

The final three communities — Bronze, Silver and Gold groups — are generally income and age related. Thus, we do begin to see how some of the traditional forms of market segmentation become relevant. However, these factors only become apparent when the entire group of consumers is considered.

Figure 46 illustrates how the Bronze community (with incomes of $20,000 or less) reports the influence of promotional activities on its shopping behaviors.

FIGURE 46: INTERNAL AND EXTERNAL-TO-THE-STORE SHOPPER INFLUENCES — BRONZE

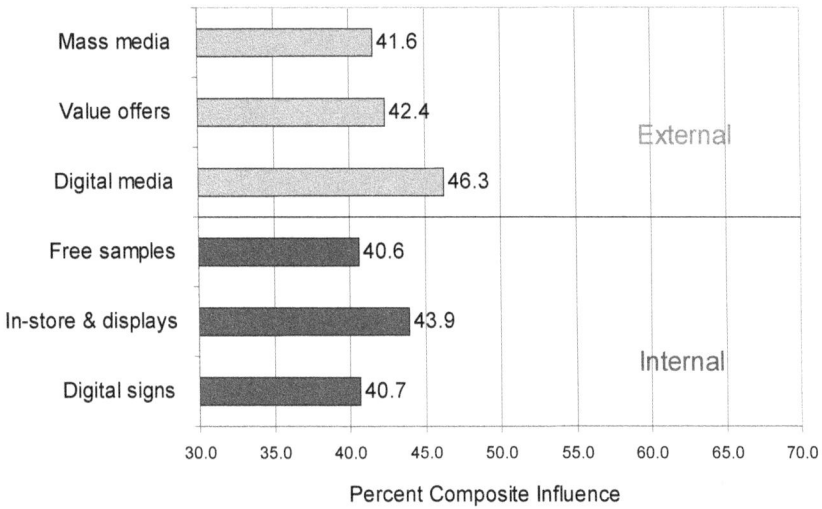

Source: BIGresearch

The Bronze group shows the least preference for either internal or external promotional activities and the three categories of activities that make up each of them. The most influential activity reported is digital media (external), which seems counterintuitive since this community is, by definition, lower in income than the Silvers or Golds. However, it is exactly this type of insight that helps the retailer develop effective promotional programs, often challenging traditional wisdom and what has been done in the past.

The Silver community (with incomes of $20,001 to $50,000), shown in Figure 47, has a unique pattern as well. These seemingly middle-of-the-road consumers strongly prefer in-store & displays (internal) and value offers (external), which seems to fit with their middle-income life situation.

FIGURE 47: INTERNAL AND EXTERNAL-TO-THE-STORE SHOPPER INFLUENCES — SILVER

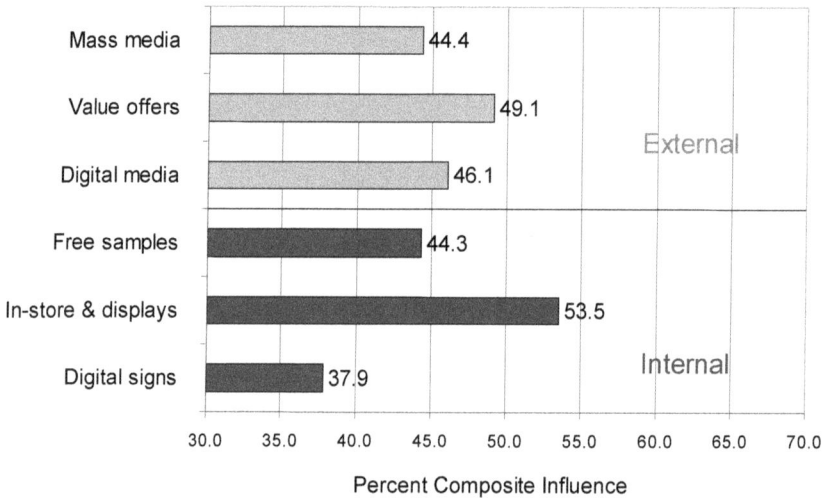

Percent Composite Influence

Source: BIGresearch

The Silvers also demonstrate their seeming indifference to in-store digital signage, a feeling that also is evident in the Bronze group. We will see later, the Gold community has the same views. External digital media does, however, seem to appeal to the Silvers.

The Gold consumer community (with incomes of $50,001 or more) provides some very interesting insights into its preferences for promotional media (see Figure 48 on the next page).

FIGURE 48: INTERNAL AND EXTERNAL-TO-THE-STORE
SHOPPER INFLUENCES — GOLD

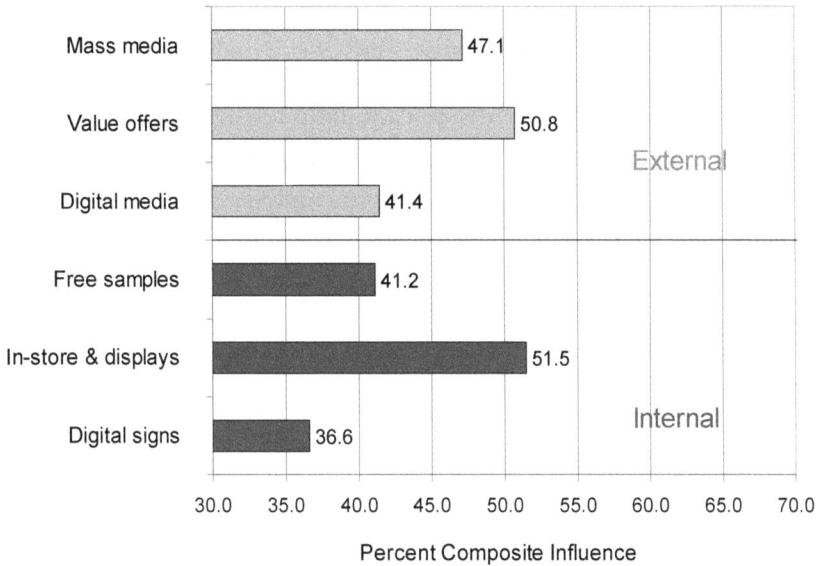

Percent Composite Influence

Source: BIGresearch

This community seems less influenced by in-store (internal) promotion than they are by the external-to-the-store media forms.
With the exception of in-store and displays, external media forms,
namely, mass media and digital media, are more preferred than digital signs and rated about the same as free samples. Again, when we
combine the external and the internal factors, the Golds are clearly
promotionally oriented. It would appear price offers would be the
most effective promotional activity to influence them — value offers
(external) and in-store & displays (internal). Again, these findings
are somewhat counterintuitive. The Golds are the oldest and highest income group of the seven communities. One would, therefore,
assume that they would be less susceptible to promotional activities
than the Shopper Mindset data suggests they are.

From this quick view of promotional preferences of the seven consumer communities developed from the Shopper Mindset data, some summary comments seem appropriate.

1. The Bronze group seems to have the least preference for any type of promotional activity—either external or internal.

2. The Singles community seems to have relatively low preference for digital media and digital signs, in spite of the fact that they are often portrayed as being "digital natives."

3. Mass media still seems to have a relatively high preference among Singles, Twenties and Pairs. This, in spite of the fact that they are often assumed to be lower consumers of the various traditional media forms.

4. Free samples are a greater preference among the Singles, Twenties, Pairs and Families than among the Bronze, Silver and Gold communities.

5. In-Store and Displays are disproportionately appealing to the Singles, Silvers and Golds than to the other communities.

Nevertheless, these top-line analyses remain just that, glimpses of the appeal and preferences of the twenty internal and thirty-one external communication and promotional alternatives found in the Shopper Mindset and SIMM data. Much more analysis is needed to make them relevant to specific retailers. Yet, the necessary information is in the two data sets and can be easily extracted.

This short description of the findings demonstrates that the capability to combine both external-to-the-store and in-store factors to create a more effective and efficient retail promotional mix is possible and practical. The value of our analysis, thus far, is more to indicate future directions and possibilities than to provide specifics to any one retailer or manufacturer.

With these analytical examples as the basis for our discussion, we can now move to a more complete view of retailing by including the on-line portion of the retailing mix.

Chapter

7

Consumer Communities in Online Shopping

Nothing has changed the face of retailing more than the advent of digital media. Strictly online retailers have emerged as significant competitors in many product categories, and virtually all retailers maintain and depend upon Web sites to enhance and supplement their business. The retail customer now commonly enters a retail store carrying one or more portable digital devices, while the in-store retail environment itself is filled with digital and video technology.

The contemporary retailer, whether it chooses to or not, is being forced to become a media enterprise itself. Digital media subscriptions, as shown in Figure 49, dominate American households. Cable subscriptions are enjoyed by over 62% of households, with another 30% subscribing to satellite TV, while 7% report subscribing to both. This gives a total of nearly 93% of households that subscribe to either cable or satellite TV.

Over 73% say they have high-speed Internet access (DSL or cable), with another 10% having fiber optic Internet service (and 5% say both). Other digital subscription services, such as streaming video and voice over Internet protocol (VoIP), are reported at much lower levels.

FIGURE 49: Digital Media Subscriptions by Retail Segments (June 2009)

	Twenties	Families	Singles	Pairs	Bronze	Silver	Gold	Total
Cable TV	63.6	63.7	66.6	64.2	58.8	61.2	67.5	62.8
Satellite TV	24.0	34.9	22.2	31.6	31.0	32.4	32.5	30.0
Satellite radio	7.0	15.8	9.9	15.1	5.1	7.0	16.6	12.8
High-speed Internet	60.4	80.8	74.1	78.4	69.1	76.4	80.5	73.2
Fiber Internet access	7.5	11.4	8.2	9.8	7.6	8.1	14.2	10.1
Streaming video	5.0	4.5	3.7	3.5	1.1	1.7	3.1	3.6
VoIP	3.4	5.9	5.1	4.8	3.2	2.7	6.3	4.8

Source: BIGresearch

Another sign of the increasing significance of digital media is the regular use of portable devices being reported. Regularly means routinely as a set pattern, as opposed to occasional use, which, if included, would dramatically increase the percentages shown in Figure 50. For example, almost exactly half report regularly using a cell phone, whereas almost 93% report having one. Bearing in mind this same conservative regular usage estimate, we find regular use of iPhones, iPods and MP3 players is higher among the Twenties segment, whereas PDAs are more prevalent among the middle-aged segments.

Digital services are also regularly used by consumers, but with quite different patterns by retail segments. TiVo and DVRs are regularly used by nearly one out of four, but the usage is highest among the middle-aged segments, especially Families and Pairs (see Figure 51). Text messaging and instant messaging are most used by the younger Twenties segment. Video downloading—both on computer and the cell phone—as well as video gaming are also highest among the Twenties.

FIGURE 50: DEVICES REGULARLY USED BY RETAIL SEGMENTS (JUNE 2009)

	Twenties	Families	Singles	Pairs	Bronze	Silver	Gold	Total
Cell phone	44.7	60.7	53.7	57.2	26.2	37.7	49.4	50.1
PDA	5.2	8.4	8.0	7.2	1.6	2.0	6.2	6.3
iPhone	5.3	4.3	4.2	3.5	0.5	1.1	2.5	3.5
iPod/MP3 player	23.2	18.0	19.9	17.1	2.5	4.1	9.4	15.1

Source: BIGresearch

FIGURE 51: DIGITAL SERVICES REGULARLY USED BY RETAIL SEGMENTS (JUNE 2009)

	Twenties	Families	Singles	Pairs	Bronze	Silver	Gold	Total
TiVo/ReplayTV/DVR	15.6	28.5	24.6	28.1	11.2	14.1	23.9	22.6
Text messaging	32.8	28.4	26.6	22.0	3.8	5.2	9.7	20.8
Instant messaging	20.3	12.6	16.6	10.7	8.3	5.9	6.3	11.3
Satellite radio	5.0	12.0	11.9	12.5	3.8	6.8	16.9	10.9
Video gaming	18.3	12.7	11.4	10.6	6.1	7.8	6.5	10.7
Download video/TV	19.2	10.9	13.2	9.9	5.1	3.7	5.4	9.8
Picture phone	14.4	10.1	8.2	8.3	2.2	2.2	3.6	7.7
Web radio	6.5	5.8	6.3	5.7	1.6	1.7	3.4	4.8
Blogs	7.8	4.3	5.1	3.9	2.9	1.8	2.1	4.0
Video on cell phone	4.1	2.4	1.4	1.1	0.4	0.4	0.5	1.7

Source: BIGresearch

Four Screens

From a technological point of view, the concept of the "four screens" of digital video media — television, Internet, cell phones and in-store video displays — is very compelling. It certainly seems that all the digital video media ought to be able to work in an integrated manner for the benefit of the consumer. Figure 52 shows the relative average influence of each of the four screens. Television easily leads the way with about 20%, with cell phones trailing at about 1%. How compelling advertising may be on each of the screens is shown by the attention percentage. Nearly 9% say they attend to the advertising on TV, whereas, only about 5% say they regularly pay attention to Internet advertising and just under 2% on the cell phone.

FIGURE 52: COMPARISON OF FOUR SCREEN INFLUENCE

	Influence	Attention
TV	20.6%	8.9%
Internet	10.5	5.4
Cell phone	1.2	1.7
In-store video	3.4	NA

Source: BIGresearch

At least in the United States, the cell phone appears to be the weak link in development of the four screen concept. Consumer attitudes are generally very negative toward advertising material on the cell phone, as shown in Figure 53. Over half say that advertisers should need permission and that ads on a cell phone are an invasion of privacy. Only a very small proportion, 3%, say that ads are okay as long as content is received, and less than 2%

say that the ads can be helpful in making purchase decisions. The ratio of those saying they like receiving some form of cell phone advertising to those who don't like receiving it is approximately thirty to one.

We can conclude—despite speculation and hope to the contrary—that consumers in the U.S. have some way to go before they will be willing to accept the cell phone as a marketing device. No doubt there is a future for mobile, but it will depend on related technologies such as the widespread use of QR codes, as found in Japan.

FIGURE 53: Consumer Cell Phone Advertising Opinions

	Percent
I don't have a cell phone	7.4
Advertisers should need my permission	56.7
I think they are an invasion of privacy	51.5
I pay per text and feel cheated	31.6
They're okay as long as I get content in return	3.1
They can be helpful in making purchase decisions	1.9
I like receiving text ads	2.0
I don't like receiving text ads	65.4
I like receiving text voicemail ads	2.0
I don't like receiving text voicemail ads	59.1
I like receiving video ads	1.7
I don't like receiving video ads	58.6

Source: BIGresearch

Social Media and Blogs

Social media, such as Facebook and MySpace, are often mentioned as a way of reaching customers in an environment where they choose to participate. Only two such sites — Facebook, which is regularly accessed by about one in four, and MySpace, regularly accessed by about one in ten — would seem to be large enough to consider (see Figure 54). It should be pointed out that the youngest segment, Twenties, has many more users of such sites, which may speak to the future if they still regularly use the technology as they age. Twitter, as of mid-2009, has a fairly small user base, which is less than one in twenty-five. And other social media sites are small, in terms of their user bases. Social media, because it is entirely user generated, can be difficult to use as a marketing tool. However, at the very least, the more popular sites deserve to be monitored by the retailer.

FIGURE 54: Subscribing to Social Media Sites by Retail Segments (June 2009)

	Facebook	MySpace	Twitter	LinkedIn	Classmates
Twenties	51.5	29.3	8.6	3.3	2.5
Families	29.9	10.6	3.7	4.6	3.3
Single	28.5	9.3	3.7	4.1	2.2
Pairs	25.0	8.1	4.0	3.5	3.7
Bronze	9.4	5.5	1.8	0.6	3.3
Silver	11.3	3.3	1.0	0.4	3.8
Gold	12.1	2.7	1.5	2.4	3.4
Total	25.6	9.8	3.6	3.4	3.2

Source: BIGresearch

Blogs are often mentioned as another possible marketing tool. Again, the problem is that they are user generated and difficult for a marketer to control. The best the marketer can do, typically, is to participate. As shown in Figure 55, the rate of participation in blogs is relatively small. Only about 8% say they regularly read blogs, with this rate being higher for Twenties and Singles. The rates of posting to blogs or maintaining a blog are quite small, with an overall rate of 3% for each.

FIGURE 55: PARTICIPATION IN BLOGS BY RETAIL SEGMENTS (JUNE 2009)

	Read blogs	Post to blogs	Maintain a blog
Twenties	12.9	5.3	5.6
Families	9.2	3.6	2.8
Single	11.0	3.7	3.2
Pairs	8.8	3.0	2.6
Bronze	5.1	1.8	1.4
Silver	4.1	1.2	1.2
Gold	5.3	1.7	1.0
Total	8.2	3.0	2.6

Source: BIGresearch

Online Activity

Consumers say they engage in a wide variety of activities when they go online. As shown in Figure 56, the most popular single online activity in mid-2009 is shopping, closely followed by seeking weather information. Given the long list of 25 activities it makes sense to try to understand similarities among them.

FIGURE 56: Participation in Online Activities (June 2009)

	Total
Shopping	38.2
Weather	38.0
Movie reviews/schedules	27.6
View photos from friends	26.3
Sports news & scores	22.9
Research/get ideas for hobbies	21.8
Video games	18.7
Watch TV shows	18.1
Online auctions	16.9
Instant message/chat	15.7
Celebrity gossip	15.1
TV reviews/schedules	14.7
Music news	13.8
Locate old friends/classmates	13.4
Visit video sharing sites (e.g. YouTube)	13.2
Stock market/business news	13.0
Share stories with friends	11.2
Adult entertainment	10.6
Horoscopes/astrology	9.4
Genealogy research	5.9
Fantasy sports	5.9
Gambling	5.1
Get advice from friends	4.7
Online dating	3.3
Virtual world (e.g. Second Life)	1.3

Source: BIGresearch

A factor analysis across the online activity participations yields seven groupings. As shown in Figure 57, the first grouping, "friends," includes such activities as sharing stories with friends, getting advice from friends, viewing photos from friends and locating old friends and classmates. The coefficients show how strongly each activity is associated with the group (1.0 is perfect). The other groups are "news," "video," "features," "search," "adult" and "fantasy." Based upon the online activity groups, particular interests can be used to attract consumers of particular types.

FIGURE 57: FACTOR ANALYSIS OF ONLINE ACTIVITIES (JUNE 2009)

	Friends	News	Video	Features	Search	Adult	Fantasy
Share stories with friends	0.71						
Get advice from friends	0.60						
View photos from friends	0.59						
Locate old friends/classmates	0.50						
Sports news & scores		0.74					
Stock market/business news		0.58					
Visit video sharing sites		0.60					
Watch TV shows			0.57				
Video games				0.57			
Celebrity gossip				0.69			
Horoscopes/astrology				0.52			
Music news					0.46		
Movie reviews/schedules				0.45			
Online auctions					0.60		
Research for hobbies					0.57		
Shopping						0.52	
Weather					0.40		
Online dating						0.74	
Adult entertainment						0.57	
Gambling							0.64
Fantasy sports		0.44					0.48

Source: BIGresearch

FIGURE 58: ONLINE ACTIVITIES BY RETAIL SEGMENTS INDICES (JUNE 2009)

	Twenties	Families	Singles	Pair	Bronze	Silver	Gold
Share stories	117	97	102	93	104	128	109
Get advice from friends	187	98	111	81	92	89	73
View photos from friends	109	105	90	102	86	104	106
Locate old friends	79	126	105	105	69	86	89
Sports news & scores	69	111	109	97	65	76	119
Stock market news	45	93	106	91	48	88	185
Video sharing sites	178	111	113	99	60	57	59
Watch TV shows	146	106	123	99	88	73	71
Video games	146	111	94	102	86	94	70
Celebrity gossip	129	126	114	115	59	46	57
Horoscopes/astrology	120	106	164	107	117	94	61
Music news	134	112	124	108	67	60	57
Movie reviews/schedules	102	116	122	107	63	66	87
Online auctions	80	116	93	114	81	90	97
Research for hobbies	99	110	93	111	88	95	93
Shopping	89	111	114	111	81	92	99
Weather	51	107	101	108	99	114	123
Online dating	115	64	387	94	141	85	46
Adult entertainment	125	93	169	106	63	72	77
Gambling	118	98	102	91	157	102	99
Fantasy sports	125	123	118	97	43	49	60
Genealogy research	52	97	57	83	172	179	156
Instant message/chat	191	99	142	98	83	64	50
TV reviews/schedules	83	102	146	108	116	104	102
Virtual world	260	110	84	73	57	25	48

Source: BIGresearch

Figure 58 shows indices of particular activities by their retail segments. Twenties, for example, are very high on getting advice from friends, video games and watching TV shows online. Families are high among locating old friends and celebrity gossip. Singles are very high on online dating. The older segments are high on genealogy research. While different activities appeal to different retail segments, shopping is, however, reasonably consistent across all segments except the Bronze segment, the older lower-income consumers. It is also interesting to note that Twenties, who are the most active shoppers, index lower on online shopping.

Online Purchasing

About one in four consumers say they regularly shop online (see Figure 59). The rate of regular shopping is highest among Pairs and Gold (the older high income segment). Add to this, the three out of five who say they occasionally shop online, and nearly everyone claims to shop online some of the time.

FIGURE 59: ONLINE PURCHASE FREQUENCY BY RETAIL SEGMENTS (JUNE 2009)

	Twenties	Families	Singles	Pair	Bronze	Silver	Gold	Total
Regularly	21.8	25.6	26.3	31.1	11.3	18.0	30.0	25.1
Occasionally	59.6	60.3	62.2	59.6	64.0	68.5	61.8	60.5

Source: BIGresearch

The middle-aged segments, Families, Singles and Pairs, all show higher rates of regular shopping (see Figure 60). The Gold segment also is higher.

FIGURE 60: MAKING ONLINE PURCHASES BY RETAIL SEGMENTS (JUNE 2009)

	Regularly	Index	Occasionally	Never
Twenties	25.5	93.6	66.8	7.6
Families	29.1	106.6	63.7	7.2
Single	29.2	107.0	61.4	9.4
Pairs	30.2	110.9	61.5	8.3
Bronze	15.2	55.6	67.3	17.5
Silver	19.1	70.0	68.4	12.5
Gold	30.8	112.9	62.5	6.7
Total	27.3	100.0	64.1	8.6

Source: BIGresearch

The overall reported rate of regularly shopping online has increased over the past four years. Figure 61 shows the trend from the last nine SIMM studies. It is interesting that the rate appears to fall every December, but increase every June. The trend, however, is strongly on the upswing.

FIGURE 61: REGULARLY MAKING ONLINE PURCHASES TREND

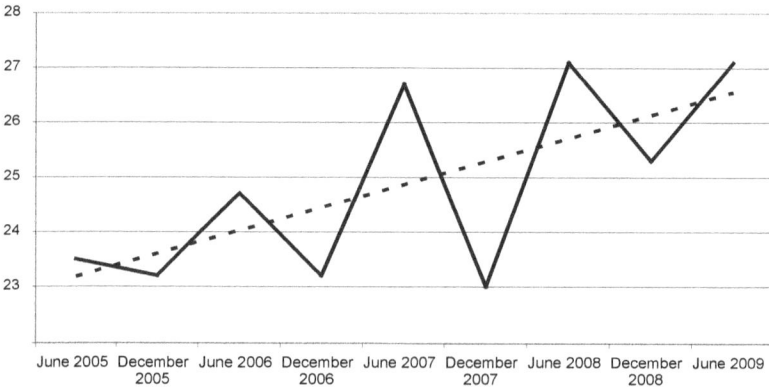

Source: BIGresearch

Search Marketing

Search marketing is a critical tool for the retailer given the relative importance of online shopping. Figure 62 shows the categories of search by retail segments. Overwhelming, the most searched items are maps and directions. This is followed by product information. There are notable differences by retail segment such as the relatively high rates for automobiles among Twenties.

FIGURE 62: CATEGORIES FOR ONLINE SEARCH BY RETAIL SEGMENTS

	Twenties	Families	Singles	Pairs	Bronze	Silver	Gold	Total
Maps/directions	39.4	51.5	43.9	51.3	22.7	38.5	50.9	46.6
Product information	24.3	30.5	29.2	31.8	12.5	20.4	28.8	27.9
Travel	19.7	28.1	24.1	32.2	10.8	20.0	34.6	26.3
Movies	36.0	26.5	23.3	23.0	8.2	14.5	15.9	26.0
Clothing/shoes	30.4	21.2	19.7	19.9	9.3	11.1	13.5	21.5
Sports	22.8	22.5	18.7	19.4	9.1	13.0	20.1	20.6
Online entertainment	36.6	18.6	18.9	15.7	6.2	8.6	7.7	20.6
Restaurants	20.9	20.8	17.3	19.6	7.6	12.2	18.5	19.5
Medical	11.3	12.7	10.1	12.6	11.9	14.5	11.2	12.1
Financial	14.1	10.7	11.3	9.9	6.5	7.5	13.2	11.3
Automobiles/trucks	12.6	8.9	6.0	7.2	3.4	5.4	10.3	9.1
Real estate	9.8	9.5	6.1	8.3	3.7	5.0	5.6	8.5

Source: BIGresearch

There are important differences among potential triggers to online search. As shown in Figure 63, magazines are the leading reported trigger. TV and newspaper are also important triggers. Online communities and blogs, except among the Twenties segment, are relatively unimportant triggers.

FIGURE 63: SEARCH TRIGGERS BY RETAIL SEGMENTS

	Twenties	Families	Singles	Pairs	Bronze	Silver	Gold	Total
Magazine	37.5	42.3	42.6	46.9	30.0	41.3	50.2	42.1
Read an article	28.8	38.4	43.0	45.5	33.1	45.4	49.4	38.6
TV/broadcast	31.9	37.9	42.8	43.5	32.0	42.3	41.9	37.8
Newspaper	25.7	37.3	36.9	41.2	33.7	46.6	49.1	36.4
Coupons	32.2	38.0	30.3	37.4	29.2	35.0	31.1	34.8
Face to face	38.5	31.1	34.9	34.0	19.3	25.2	28.5	32.8
Cable TV	40.7	30.5	32.3	32.3	25.2	25.1	25.5	32.4
Radio	28.1	30.4	28.8	31.0	12.7	22.3	28.8	28.7
Direct mail	23.2	27.7	24.8	29.5	26.3	31.3	28.9	26.7
Advertising inserts	18.6	25.4	22.2	25.0	15.6	25.1	23.1	23.0
E-mail advertising	23.9	23.9	22.7	22.6	19.5	21.3	20.9	22.8
In-store promotions	24.2	23.1	19.9	22.9	22.1	23.1	18.6	22.5
Internet advertising	26.3	20.5	21.1	20.4	15.6	17.2	17.2	21.0
Outdoor billboard	13.6	11.2	8.6	9.7	5.1	7.7	7.5	10.5
Online communities	21.4	7.5	7.7	6.2	4.5	4.3	1.9	9.8
Blogs	14.3	5.5	7.1	5.1	3.4	2.7	4.0	7.3
Yellow pages	6.5	4.9	6.4	5.0	8.5	6.7	6.3	5.7
Instant messaging	14.7	3.0	3.2	2.6	4.0	3.1	1.6	5.6
Cell phone	11.8	2.7	3.0	1.9	2.5	1.5	1.0	4.5
Text messaging	8.8	2.0	2.0	1.1	2.3	1.5	0.8	3.3
Picture/video phone	7.9	1.8	1.9	1.0	2.0	1.1	0.6	3.0

Source: BIGresearch

The product categories searched also vary considerably (see Figure 64). Electronics is the dominant product category searched for, followed by apparel, appliances, shoes, and food and groceries. Cars and trucks are far down the list. No doubt, some of the differences seen can be attributed to the purchase frequency within the category, although appliances ranks fairly high, which may be a function of the complexity of the product category.

FIGURE 64 PRODUCT CATEGORIES SEARCHED BY RETAIL SEGMENTS

	Twenties	Families	Singles	Pairs	Bronze	Silver	Gold	Total
Electronics	48.8	47.9	42.5	46.6	22.7	36.5	46.7	46.2
Apparel	36.4	31.1	26.7	29.5	14.4	22.7	25.6	30.6
Appliances	23.5	27.0	18.0	25.2	12.2	18.1	27.6	24.7
Shoes	28.1	21.3	18.2	19.0	11.3	15.2	17.1	21.3
Food/groceries	20.3	22.2	22.9	22.7	15.6	18.0	17.8	21.1
Home improvement	13.3	23.4	17.1	25.7	10.5	20.8	27.2	20.9
Beauty care	22.1	19.0	17.3	18.1	8.5	13.8	12.3	18.3
Medicines	14.5	18.4	18.6	19.6	18.1	21.6	20.8	18.0
Home decor	14.9	13.8	11.6	15.7	7.6	9.1	10.5	13.6
Sporting goods	14.0	14.3	9.2	11.0	4.8	7.4	12.6	12.6
Tires/batteries	10.8	14.6	10.6	12.3	8.5	10.7	13.1	12.6
Car/truck	13.9	13.2	7.3	10.8	5.1	9.1	13.5	12.2
Furniture	14.5	12.8	10.3	11.6	4.5	6.8	8.6	12.0
Jewelry/watches	15.0	11.0	9.3	9.8	6.2	6.6	8.7	11.1
House/land	6.5	4.8	3.6	3.7	2.8	2.0	3.8	4.6

Source: BIGresearch

Online search, interestingly, drives face to face and e-mail communication (see Figure 65). While, online communities and blogs remain a small post-search activity for all segments except the Twenties.

FIGURE 65: POST-SEARCH COMMUNICATION BY RETAIL SEGMENTS

	Twenties	Families	Singles	Pairs	Bronze	Silver	Gold	Total
Face to face	66.0	68.3	68.2	70.6	48.2	62.0	66.0	66.9
E-mail	41.9	50.6	49.1	52.7	41.9	50.5	53.3	48.6
Telephone	33.9	43.2	42.8	45.0	48.4	53.0	47.6	42.0
Cell phone	39.3	24.0	23.3	21.8	13.3	14.8	18.0	26.0
Instant messaging	27.7	8.4	9.0	7.8	9.9	5.0	3.1	12.3
Text messaging	25.6	9.0	8.8	7.5	3.4	3.5	2.8	11.7
Online communities	21.4	6.3	5.8	5.5	3.4	2.7	1.7	9.0
Blogging	10.7	3.5	3.1	2.4	2.8	1.3	1.5	4.7

Source: BIGresearch

Chapter

8

Understanding Customer Store Loyalty

Customer store loyalty is a critical issue for any retailer. Long-term retail success generally comes from having a core group of customers who shop at the retail outlet time after time. In this chapter, we will look at store loyalty in two ways. First, store loyalty in terms of the consumer's purchase purposes and interactions. Those were identified in Chapter 3 as stock up, one bag, leisure, special and eating out. Then, we discuss an alternative view of loyalty based on a combination of CIA, SIMM and Shopper Mindset data. This utilizes a new analytic technique that separates shoppers into four categories, Loyals, Gains, Losses and Prospects, which track their actual shopping behaviors. We start first with the data from the Shopper Mindset study that provides a consumer view of store loyalty in terms of satisfaction with shopping experiences in retail locations.

I. Customer Reported Store Loyalty and Satisfaction

In the SIMM studies, store loyalty is captured on a five-point scale, with 1 being very loyal and 5 not being loyal at all. As shown in Figure 66, the overall average store loyalty to the store shopped on the last trip is 1.8. A similar five-point scale is used to measure the satisfaction with last shopping trip, with 5 being very satisfied. Overall, the consumer shopping satisfaction level is quite high, at 4.3. Thus, we might say there is fairly high loyalty and satisfaction with the stores at which consumers shopped in these two SIMM waves. Also shown in the figure is the number of stores visited on the last trip, with the overall average being 1.4.

As shown, shoppers claim a higher loyalty to stores on stock up or one bag trips and, consequently, lower store loyalty for the other types. Satisfaction is reported to be about the same by type of trip. As might be expected, those shoppers on a leisure time trip report visiting more stores probably looking for variety.

FIGURE 66: LOYALTY, SATISFACTION AND STORES VISITED BY TRIP TYPE (MEAN OF FIVE-POINT SCALE)

	Stock Up	One Bag	Leisure	Special	Eating Out	Total
Loyalty (1=very loyal)	1.7	1.6	2.1	2.0	2.0	1.8
Satisfaction (5=very satistifed)	4.4	4.4	4.2	4.3	4.3	4.3
Stores (number shopped)	1.5	1.3	2.1	1.5	1.4	1.4

Source: BIGresearch

The class of trade with highest reported loyalty, as shown in Figure 67, is the grocery store (1= most loyal). Yet, satisfaction is not the highest (5=very satistifed), whereas, convenience stores have lower loyalty but higher satisfaction. The classes of trade with the lowest loyalty are department stores, electronics stores, specialty stores and office supply stores, which is also reflected in the satisfaction scores. Organic grocery stores show the highest satisfaction. Dining restaurants overall have the lowest satisfaction.

FIGURE 67: LOYALTY, SATISFACTION AND STORES VISITED BY CLASS OF TRADE

	Loyalty	Satisfaction
Convenience store	1.8	4.7
Department store	2.2	4.3
Discount store	1.8	4.3
Dollar store	1.7	4.3
Drugstore	1.8	4.3
Grocery store	1.6	4.4
Organic grocery store	1.8	4.8
Electronics/office supply	2.2	4.4
Home improvement store	2.0	4.5
Membership warehouse	2.1	4.4
Dining restaurants	2.0	3.8
Quick service restaurants	1.8	4.2
Specialty store	2.2	4.3
Total	1.8	4.3

Source: BIGresearch

Comparing the class of trade and store loyalty yields some interesting interactions. Figure 68 shows the percent saying they are very satisfied with last trip by class of trade and loyalty.

Those classes of trade that seem to enjoy the highest satisfaction levels among their loyal customers are restaurants, drugstores, department stores, dollar stores, specialty stores and membership warehouse stores. Home improvement stores, discount stores, consumer electronics, and office supply stores have lower satisfaction, especially among those who say they are not very loyal.

FIGURE 68: PERCENT SATISFIED WITH LAST SHOPPING TRIP BY CLASS OF TRADE AND STORE LOYALTY

	Very Loyal	Others	Total
Dollar store, specialty store, membership warehouse, other	76.3	59.6	64.1
Quick service restaurants, dining restaurants	79.5	56.4	62.2
Grocery store, organic grocery store	70.6	52.2	62.0
Drugstores	77.1	51.8	61.5
Department store	75.0	55.0	56.4
Home improvement store, discount store, consumer electronics, office supply	61.2	45.8	52.3
No preference, online retail	45.2	25.9	34.6
Total	68.1	51.4	58.5

Source: BIGresearch

With this overview of what consumers say about how they view store loyalty, we now turn to a different view, that of what consumers actually do in terms of their store loyalty behaviors.

II. Building Consumer Demonstrated Behavioral Loyalty

Traditional methods of creating or improving store loyalty have often revolved around some type of reward system based on either sales volume or store patronage. For the most part, these programs have been based on an "after-the-fact" analysis. That is, the consumer is rewarded after the shopping experience. There have been few approaches that have attempted to identify consumer behaviors in an integrated way, namely, how and in what way consumers have, through their behaviors, demonstrated their store loyalty.

A unique feature of the BIGresearch data is that the three databases — the CIA, SIMM and Shopper Mindset data — can be merged to provide a unique view of consumer loyalty based on their media usage, something not possible even with the most sophisticated media management or point-of-sale analytical systems.

As discussed in Chapter 1, BIGresearch conducts a monthly study of consumers — where they shopped, what they purchased, what they intend purchasing in the future, and so on. From that data, we have identified the communities consumers have created by their behaviors. It is now possible to marry that purchase data with the simultaneous media usage data found in the SIMM database. Because the CIA data is essentially panel data, that is, the same customers report on their purchases and intentions over time, it is possible to identify various types and forms of customer loyalty. In the sections below, a simplified approach to understanding consumer loyalty is illustrated.

A. Customer Classifications Based on Shopping Behaviors

In the figures that follow, we have taken two SIMM data sets and identified customers for a major mass merchandising organization. In the first SIMM data set (June 2007), we have noted which of the respondents said they shopped at the specific retailer. Those shoppers were then compared with those who said they shopped with the retailer in the subsequent SIMM report (December 2007). When the consumer shopped with the retailer in both CIA studies, we classified them as Loyals. If they shopped at the retailer in the first CIA study but not the second, they were termed Losses (that is, the retailer lost the customer in the subsequent CIA study). Where the shopper did not purchase at the identified retailer in the first CIA study but did in the second, we have classified them as Gains — they are either new or returning customers. Those consumers who did not shop at the specified retailer in either of the two CIA studies are considered Prospects, since we know from the CIA studies that they purchased in the category during the time period, but not at the specified retailer. Thus, we have another customer aggregation or set of consumer communities: Loyals, Gains, Losses and Prospects. We use this consumer community development approach to discuss the media consumption habits for this particular retailer. We believe these consumer communities provide unique insights into what shoppers are doing across the marketplace, not merely what they are doing in one store or with one retailer.

B. Media Behaviors

As we did with the previous seven retail segments, we investigate customer loyalty based on media usage by customer status in minutes per day (see Figure 69).

In Figure 69, we have shown the top twelve media forms from the thirty-one in the SIMM studies. The first noticeable difference is that these media forms are not the same as those in the "seven communities" approach shown earlier. Three types of radio appear in the most used media category — regular broadcast radio, satellite radio and Web radio. Further, few of the promotional media forms such as coupons and inserts are among those most widely used by these groups. Television, e-mail and the Internet are heavily used by these consumers and there is quite a drop off to the next medium, which is broadcast radio.

FIGURE 69: MEDIA CONSUMPTION BY CUSTOMER STATUS
AVERAGE MINUTES PER DAY

	Prospect	Loss	Gain	Loyal	Total
TV	122.4	125.9	146.3	148.8	135.0
E-mail	118.0	118.7	122.2	122.1	120.1
Internet	112.4	113.5	123.7	122.7	117.8
Broadcast radio	71.8	71.2	70.8	75.5	72.1
Direct	55.5	55.5	57.8	57.0	56.4
Magazines	53.0	52.2	49.8	50.0	51.4
Newspaper	48.2	49.1	45.5	47.0	47.5
Instant Message	34.3	35.5	35.2	34.3	34.8
Video game	31.0	30.6	36.6	36.6	33.5
Blog	21.0	21.2	21.8	21.2	21.3
Satellite radio	21.6	22.4	15.8	16.4	19.2
Web radio	13.3	12.3	10.7	11.3	12.0

Source: BIGresearch

The other major finding is the big difference between the amount of media consumption by Loyals and Prospects. Loyals are generally much heavier users of all media forms than are the Prospect group. The same also appears to be true with the Gain and Loss groups. Gains spend more time with media than do the Losses.

One of the key elements in this type of media usage analysis is the ability of the retailer and the firm's manufacturer partners to compare the media plan being used with the importance the various groups give the media form. For example, if the retailer were to review the most recent media plan and determine that it had invested heavily in television, that might explain how it reached Loyal customers and what we have termed the Gains, but it would conclude that the investment was not as effective with the Losses group. Thus, being able to adjust media plans based on these consumer categories and the communities the consumers have created through their behavior could help the retailer and manufacturer initially develop and also fine-tune their media allocations.

C. Indexing Media Usage

This media usage analysis can be taken to the next step, by creating an index of the customer status media usage data (see Figure 70).

FIGURE 70: MEDIA USAGE BY CUSTOMER STATUS INDEX

	Prospect	Loss	Gain	Loyal
Coupons	96.9	97.5	102.1	104.7
Inserts	92.2	91.7	106.4	112.4
TV	91.8	90.3	107.5	113.3
Newspaper	99.3	98.4	103.1	99.0
Direct	94.5	94.7	105.9	106.4
In-store	91.4	91.0	107.6	112.8
Magazines	101.2	100.8	98.1	99.8
Cable TV	94.6	90.6	106.7	109.9
E-mail	96.4	95.9	101.7	107.6
Internet	93.3	94.2	105.3	109.3

Source: BIGresearch

Once this index has been created, it is easy to see that Prospects are heavier users of magazines, newspapers and lighter users of television and video games than average. Among the Losses group, the favored media forms are magazines and newspapers. Those media forms scoring lower with this group is television. Among the Loyals group, the favored media forms are television and Internet and the less favored media forms are Web. This type of data should be very helpful to both manufacturers and retailers in developing their media programs based on the type of customer they want to reach.

D. Media Influence

In the next two figures, we have conducted the same type of analysis only looking at the media influence by customer status and then, for ease of use, creating an index for that media influence. For a large retailer customers were asked to report their first choice. A Prospect is a customer that for two time periods selected another retailer. A loss is a customer who selected the retailer in time period one, but not two. A gain is a customer who selected another retailer in period one, but the retailer in question in pertiod two. The loyal customer selected the retailer both times.

Figure 71 shows the media influence by customer status for the top ten media forms found in the SIMM data.

FIGURE 71: MEDIA INFLUENCE BY CUSTOMER STATUS

	Prospect	Loss	Gain	Loyal	Total
Coupons	25.7	25.8	27.1	27.8	26.5
Inserts	22.0	21.9	25.4	26.8	23.8
TV	18.0	17.7	21.1	22.2	19.6
Newspaper	18.9	18.7	19.6	18.8	19.0
Direct	18.0	18.0	20.2	20.2	19.0
In-store	17.2	17.1	20.2	21.2	18.8
Magazines	17.0	16.9	16.5	16.8	16.8
Cable TV	11.6	11.1	13.1	13.5	12.3
E-mail	10.4	10.3	10.9	11.6	10.7
Internet	9.8	9.9	11.0	11.4	10.5

Source: BIGresearch

The first thing one notices in Figure 71 is the larger number of media forms than appeared in previous analyses. That's because consumers are saying, "These are the media forms that influence me," not only how much time they spend with them. Thus, some media forms could be quite influential, yet, not account for a large amount of media consumption time by the consumer, for example, using the Internet or search engines.

The second thing is the re-appearance of word of mouth (WOM) when influence is involved. WOM, with the exception of perhaps social media, is not something to which people devote a great deal of their time, at least not their shopping time. However, even social media often comes in bits and pieces and, while perhaps very influential on consumer purchase decisions, does not normally consume a great deal of time, the way more traditional media forms do. The third noticeable thing is that coupons, inserts and read an article (PR), along with WOM rank as high or higher than all traditional media forms. Again, the question of the believability of advertising rears its ugly head.

FIGURE 72: MEDIA INFLUENCE BY CUSTOMER STATUS INDEXED

	Prospect	Loss	Gain	Loyal
Coupons	96.9	97.5	102.1	104.7
Inserts	92.2	91.7	106.4	112.4
TV	91.8	90.3	107.5	113.3
Newspaper	99.3	98.4	103.1	99.0
Direct	94.5	94.7	105.9	106.4
In-store	91.4	91.0	107.6	112.8
Magazines	101.2	100.8	98.1	99.8
CableTV	94.6	90.6	106.7	109.9
E-mail	96.4	95.9	101.7	107.6
Internet	93.3	94.2	105.3	109.3

Source: BIGresearch

The other interesting thing about the data is the big differences in media influence among the four customer communities—Loyals, Gains, Losses and Prospects. That becomes more evident in Figure 72 above, which shows the media influence by customer status indexed. The indexing of the media forms by influence is quite revealing. For example, Loyal customers say almost all the media forms have some influence on them with the exception of blogs and perhaps text messaging. All the rest are either on par or above in terms of their influence. Thus, it is clear that Loyal customers, for this retail firm, are acquainted with the various media forms and rely on them extensively. In fact, we might say, they are skilled and experienced shoppers.

Alternatively, Prospect customers index higher only on magazines. By the same token, television, in-store, product placement and yellow pages rate much below average. Thus, it would seem that a media plan designed to hold on to present Loyal customers would not have much impact in attracting Prospects; something not often considered by retailers.

Similarly, when we look at Loss and Gain customers, we begin to see a pattern as well. Loss customers index much lower on overall media influence with only magazine about average. Thus, it appears that this group of people could not be effectively or efficiently reached with traditional media programs. Something else would likely be needed.

Gain customers are quite different. They index highly on almost all media forms, particularly product placement, in-store and inserts. Thus, it would seem that these are real shoppers who make use of the retail offers being developed by the merchants as much or more than they rely on traditional media activities.

E. No Single Media Plan Fits All

What is clear is that there are media preferences and differences in terms of media influence among the four identified groups from the CIA and SIMM data. More emphatically than ever, we can say that there is no one media plan that fits everyone, either mass or targeted. Thus, we can summarize by saying that to develop effective marketing communication and promotional plans prior to the customer entering the store, the manufacturer and retailer both must know a great deal more about consumers than has been assumed in the past. Fortunately, emerging data, such as that found in the CIA and SIMM databases, is beginning to become more available. Through the use of that type of data, marketers can begin to improve their external-to-the-store investment and return strategies.

Chapter

9

Environmental Factors in Retailing

Retail businesses are strongly influenced by the prevailing economic climate and consumer attitudes that people generate toward their own personal situation. The external environment, particularly the economy in the broadest sense of the word such as employment rates, ability to pay debt and mortgages, have a major impact on how people feel, what they do and their purchasing behaviors in retail outlets.

In this chapter, three major external factors that impact retail sales and profits are discussed:

1. The economic climate and consumers' perceptions of whether the economy and their own personal situation will change in the months ahead.

2. Competitive factors such as what other retailers are doing in the marketplace.

3. Forecasting or the ability of the retailer and marketing partners to pull all these various views and situations together to develop some type of informed decision calculus going forward.

Much of the following discussion will be on the first two elements — the economic climate and the competition. We can reasonably conclude that if retailers and their manufacturer partners do not understand the global economic situations, which are changing at lightning speed in the current marketplace, forecasting is all but impossible. Thus, while we recognize the need for forecasting — much of which can be found using the CIA data — we wish to focus here on the economy and competition, and leave a detailed discussion of forecasting for another text.

In terms of the competitive framework, we will focus our comments at the strategic level. While much retailer attention is focused on the actions and activities of competitors — what they are doing, what they are saying, how they are operating in the marketplace — if the customer view is taken in developing retailing programs, as we do in this text, competitors become less important in the overall operations of a retail firm. This is not to say competitors are unimportant. It is only to stress the fact that retailers have no control over what competitors do or don't do. Therefore, our research would indicate that a clear, concise, finely tuned, customer-focused retail strategy directed towards an identified group of consumers can obviate much competitive activity.

With these two provisos in mind, we move to a discussion of how consumer-focused research can provide the impetus needed to develop effective retail marketing programs.

I. The Importance of Consumer Data and Understanding

As has been stressed throughout this text, it is the consumers and the communities they create that matter. It makes no difference what the economic climate is. An external store focus is critical. The economy should also be taken as an external environment situation. It is there. The retailer has little control over it. So, reorganize both and plan accordingly.

A. Trending Consumer Confidence Data Is the Key

BIGresearch, in its monthly CIA survey, measures perceptions and attitudes toward the economic climate and consumer plans and intentions that develop as a result of those perceptions. A series of questions has been asked in the CIA studies since May 2007. These questions give a time series view of U.S. consumer attitudes and perceptions about the economy, which can then be related directly to their retail purchasing behaviors and plans. The information used in the analysis that follows consists of twenty months of data, from May 2007 through December 2008.

Figure 73 shows the trend in the U.S. consumer's perception of the chances for a strong national economy going forward. A score of four represents "very confident," therefore, the lower the number, the less overall confidence. The trend for the last twenty months shows a steady decline, that's the solid line in the chart below. The dotted line reflects the overall linear trend over the period.

FIGURE 73: Chances for a Strong Economy
(4=Very Confident, 3=Confident, 2=Little Confidence, 1=No Confidence)

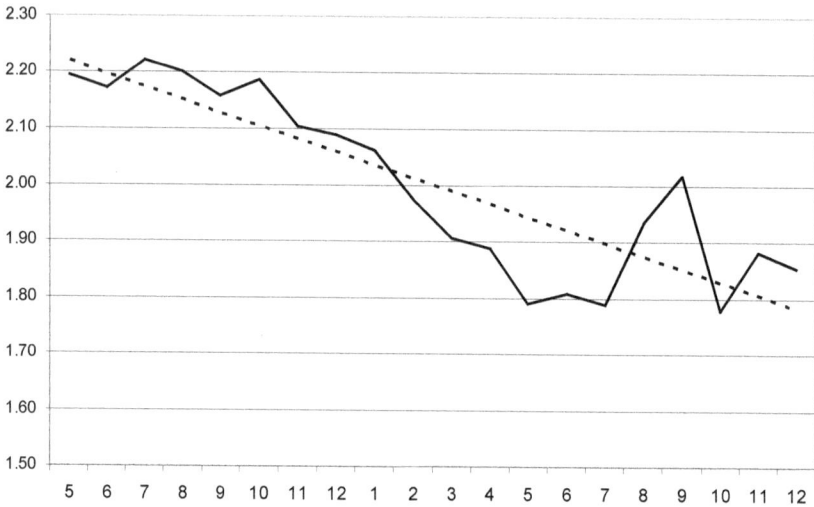

Source: BIGresearch

This does not present a very pretty picture for any type of retailer. When confidence goes down, consumer purchasing generally goes down with it and retail follows the same pattern.

Looking at the chart, some things appear obvious. The months between February and August 2008 (periods 2 through 7 on the right-hand side of the chart) likely reflect consumer reaction to the rapidly rising gasoline prices in the U.S. during that period. The drop in October 2008 (period 10 on the right-hand side of the chart), likely reflects the initial stages of the quickly developing recession. We suspect the data for the first half of 2009 has continued that downward trend.

The confidence levels vary by the retail consumer communities created from the Shopper Mindset data (described in earlier chapters). Figure 74 shows the confidence level is higher among the Twenties community (mean=2.08), the older, higher income Gold (mean=2.10) and Silver (mean=2.04) groups. It is interesting that the lowest confidence levels are mainly among the younger groups—Pairs, Singles and Families — perhaps because they have been most immediately impacted by the economic downturn. But it is the lower-income Bronze group that has the most pessimistic view of all.

While this consumer confidence material is useful, the real question is: what is the marketplace reaction of the consumer communities based on these economic views and perceptions?

FIGURE 74: CONFIDENCE IN ECONOMY BY RETAIL SEGMENTS

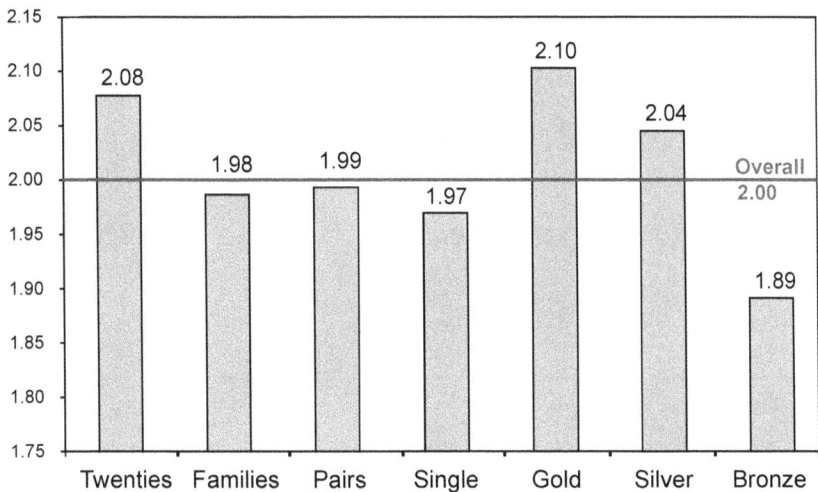

Source: BIGresearch

B. Changing Consumer Behaviors Due to Confidence Levels

One of the most clear-cut reactions of consumers to a perceived decline of confidence in the economy is to defer purchases. This phenomenon is discussed in the following paragraphs.

Over the last twenty months, as confidence in the economy has generally declined, consumers have reported different levels of planned purchase deferrals in different product categories — some quite dramatic, others less so.

Figure 75 shows that going out to eat is the highest deferred purchase among all consumer communities. Nearly 57% of all Shopper Mindset respondents said they planned to defer or delay going out to eat in the next thirty days—making it their most immediate reported reaction to the changes in the economy. Vacation travel also takes a hit as a result of declining confidence. Almost half of the Shopper Mindset respondents said they planned to defer vacation travel in the next thirty days. Deferring automobile purchases, as a money-conserving choice, was relatively low. No doubt, the level of this response is impacted because only a low proportion of the Shopper Mindset panel would be considering an automobile purchase at all in any given thirty-day period. However, we can see that short-term purchase deferral is a common consumer response to consumers' views of a worsening economy.

FIGURE 75: PERCENT DEFERRING PURCHASE IN THE NEXT 30 DAYS BY PRODUCT CATEGORY

	Percent
Going out to eat	56.7
Vacation travel	48.3
Home improvement projects	41.8
Entertainment	41.2
Apparel	39.7
Electronics	36.4
Auto purchases	23.7

Source: BIGresearch

Short-term planned purchase deferral rates generally vary over time based on the differing levels of consumer confidence in the U.S. economy. Figure 76 shows the twenty-month trends for six consumer purchase categories.

In general, the levels of planned deferrals increase for all categories during the time confidence is declining. That was previously shown in Figure 73. Vacation travel deferral plans seem to have occurred the most in the last few months of the reported data, though it had been falling during other periods as well. Perhaps there had been some sort of "get away" mentality earlier that had grown with declining consumer confidence. At some point, however, it appears to hit a reality check that says, "This is a serious situation," and the spigot got turned off.

As shown, apparel sales are also beginning to decline substantially near the end of the reporting period, which likely has something to do with the "make do" feelings that seem to have started in almost all consumer communities.

It is also interesting that eating out leads all categories in terms of deferrals. This consumer choice exhibits a volatile pattern during the entire data set, lending further credence to the notion that dining out is considered a non-essential by almost all consumer communities.

FIGURE 76: PERCENT DEFERING PURCHASE BY MONTH BY SELECTED PRODUCT CATEGORY

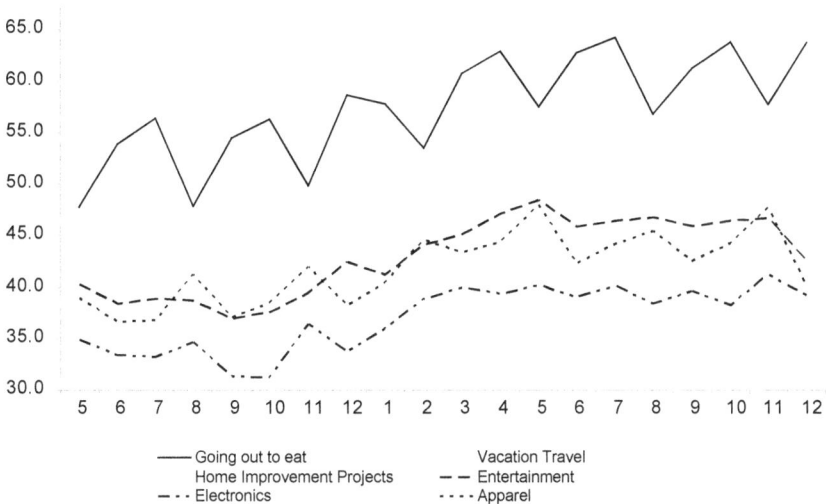

Source: BIGresearch

A better way to illustrate the relationship between consumer confidence and purchase deferral is through the average change (illustrated
by the unstandardized regression coefficients), as shown in Figure 77.

In that calculation, the results show that going out to eat has an
average monthly change of .44%. This is the highest average increase. :
It is followed by the electronics category, which includes DVDs, CDs
and videos, at .35%. While all categories increase, these are the two
highest rates of planned short-term deferral found in the data set. The
lowest categories are auto purchases, home improvement projects and
apparel.

All of the product categories have a negative linear correlation
with the confidence in the economy ratings. That means, as confidence
declines, planned short-term deferrals increase. That is clearly evident
in Figure 77. Those categories most associated with an impact of
change in confidence in the economy are those that are relatively low
cost and frequently purchased, and, as shown, include entertainment,
electronics and going out to eat.

FIGURE 77: CHANGE IN SHORT-TERM PURCHASE DEFERRAL
BY PRODUCT CATEGORY AND ASSOCIATION WITH
CONFIDENCE IN THE ECONOMY

	Percent	Correlation	Change
Going out to eat	56.7	−0.73	0.44
Vacation travel	48.3	−0.44	0.23
Home improvement projects	41.8	−0.65	0.13
Entertainment	41.2	−0.82	0.27
Apparel	39.7	−0.52	0.15
Electronics	36.4	−0.86	0.35
Auto purchases	23.7	−0.45	0.07

Source: BIGresearch

C. Longer Term Product Purchase Deferrals

Longer-term purchase deferrals, that is, within the next ninety days, show a slightly different pattern. Figure 78 illustrates that the more expensive items—such as home furniture, sporting goods, linens and apparel—are near the top of the list, whereas, they were further down the list in the short term. Going out to eat was at the top of the short-term list at 56.7%, but falls to the middle of the long-term list at 44.6%. Categories such as health and beauty aids and groceries are at the very bottom of the long-term deferral calculation. These categories, we can conclude, have a "sustenance nature" for the consumer. They simply can't be deferred for too long, no matter what the economic outlook.

Three shopping categories shown on the Figure 78 list deserve special attention. As shown, the most commonly deferred types of purchasing behaviors are TV home shopping at 49.6%, followed by catalog shopping at 43.4%. Internet shopping, however, is almost at the bottom of list—it is planned to be deferred by only 28.5% of respondents. Thus, there clearly is a primary difference in the minds of consumers between home/catalog shopping and Internet shopping. It may well be that the first two are considered optional, while the Internet is being used to gather information to make more informed shopping decisions or to take advantage of short-term promotional offers.

It is worth noting that 16.1% of Shopper Mindset respondents say they plan to purchase more on the Internet, which is the highest level of planned increase. Again, the anomaly of what consumers believe can be delayed and what they plan to do becomes apparent.

Interestingly, home improvement and children's apparel are the two other areas where double-digit increases are found, which doubtless reflects the inward-turning nature of consumers as the economy becomes more challenging.

FIGURE 78: PERCENT 90-DAY PLANNED PURCHASE DEFERRAL BY PRODUCT CATEGORY

	Less	Same	More
Decorative home furnishings	54.7	38.7	6.6
Home furniture	54.3	36.5	9.2
Sporting goods	51.3	45.1	3.5
Linens/bedding/draperies	51.0	44.5	4.5
TV home shopping	49.6	46.4	4.0
Women's dress	48.7	46.4	4.9
Electronics	48.6	43.6	7.8
Men's dress	48.5	47.3	4.2
Toys	45.8	44.4	9.9
Candy	45.3	51.1	3.6
Home improvement and hardware supplies	44.7	47.9	10.8
Lawn and garden supplies	44.7	46.1	9.2
Going out to eat	44.6	52.0	3.5
Catalogue shopping	43.4	50.8	5.8
CDs/DVDs/videos/books	42.4	52.0	5.6
Women's casual	40.1	54.5	5.4
Men's casual	39.0	56.3	4.8
Shoes	38.3	55.4	6.3
Children's apparel	31.7	53.1	15.2
Beer/wine/alcohol	30.1	64.6	5.3
Internet shopping	28.5	55.4	16.1
Health and beauty aids	22.5	75.0	2.5
Groceries	17.3	74.2	8.5

Source: BIGresearch

II. Changes in Shopping Attitudes

Planned changes in purchasing behaviors are often reflected in the attitudes consumers report in the Shopper Mindset data.

Consumers say that there are a number of adjustments they plan to make in response to their declining confidence in the economy. Figure 79 shows the highest levels of agreement on (a) buying what is needed, (b) being practical and (c) being more budget conscious. We can also deduce that lifestyle changes, in response to declining confidence in the economy, are becoming more prevalent as well, for example, eating more home-cooked meals, being more environmentally responsible, shopping less at malls and reordering priorities in daily life. We see that three top areas dominate consumer responses in the Shopper Mindset questionnaire: needs versus wants, purchasing practicality and budget consciousnesses.

FIGURE 79: PERCENT AGREEMENT WITH PURCHASE ATTITUDE ITEMS

	Percent
I focus more on what I need rather than what I want	59.4
I have become more practical in my purchases	49.6
I have become more budget conscious	45.0
I worry more about political issues	26.8
I have become more conscious about food safety	24.3
I am spending more time with my family	22.5
I have not made any changes	20.6
I have reordered priorities in my daily life	19.6
I am shopping less at malls	14.9
I am spending more money on decorating my home	8.5
I have become more environmentally responsible	7.3
I am eating home-cooked meals more often	5.5
I have become more impulsive in my purchases	2.4

Source: BIGresearch

The apparel category provides some interesting additional insights. Figure 80 shows the change in the percent of those saying that they buy familiar labels when buying clothing compared with the general level of confidence in the economy. Broadly, as the confidence in the economy has declined, the proportion saying they buy familiar labels has increased. The relationship looks especially strong toward the end of the survey period.

FIGURE 80: PERCENT BUYING FAMILIAR APPAREL LABELS VS CONFIDENCE IN THE ECONOMY

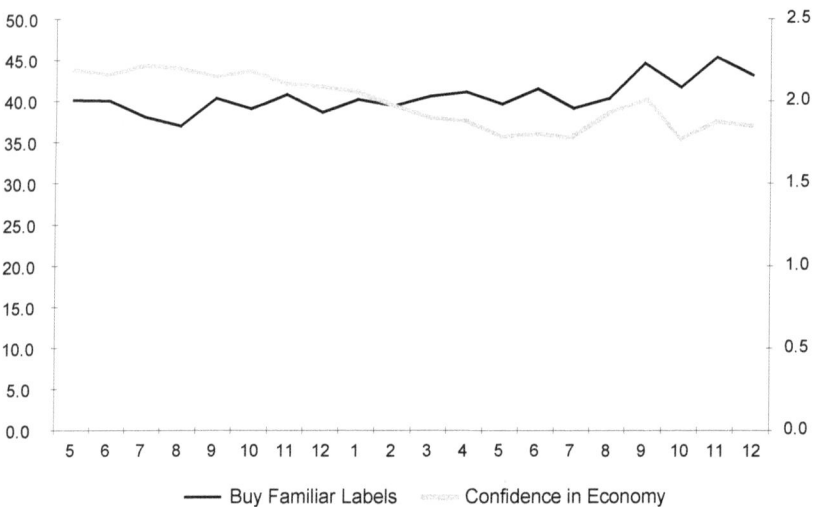

Source: BIGresearch

Figure 81 shows a similar relationship between confidence in the economy and the proportion of consumers saying they always buy apparel on sale. The rising "buying on sale" response appears to indicate a greater concern for (low) price, as might be expected from the shopper attitudes shown in Figure 79, in response to the declining confidence levels. Again, the relationship looks especially strong in the most recent months.

FIGURE 81: PERCENT ALWAYS BUYING APPAREL ON SALE VS CONFIDENCE IN THE ECONOMY

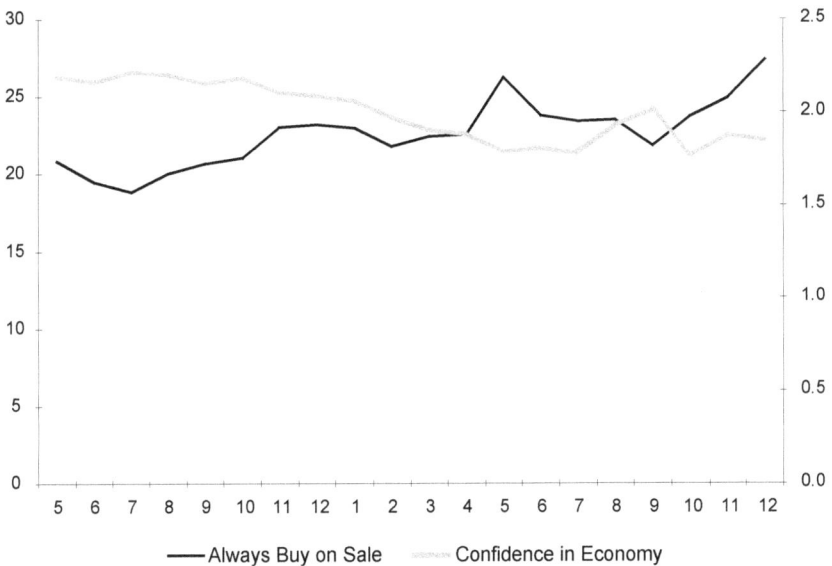

——Always Buy on Sale   Confidence in Economy

Source: BIGresearch

In the apparel category, at least, the downturn in the economy impacts buying clothing on sale and buying familiar labels. Figure 82 shows a strong correlation, -.79, with buying clothes only when on sale and confidence in the economy. A moderate correlation is shown with buying familiar labels, -.46. Other apparel-related attitudes — such as the newest styles being important, preferring a traditional conservative look and fashion being important — are much less associated with the change in confidence in the economy.

FIGURE 82: SELECTED APPAREL-RELATED ATTITUDES AND CONFIDENCE IN THE ECONOMY

	Percent	Correlation
Familiar labels are important to me	40.6	−0.46
Newest styles are important to me	8.5	0.17
Prefer a traditional conservative look	33.8	−0.26
Fashion is less important than value	57.7	0.15
I only buy clothing when on sale	22.5	−0.79

Source: BIGresearch

With this view of how consumers react to the external economic environment, we now turn briefly to retail competition.

III. The Impact of Retail Competition

A proxy for retail competition is the relative concentration among retail classes of trade in a particular product category. Relative concentration within a category can be estimated using what is called a Herfindahl index (sum of the squares of proportions that can be extracted from the Shopper Mindset data).

For example, the proportion of shoppers selecting a discount store could also be seen as a proxy for interest in value and price. The proportion selecting "no preference" within a product category might also be a proxy for manufacturer brand strength or loyalty, that is, the retailer becomes less important as more confidence is placed in national brands and their availability. A no preference choice might also be interpreted as being indifferent to the retailer or even that the consumer is in a store-switching mode.

Figure 83 shows the trends in retail class of trade preferences in the grocery product category. The grocery store is the leading category and shows a slight increase in preference during the survey period. Discount stores also show a similar increase over the twenty-month survey period. The no preference category, however, declines. This means that consumers are saying they are relying more on known classes of trade — here, on the grocery store and the discount store — rather than on the presence of national brands. Other product categories in the Shopper Mindset data show similar patterns.

FIGURE 83: CLASS OF TRADE PREFERENCE FOR THE GROCERY CATEGORY

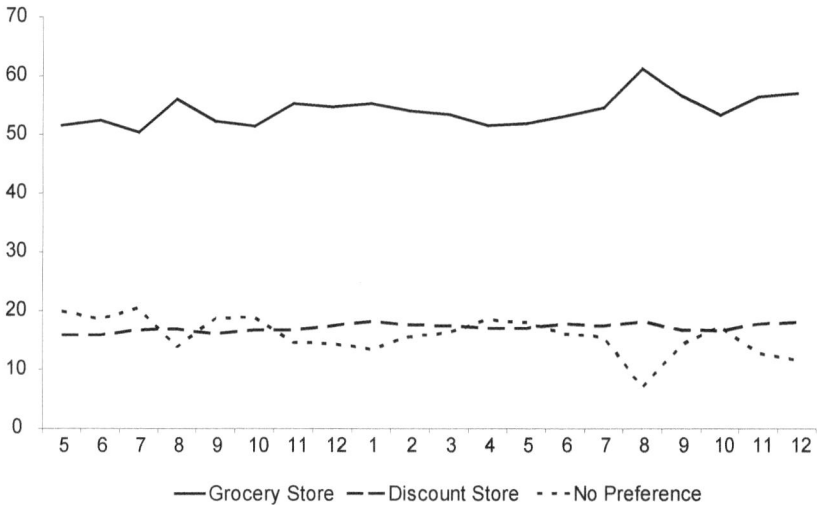

Grocery Store — — Discount Store - - -No Preference

Source: BIGresearch

The pattern of trade categories varies considerably by product category. Figure 84 shows that 54% of the grocery product category sales are through a grocery store, in other words, few products generally purchased in a grocery store are purchased somewhere else.

A relatively concentrated category is home improvement, with 65% of all volume sold through specialty stores. Children's categories, both clothing and toys, have relatively high proportions of no preference, in other words, the shopping is for the product, not for the retailer.

FIGURE 84: PREFERRED CLASS OF TRADE BY PRODUCT CATEGORY

	Grocery	Department	Discount	Specialty	Drug	No Preference
Women's clothing	0	30	20	13	0	30
Men's clothing	0	32	22	8	0	29
Children's clothing	0	12	19	5	0	61
Children's toys	0	1	24	12	0	59
Shoes	0	17	17	24	0	27
Electronics	0	3	18	43	0	27
Linens	0	18	25	10	0	32
Home improvement	0	1	4	65	0	27
Prescription drugs	9	0	12	0	36	24
Groceries	54	0	17	0	0	16
Health & beauty aids	9	0	38	0	21	20

Source: BIGresearch

The concentration (normalized Herfindahl) ratios for the various product categories are shown in Figure 85. The conventional interpretation is that ratios of less than 0.10 mean the market is un-concentrated, between 0.10 and 0.18 equal moderate concentration, and ratios above 0.18 indicate high concentration. Figure 85 shows that children's products, home improvement and groceries are concentrated. Shoes are the least concentrated.

The value of this type of information is that it should help the retailer to understand when to promote branded products as part of the firm's assortment and when to promote the retail store itself as the factor that will likely encourage consumer shopping interest.

Also shown in Figure 85 are the linear changes in both the discount store preference rate and the no preference rate (these, as before, are un-standardized regression coefficients). The greatest change in discount store preference is in the decline in women's clothing, meaning the brand being sold in the store is more important than the store itself. The greatest change in no preference is the decline in groceries, meaning the retail store is becoming more important in the mind of the shopper than the brands being sold in the store. This is important news for retailers, but likely somewhat disconcerting for manufacturers.

FIGURE 85: PREFERRED CLASS OF TRADE BY GROWTH AND CONCENTRATION RATIO

	Concentration Ratio	Discount		No Preference	
		Pct	Change	Pct	Change
Women's clothing	0.16	20	−0.18	30	0.06
Men's clothing	0.17	22	−0.15	29	−0.20
Children's clothing	0.37	19	−0.10	61	0.03
Children's toys	0.37	24	0.03	59	−0.06
Shoes	0.12	17	−0.16	27	−0.06
Electronics	0.22	18	−0.17	27	−0.17
Linens	0.15	25	−0.15	32	0.05
Home improvement	0.44	4	−0.06	27	−0.14
Prescription drugs	0.17	12	0.06	24	−0.04
Groceries	0.29	17	0.08	16	−0.31
Health & beauty	0.17	38	0.04	20	−0.18

Source: BIGresearch

Figure 86 shows the change in no preference and concentration. In general, as the concentration ratio increases, the no preference selection rate decreases. In other words, where there is less competition, consumers are more willing to express preferences for existing classes of trade. Where there is less concentration, or more competition, the opposite is the case.

FIGURE 86: CLASS OF TRADE CONCENTRATION BY NO PREFERENCE CHANGE FOR SELECTED PRODUCT CATEGORIES

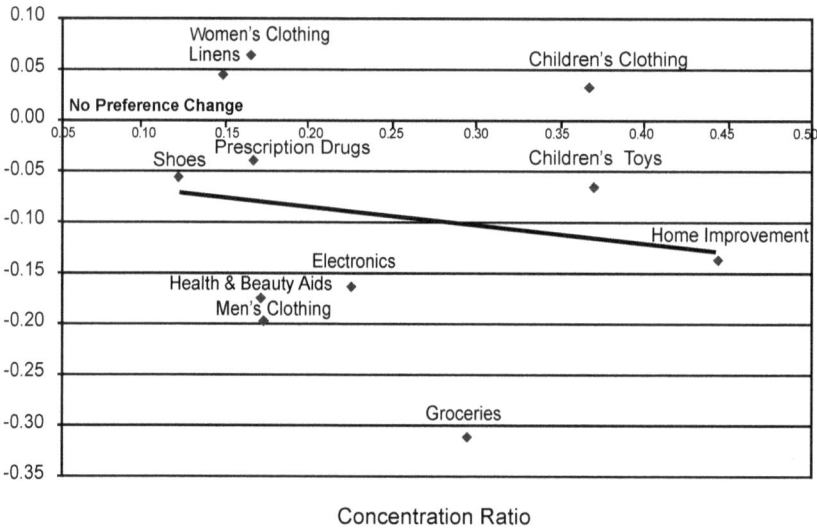

Concentration Ratio

Source: BIGresearch

Figure 87 shows an increase in the rate of the selection of discount stores as the concentration ratio increases. In other words, as competition increases, consumers are less likely to select the discount store option.

In both cases, the response to the declining confidence in the economy reinforces the points made before. Consumers tend to fall back on the trusted and well-recognized retailers, and tend to favor the low-price and high-value discount store. Both of these responses are mediated by the relative amount of competition. The statistical associations here are weak, but they are significant.

FIGURE 87: CLASS OF TRADE CONCENTRATION BY DISCOUNT STORE CHANGE FOR SELECTED PRODUCT CATEGORIES

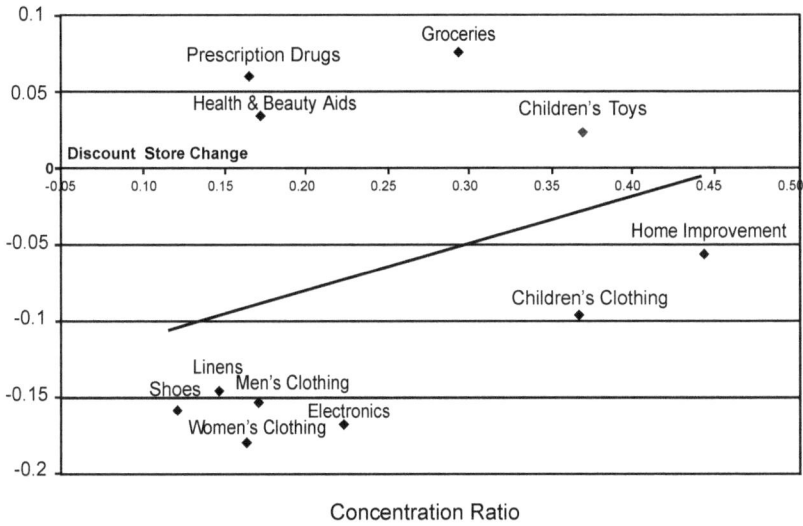

Concentration Ratio

Source: BIGresearch

Consumers are falling back on trusted retailers in down economies, apparently recognizing the outlets' ability to fulfill their needs at reasonable prices. This would explain the success of Walmart, McDonald's, Amazon and the like, while the newer, trendier specialty retailers seem to be falling by the wayside.

With this view of the current retailing situation in a down economy, we close this view of consumer communities and their impact on retailing. The last chapter provides a summary of all the primary points made in this text.

Chapter

10

Retail Communities in a Transformational Marketplace: The Baker's Dozen Requirements for Success

Throughout this text, we have identified customers and consumers as the key elements for retailing success—now and into the future. Many will say that's only common sense. But, when we survey the collective wisdom of the field of retailing, we find this focus on consumers is a pioneering and radical approach.

For the most part, retail pundits, both professional and academic, have suggested that retail success comes from what the retailer does, not what consumers do. All these experts have assumed there is always a large and generally malleable group of consumers waiting to be influenced, and perhaps even manipulated, by skilled retailers. These retailers—using various types of store format, location, product as-sortment, in-store ambience and other factors—are said to be able to influence the purchase activity of the general marketplace and the buyers in it. The experts seem to assume the retailer is in control—in control of the system, in control of the marketplace and, therefore, in control of the customers and consumers as well.

That was then, and this is now.

We believe that the evidence from the CIA, SIMM and Shopper Mindset databases amply demonstrates how the consumer drives the marketplace and our analyses of that data have put the consumer in a totally new perspective, for both retailers and manufacturers. In short, it is the consumer who drives today's marketplace. It is the retailer who must be aware and cognizant of that power and adjust its operations accordingly.

In this text, we have argued that retailing, like so many other traditional marketing and communication activities, is going through transformational change. Some of the changes are obvious: globaliza-tion, enhanced supply chains, consolidation as large retailers become even larger and small retailers drop by the wayside, digital communica-tion and the like. All are evident and easily measured and evaluated. What's not so obvious is what the consumer is doing. That's what is being continually measured through the CIA, SIMM and Shopper Mindset research studies. And, that's what has provided our views of retailing in this transformational age.

Many of the systemic retailing changes are having an impact as well. Some of those referenced in this text include the rise of own and private label merchandise to the detriment of national brands, the growth and availability of consumer retail purchase data—which has enabled retailers to know and understand their customers, whether they be in the hundreds or millions—and the increasing development and identification of retail and consumer communities. All these have combined to create what could be seen as a "perfect storm" in retailing. Some establishments will be blown away by the changes, others will manage to adapt and adjust to the new realities, while some will likely prosper beyond the wildest dreams of their owners and managers. It all depends on the view they take of the marketplace.

In the preceding pages, we've identified a number of the factors we believe to be governing the market today, and, here, we summarize and focus on the critical elements that we believe are, or will be, the base for retailing in the years ahead. We've identified thirteen factors we think all retailers, and their manufacturer-suppliers, will have to consider if they hope to be successful. In true retail fashion, this lagniappe for readers we call a "Baker's Dozen Factors for Retail Success."

1. **Retailing is undergoing transformational change.** What we've experienced in the past is likely never to be repeated. Those who argue that "once things return to normal, we'll be able to regroup and recover" are, we believe, in for a rude awakening. Today is the new normal and it will be the new normal in all the weeks and months to come. As we illustrated in Chapter 1, this is a period of discontinuous change. A time when the future is often not foreseeable to anyone. That makes it almost impossible to predict what changes will occur and what retailing systems will succeed or fail. Those changes, though, are in the hands of consumers and customers — as they always have been. All we know is that our future won't be like the past. While that is disconcerting for many, it gives those who can leave the past behind and help create the future, not be created by it, great opportunities.

2. **The overall economy and resulting customer expectations have an impact on retail.** That's obvious. Economic conditions impact consumer retail shopping behaviors. They always have and always will. What is different today is that with contemporary technology, database analytical capabilities, observational research and other data-gathering tools, we've

been able to document not just what feelings are or were in the face of economic declines and uncertainty, we've been able to document consumer behaviors as well. The dramatic events of the past couple of years have demonstrated that more vividly than ever. In this text, we've focused heavily on consumer confidence, or what consumers believe is happening now and will happen in the near future. Our data has shown that there is a direct correlation between consumer confidence in the economy and their purchasing behaviors in category after category. With dramatic economic changes, consumers have to make choices: what to buy, what to postpone, what to consider lost opportunities, how to satisfy current needs and wants, and so on. Some new and innovative research techniques now make it possible to predict some of the future consumer behaviors that might occur during times of economic difficulty. And, if you believe, as we do, that the future will be a series of continuing economic upheavals and adjustments, then understanding how consumers react to those changes will at least give retailers some clues as to what to do. Therefore, while the past will likely never resemble the future, we can be much better prepared to identify the potential economic potholes, and the consumer reaction to them, than we have been in the past.

3. **Retailers and customers together create retail communities.** Retailers cannot create identifiable retail communities alone, and, equally, consumers don't create them either. It is the two of them, together, that create the value for each other. That is what keeps the marketplace humming. When these retail communities are created, huge marketing opportunities come along with them. Both the buyer and the seller want to succeed. Therefore, it is the combination of the two that creates marketplace success. That's what we term reciprocity or shared value. When the retailer and

consumer have their needs and requirements met profitably by each other that creates the best of all retailing worlds. There must, however, be shared value or reciprocity in the marketplace for there to be marketplace equilibrium. Today, these retail communities can be identified through participant behaviors. That's why listening to and hearing consumers is so critical to retailer success in the years ahead.

4. **Consumer behaviors are what drive retailers' marketplace success.** It is not so much what the retailer buys and stocks, or even what is promoted, that counts. It's what customers and consumers do as a result of the retailer's actions. Too often in the past, retailers have tried to create customer segmentation schemes based on consumer feelings, attitudes, demographics, lifestyles and the like. As we have demonstrated in this text, actual consumer behaviors are a much better method of understanding consumers—how they create their own communities, who belongs, how they influence each other and how their behaviors can be used to make more accurate predictions of what they likely will do in the future. So, a corollary to the previous point (3) is that customer aggregation, that is, customer-created groups, is a far superior way to develop retail groupings than traditional segmentation approaches. The task of the retailer, then, is to identify the naturally occurring groups consumers create based on how they behave, how they live their lives, what products they buy and use, how they shop, the types of stores that appeal to them and so on. When we have consumer or customer behavioral data, such as is found in the CIA, SIMM and Shopper Mindset databases, it is much easier to develop effective marketing and communication programs.

5. **Retail theater drives sales.** "Retail theater" is the combination of the external environment and the marketing efforts of the manufacturer/supplier and retailer. Those three things come

together in a retail location and impact and affect consumer purchases. Retail theater is not in-store promotion alone, nor is it the external environment only, rather it is their combination *plus* the existing knowledge consumers bring into the retail environment from their exposure to various marketing and communication activities in the marketplace. Retail theater is a relatively new concept but a logical one. We must begin to think holistically, not individually. Consumers are impacted by the world around them. Retail theater simply consolidates those experiences into an overall concept, which we believe will have a major impact on retailing in the years ahead.

6. **Manufacturers are brand focused.** The goal of the manufacturer with its brand promotional efforts is to encourage consumers to seek out or buy the promoted brand at retail. Thus, the use of mass media advertising such as television, magazines and radio have only one goal: to create consumer brand preference at retail, no matter which retailer store or venue the retail sale occurs in. Thus, the manufacturer's goal is to implant brand messages in the consumer's mind or put brand incentives in the prospect's hands that will influence them in the retail store. We can measure the consumption of those brand messages, as we have shown in this text. Thus, knowing consumer exposure to manufacturers' brand messages should help retailers develop and implement better in-store merchandising and promotion. Then, manufacturers and retailers must work together to optimize both parties' investments to maximize marketplace success. That's quite different from the adversarial relationship that occurs in far too many situations today.

7. **Retailers focus on category movement.** Retailers don't particularly care what brand the consumer buys, as long as they buy in the retailer's store or location. Retailers know this, but they often ignore the prior knowledge that consumers have

when they enter the retail environment. Retailers succeed when they take advantage of the brand manufacturer's previous communication efforts and bring that down to the retail store level. Category movement comes about through a combination of external-to-the-store manufacturer efforts and retailer in-store merchandising programs. They are intertwined and interdependent. It is the combination of efforts that create success, not an independent one.

8. **Retailers need more customer knowledge.** Everyone harks back to the "good old days when retailers actually knew customers" not simply their frequent shopper card number. With rare exceptions, those days of retailer-customer interaction are gone forever. Yet, to be successful retailers simply must know more about their current shoppers, their prospects and those customers they have lost. Thus, the successful retailer of the future must rely on better customer data capture, better customer analysis and better customer relationships. That means the customer database becomes as important as the product supply chain and inventory control. Today, retailers have tons of customer data. The problem is that they do, or have done, little with it. Customer listening, customer analysis and customer insights must drive retailing in the future.

9. **Shopping trip purpose and amount spent are critical customer variables.** As we demonstrated throughout this text, the key variables in understanding retail shopping are (a) the purpose of the shopping trip and (b) the amount spent. For the most part, retailers still continue to rely on total store and category volume, like period sales, inventory turnover and other mechanistic measures of retail success. While those will continue to be important, we have amply demonstrated the importance of understanding how the consumer approaches shopping visits, the trip purpose, the amount spent, whether

shopping occurs alone or with others and other factors. These help retailers understand their aggregate measures, why sales go up and down, why "can't miss" features fail to move, how cross-selling and up-selling can be improved, and so on. Today, retailers simply don't know enough about their customers at any level. That's one retail skill that simply must be improved going forward.

10. **Understanding media consumption is the key to retail promotional success.** We know, for example, consumers who shop primarily at some stores have differing media consumption patterns from those who shop at other stores. For too long, retailers have judged media forms based primarily on efficient delivery. Today, they must focus on media effectiveness. How and in what way consumers use and consume media, in what combinations and with what impact are the key elements in retail promotion going forward. Knowing how online and offline media forms work together and, from that, developing an effective media allocation system is the key challenge of retail marketers.

11. **SIMM studies, when combined with CIA and Shopper Mindset data, provide holistic views of the consumer's media usage and purchase behavior.** For the first time, retailers now have holistic measures that bring together thirty-one external-to-the-store and twenty in-store merchandising factors to provide a view of how consumers see retail efforts—not just how retailers plan and execute them. It is this consumer and customer view that is so new and different. And, it suggests a different approach to retail marketing from that which has existed in the past. The forms, formats and approaches presented in this text are, we believe, the future of retail promotional analysis. The marketplace is complex today, and will only get more complex in the future. The new tools and techniques presented in this book

can do much to help the retail marketer develop more effective marketing and promotional programs. The future is here and it's available to all.

12. **Retail forecasting, often one of the most challenging of all management skills, is now possible based on consumer, not economic, data.** Consumers are the source of all retail sales. If the retailer knows, understands and can forecast the future based on the information contained in a customer base, gigantic improvements can be made in retail sales forecasting. Historically, retailers have relied on economic factors to predict future sales. Today, we argue, it is the ability to estimate what consumers and customers are likely to do going forward that is the key element in retail forecasting success. The data is available but the processes often are not. Therefore, one of the key challenges of all retail firms is to have the ability to know, understand and predict the future behaviors of those customers that result in relevant future projections. Use of the tools presented in this text can help immeasurably in that task.

13. **Digital communication is key to retailing in the future.** As more communication moves from fixed location outlets to handheld mobile distribution systems, retail promotion will change dramatically. Being able to deliver retail offers in real time to real people in real retail situations will be the breakthrough ingredient in future retail success. The U.S. lags in mobile and handheld promotional activities, but they are relevant in many overseas markets. The value of the SIMM data is that it provides a predictive measure of how quickly mobile activity could make a significant impact. In-store merchandising will be become in-hand merchandising. When that happens, retailing will become truly interactive and totally focused on the idea of customers and retailers creating reciprocal value for each other. That's the most exciting view of all.

With this thirteen-point summary, we complete our discussion of retail communities. We believe the information contained here (in our "baker's dozen") and throughout *Retail Communities* can and will be useful to retailers in multiple types of businesses and industries. But, we also believe that we have merely scratched the surface of what needs to be done and what can be done. The future of retailing is bright, but it can be brighter still if we simply employ the tools already in hand. That's what we've tried to do in this text. We hope you will agree that the effort has been worthwhile.

About the Authors

Don E. Schultz is Professor (Emeritus-in-Service) of Integrated Marketing Communications at Northwestern University, Evanston, IL. He is also President of Agora, Inc., a global marketing, communication and branding consulting firm also headquartered in Evanston, IL. Schultz lectures, conducts seminars and conferences and consults on five continents. He is the author of twenty-four books and over 150 trade, academic and professional articles. He is a co-author of *Media Generations* (BIGresearch, 2008), and a featured columnist in MARKETING NEWS and MARKETING MANAGEMENT. He was the founding editor of THE JOURNAL OF DIRECT MARKETING. Schultz is recognized as a leading authority on new developments in marketing and communication and has helped develop the Integrated Marketing and Integrated Marketing Communication concepts around the world along with pioneering work in marketing accountability, branding, internal marketing and marketing metrics/ROI.

Martin P. Block is a Professor in the Integrated Marketing Communications Division of the Medill School at Northwestern University. He is currently sector head for Entertainment and Gaming. He teaches graduate level marketing research, sales promotion, advertising, and direct marketing courses. Previously, Martin was a Professor and Chairperson of the Department of Advertising at Michigan State University.

Martin is co-author of *Media Generations* (BIGresearch, 2008), Analyzing Sales Promotion (Dartnell, 1994), Business-to-Business Market Research, (Thomson, 2007). His recent chapter "Post Promotion Evaluation" appears in The Power of Marketing at-Retail (POPAI, 2008). He was also co-author of Cable Advertising: New Ways to New Business (Prentice-Hall, 1987). He has published in academic research journals and trade publications. He has been the principal investigator on several Federally funded research projects and has served as a consultant to the Federal Trade Commission (FTC).

BIGresearch provides U.S. and Chinese consumer intelligence and shopping behavior research in areas of retail, products, financial services, automotive and media. Through the Consumer Intentions and Actions™ (CIA™) Survey, BIGresearch interviews more than 8,000 consumers each month and delivers fresh, demand-based information on where the retail consumer is shopping and their changing behavior. The BIGresearch Simultaneous Media Usage™ Survey (SIMM®) of more than 20,000 consumers is conducted twice each year and gauges consumption across media, products and services. The BIGresearch China Quarterly monitors the purchasing behavior and media consumption of more than 15,000 Chinese consumers between the ages of 18 and 54 years old. BIGresearch's large sample sizes and methodology provides highly accurate consumer information with a margin of error of +/- 1 percent. www.bigresearch.com

pressures on and unpredictability in cash flows for businesses lacking easily defensible intellectual property rights.

Social organization is transformed within cyberspace, resulting not only in the enhancement of human labor such that productivity is higher, but also creating completely new outlets for the buying and selling of labor time, and the products of that human labor. These issues are explored in chapters 3,4, and 5 which are on the labor market and internet job searching.

In this text, Cyberspace is understood as both a product of changing social and environmental conditions and as a dynamic force changing those same social and environmental conditions. Among these changes are radical transformations in notions of identity and perception, the raw material for preferences and decision-making. Homo oeconomicus, understood as an autonomous and rational (narrowly defined) decision machine, was never a correct metaphor for human behavior. Microeconomic behavior in the world of Cyberspace diverges significantly from the predictions of the neoclassical paradigm, including the "spontaneous" growth of radical collectivities where individuals perform anonymous labor in pursuit of open source goals. This is exemplified in chapter 7, which explores the open source movement where individuals from around the globe join together to create source code for usable computer programs—without remuneration or, in most cases, recognition. The chapter delves into the motivation behind this collective sharing and reveals the current tensions over debates on licensing and monetizing some open source code projects.

Finally, Cyberspace has served as a key catalyst for accelerated globalization, connecting people and businesses across the globe. Chapters 8 and 9 delve into the positives and negatives of this as chapter 8 explores the globalization of criminal activities through the internet (a potential value destroyer), while chapter 9 offers a more positive outlook as Cyberspace contributes to the redevelopment of a war ravaged Afghanistan.

Satyananda Gabriel
Professor of Economics and Finance
Mount Holyoke College
July 2011

1

E-Commerce: Paradise or Jungle?

Cen Zhang and Lei Wah Wong

The Internet was used mainly in governments and academic institutions for two decades after its invention. In 1994, the Internet lifted its mysterious veil and was revealed to the public. Two years later, in 1996, the Internet had become a common word and was known as the World Wide Web. No one had expected back then how dramatically the Internet would change our ways of living. The Internet has influenced almost every aspect of the world, including commerce. Imagine Adam Smith living in today's world, the world of cyberspace. Not only is there an invisible hand of the market, even the market itself is invisible. Sitting in your room and having all purchases done would be a fantastic dream for Adam Smith, but is definitely a reality for you.

Cyberspace has become essential in the business world. For instance, early in 1999, IBM's Tokyo Office launched an e-business integrated marketing campaign—"e-business people," highlighting the strengths of IBM Global Services in Japan. IBM aimed to recruit experts from various backgrounds to compete in the fast-changing e-business environments (*Computing Japan, 1999*).

With the fast development of Internet technology, purchasing online has become an ordinary activity. E-Commerce seems like a dream come true; however, is it truly a paradise or it is just a jungle in disguise? In the first half of the chapter, we will give a general overview of customers' benefits and concerns regarding e-commerce through the use of two stories; one from a customer's point of view and the other from a business owner's perspective. In the second part, we discuss potential solutions for online business retailers to increase customer loyalty and clear out the "jungle."

Customers' benefits and concerns

Mary's story

After a thirteen-hour flight and a four-hour bus ride, Mary finally arrived at Mount Holyoke College. Dragging her two huge suitcases to her dorm, she immediately fell on the bed. She was exhausted, but excited, "I can't believe that I am now a first-year college student in a foreign country!" Still jet-legged, Mary was excited about her classes. There were still three days before classes started and she needed to get her books. Where to find the books? Naturally, she turned to the internet. With the help of Google, Mary found several bookstores nearby and even managed to compare prices.

Benefits: 1. More and Customized Information

The Internet gives easier access to information. Google, for example, is a search engine. It will show a list of websites related to the keywords the user provides. One category of website is the informative website. For example, Weather.com is a website providing weather broadcasting services. Morton (2006) points out that "Weather.com is much better than TV weather because of the user's control over which piece of content to view. It allows a consumer to learn weather over a time frame of her choice and a geographic location of her choice, instantly." Compared with pre-Internet information, consumers have easy access to much more information and technical supports make customization of information possible.

Without the Internet, consumers get information about nearby stores through advertisements in the newspaper, or from friends. However, the customers are in a passive position waiting for the information to reach them. With the help of the Internet, the customers take an active position in searching for information. There are also many gadgets that help the customers to reach information which was previously unavailable. For example, Google Translator provides free translation services, so that customers can easily reach information about products from foreign websites.

Mary's story

However, Mary didn't have a car, and the cheapest bookstore was far away. The public transportation system was not very sophisticated in the Pioneer Valley where Mount Holyoke College is located. It took Mary an hour and a half to reach the bookstore which was in the neighboring town center. It was a small local bookstore, and it was quite crowded with people looking for books inside. It was really hard to find a certain book because some books were sorted into the wrong categories. There were two clerks inside the bookstore who were busy at the counter. She turned to a clerk and asked for help. The clerk started searching within the pile of books, but failed to find the book Mary needed. Disappointed, she bought one book and left the store.

Since Mary spent a long time searching for books, she realized that she had missed the bus to go back to school. The next bus wouldn't take her back in time for mandatory orientation meeting. "Oh well, I have to take a cab then." Mary was very frustrated. Taking a cab back to school was quite expensive for her, but she didn't have another choice. Back to her dorm after a long day, she complained to her roommate, "Buying books is so inconvenient. We are not in the city, and there aren't many stores within walking distance. I have to spend time and money to go to stores in other towns, and it was very messy there. To find the right books isn't an easy task." While venting her frustration, Mary took her book out from her backpack; she suddenly realized that she had bought the wrong book.

"Oh, no!" Mary couldn't be more disappointed. Looking up from her desk, Lynn, her roommate, tried to comfort her, "Don't worry, you could always return the wrong book. Do you still have your receipt?" Mary searched high and low for the receipt. Finally, she gave up and shook her head in disbelief.

"Oh well, Mary, did you pay with cash or credit card?" Lynn tried to help with the problem.

"I paid with cash since I don't have a bank account here," Mary answered. It seemed like the world had just fallen on her feet as the book was quite expensive. "So without the receipt, I couldn't return the book?" Mary still hoped for a positive answer.

"I am sorry Mary. You probably couldn't. Since you lost the receipt, they don't have a record that it was you who paid for the book. If you had paid with a debit card or a credit card, you could print out the record online and show them," explained Lynn. "And I would suggest that you go get a debit card and start shopping online."

Benefits: 2. Easy to keep track of transactions

Online shopping usually involves e-money and e-banking. E-money is short for electronic money. It is also known as electronic cash, electronic currency, digital money, digital cash or digital currency. It is money that is only exchanged electronically. Using e-money always requires computer networks, Internet and digital stored value systems. E-banking or online banking allows people to make financial transactions online. Users can keep track of every deposit and withdrawal in the online bank account. Users can also transfer money to other people, or make purchases online. E-banking changes the banking industry by changing "the ways customers interact with the financial services provider" (Lustsik, 2003) with the new technologies. In Mary's case, if she used a credit card or debit card while paying for the book, the record is automatically kept online. With online banking, it is easier to keep track of transactions.

Mary's story

After receiving a debit card from a major bank, Mary started shopping online. First off on her list were textbooks. Mary then began to make a list of the books she needed: she wouldn't need to take a long bus ride to a store; she could easily search for the books she wanted because everything on the website was easy to navigate and search; she could return the wrong book because there was always a record online. With the internet and e-commerce, the problems Mary encountered previously could be easily solved.

Benefits: 3. Save time and additional cost

Shopping malls have open hours, normally from eight to ten hours a day. With the Internet, the online stores open twenty-four seven. The customers can do shopping at any time, such as two o'clock in the morning. The flexibility of time makes shopping much more convenient for customers. Also, if customers live in the suburbs, the shopping places are often far away. There is always the additional cost of transportation, fuel, and parking. With online shopping, these additional costs are reduced. Conducting business online reduces transaction costs by eliminating the time and place aspects of traditional markets. It has also allowed sellers to reach a greater number of potential buyers because of the internet framework (Bichler *et al.*, 2002).

Mary's story

Mary thought of comparing prices between the websites so she typed in name of the book and compared. She found a website named Nextag. It provided price comparison for the book from major internet sellers. It also provided book details and reviews. This became useful because Mary found that she could base the amount that she was willing to pay for the book on the prices that she found on Nextag.

Benefits: 4. Easy to compare prices

Prices on the Internet are 9-16% lower than prices in traditional markets, depending on whether taxes, shipping, and shopping costs are included in the price. Additionally, it is found that Internet retailers' price adjustments over time are up to 100 times smaller than conventional retailers' price adjustments, reflecting the lower operating costs in internet channels. On average, Internet retailer prices differ by an average of 33% for books and 25% for CDs (Brynjolfsson and Smith, 2000) Customers are likely to make a purchase at a cheaper price than the traditional market price.

Price comparison websites, such as Nextag collect price information from other websites, and usually provide services to put the items in order according to price. Users can easily spot the cheapest price. The search option also allows the user to choose a range of acceptable prices, so that the search results are customized. In the traditional way of shopping, it is extremely difficult and time consuming to compare prices; the customers have to go to different stores in different locations, which adds to transportation costs, increasing total cost.

Mary's story

Besides websites like traditional sales websites such as Barnes and Noble and price comparison websites such as Nextag, Mary also found Half.com. It is just for books, especially textbooks. The website is just a platform, which displays all the goods available at different prices from all different sellers. Buyers can browse through the catalog and buy from an individual seller. Unlike Barnes and Noble, Half.com is a matching website. The matching website often has a new purchase method: bid auction. Different buyers can bid on one item for a certain period of time. The bid auction gives the buyers the right to determine what the price should be for an item. Usually, buyers won't bid higher than market price, which means that buyers most of the time benefit from the bid auction.

Benefits: 5. Bid auction: more power in determining prices

The bid auction on Half.com and eBay.com is called online timeshift auction. The seller provides a timeshift interval, which informs the customers about the closing time of the auction. The starting price is usually much lower than the market value. In this fixed time interval, the customers type in their preferable prices and outbid each other. Whoever at the end of the time interval has the highest price gets the item. Usually, the product is sold out at a lower price than the market price, because the customers stop bidding up the price if the bid auction won't save them money.

Another way to gauge a suitable price is based on the price that the product was previously sold for. Based on the historical price, buyers will know what a reasonable price for a given item is and can avoid paying too much. Sellers can use the same information to determine appropriate minimum prices for their auctions. This creates a level playing field and establishes online auctions as a viable and satisfactory commerce alternative for a much larger consumer population (Gregg and Walczak, 2003).

Mary's story

Mary quickly selected the books and compared prices. She typed in her debit card number and billing information, and with one click, she made the purchase. She only needed to wait for the books to be shipped to her. Mary thought, "For people like me who are stuck in a place off town without a car or a sophisticated public transportation system, online shopping makes life much easier. It saves so much time and energy. Besides, it's cheaper to shop online and the variety of goods online is more diverse than stores nearby. I could even buy things from abroad!" Mary laughs, "I really love this!" However, from the day Mary signed up as a member for some websites, she kept receiving tons of e-mails of deals, commercials and updates, which she wasn't actually interested in.

Concerns: 1. Overwhelming information and e-mail spam

According to data from Madden (2006), 73 percent of American adults use the Internet, and about 84 million Americans have broadband Internet connections at home. The greatest advantage of the Internet is providing easily accessible information. Studies have been done to show that technical elements can determine and even manipulate the credibility of online information (Fogg *et al.*, 2001). The quantity of information doesn't guarantee the quality of the information. Technically, anyone can post information online easily. The users can't really know whether the source of the information is credible or not. There can be huge amounts of wrong information, and it is hard for the users to distinguish and pick out the useful information. Also, e-mail spam is another big problem. Usually, customers can choose to sign up for a mailing list of certain companies to get updates and deal alerts. However, some companies overuse e-mails as a platform for advertising, so they send out overwhelmingly huge amounts of e-mail, which causes inconvenience for the customers. Also, some companies just randomly send out e-mail spam to people who have never signed up for their mailing list, which troubles customers.

Mary's story

Unfortunately, things did not go as expected. Several days later, Mary received a package. She opened the box with excitement, like opening a Christmas present. To her surprise, one book was in extremely bad shape. The pages were not bound together and there were several pages missing. There were stains everywhere on the book. Mary couldn't believe her eyes. The description of the book online was so different from the actual book in front of her face. The online description stated that the book was second-hand but in generally good condition. Mary was not happy. She logged into her account and tried to contact the seller. Half.com allows users to send messages to each other, so Mary sent a message to ask the seller whether he had a better one. She waited for a whole day and didn't get any reply. She was quite upset and she sent out more messages. She waited and waited. Finally, she got a reply with a single word: "No!" She tried to argue by sending more messages but none were replied to again.

Concerns: 2. Product quality and shipping cost

The Internet makes shopping for geographically distant products possible, which gives customers more choices. However, buying a product from far away means the customer can not inspect the product quality and shipping is necessary. Shipping has an additional cost. Long distance and faster shipping time require more money, so with the shipping fee, it is not always cheaper to buy online than from a real store. Also, shipping might take a long time. Customers get the product immediately from the real store but they have to wait for the products to be shipped. There are also chances that the products are lost during the shipping process. Ed Foster (1999) in his article, "Shipping and handling: The big surprise on your e-commerce shopping bill," talks about some complaints about e-commerce shopping. Some websites just show "plus shipping and handling" but hide the true cost of shipping, which surprises the customer when the total is shown at checkout. Also, One of the most common complaints is that customers have to pay extra shipping fees for the mistakes of the companies, such as mis-shipments and defective products.

Mary's story

Furious by the answer and the treatment she was receiving, Mary logged a complaint with Half.com. Mary was upset, "The customer service is just so bad. If I were buying books at a real store, I could talk to the people face to face and work out a solution. The clerks in the stores are usually very friendly. However, the customer service online is so bad. I couldn't hear back the reply in time. I don't even know exactly who is selling this book to me. Also, the seller could be irresponsible in writing a fake description to attract the buyers. There really isn't a way to check whether the description is true or not unless you actually get the product."

"Oh, well, I guess e-commerce is not that perfect after all." Mary sighs.

Concerns: 3. Customer service

Gabbott and Hogg (1998) point out that a service encounter has three stages, which are pre-purchase, purchase and post-purchase. In the pre-purchase stage, the customer searches for a business; the purchase stage is when the customer makes the purchase; the last stage is the post-purchase stage, which includes follow-up support and delivery of the product or service. A pleasant shopping experience includes getting the wanted product at a good price, and also enjoyable customer services. Marian Petre, Shailey Minocha and Dave Roberts (2006) give some examples in the post-purchase stage: maintain continuity across modes of communication, provide a reliable customer services, provide a reliable delivery service and ensure that customers are in control. Customers need to accurately receive related information. Many stores decorate their stores in innovative ways to create an attractive shopping environment. However, while online shopping websites can be very fancy and interactive, it is not as powerful as the real full dimensional experience. If you need help finding a product, the clerks in the store are ready to answer questions at any time. By contrast, customers don't usually get immediate replies from internet retailers, and face-to-face conversation is much more convenient than waiting in front of a computer for responses which might never come.

Mary's story

The low quality is not the only problem. Another book Mary ordered online didn't arrive but Mary needed it to do readings for class. Mary couldn't do anything but had to wait. She began to realize that online shopping has many disadvantages as well. After a week, the book finally arrived. Mary continued using her debit card buying things from the campus store, or from the mall. She worked in the school library, and she deposited the check with an ATM machine into her checking account for further use of the debit card. Everything went great until one day when Mary logged into her online banking account as usual, and suddenly found out that the remaining number wasn't right. She checked the transaction records and found a huge purchase that she didn't make.

"What happened? I didn't buy anything from this website! It is impossible!" Mary couldn't believe the fact that she had lost a huge amount of money. She always trusted the security. She didn't tell anyone her card number and identification information such as the expiry date and billing address, and she certainly didn't give her card to anyone. "How is it possible?!" Mary asked her roommate Lynn.

After Lynn heard the situation, she realized that Mary's information must have been stolen. "Oh no, your information must be stolen. Did you log into your account in a public computer and forget to log out? That sometimes happens. If you forget to log out, the next person using that computer could use your card to make purchase. Or it might be fraud." "No way. How can it be fraud?" Mary exclaimed in disbelief.

Lynn said, "In fact, someone stole my credit card information. Thankfully the bank decided to reimburse me the full amount. You should call the bank and report the situation. I'm sure they will reimburse you after they've investigated the case." Lynn said as she searched the internet for an appropriate number to call. "It is really risky to give out any information online then. Although my online banking account always asks for my password and personalized questions before logging in, but it still feels shaky."

Mary thought aloud,"But e-commerce and e-banking are just so convenient. I really hope we could find some better way to reduce the risk!"

Concerns: 4. Privacy and security

Getting information from the Internet is convenient; however, at the same time, customers give a considerable amount of personal information for membership registration, online payment and so on. Trevor Moores (2005) argues that although e-commerce sales are very likely to grow at a rapid rate, privacy concerns will make Internet-related business lose billions of dollars. AT&T Labs (1999) presented a list of findings from an analysis of data collected from Internet users.

—Internet users tend to provide information when they are not identified.

—Users feel more comfortable to provide information of their preference than credit card numbers.

—Customers have concerns about their information being shared with others.

—Users don't want tools which automatically transfer their information to Websites.

—If there were privacy laws and policies well enforced, Internet users are willing to provide their personal information.

Thus, privacy and security are always an important issue. Technical problems, hackers and viruses can cause the system to break down and harm customers' benefits.

Businesses' benefits and concerns

Tom's story

Tom is the owner of an online photo printing firm. Before transforming his firm to an online business, he had a studio located on the main street in a small town in the Pioneer Valley. The rent was pretty high, which took up half of his monthly profits. There were three people in his firm: one person was at the reception desk and kept track of transactions; one employee took care of making purchases of raw materials from other firms; and Tom was in charge of technical issues of printing and editing photos for customers. Tom found his firm not earning much profit, so he took the advice of his economist friend and started his photo printing business online.

Now Tom works in the basement of his own house, which saves the rent of the studio. He orders raw materials online, and they are shipped directly to his house; so he doesn't need to hire an employee to take care of the logistics of raw materials. Also, he interacts with customers online directly through messages and e-mails, so that the receptionist is not needed either. He is still in charge of editing photos and printing them out. Tom's photo printing firm is now a one-person online business.

Benefits: 1. Reduction in costs

Cost structures of Internet-based business and traditional businesses differ a lot (Peter and Mandeville, 2009). Online business usually reduces costs such as rent and employees' wages. Online business doesn't require an actual store to display products, so business owners can work at home as long as they have Internet access. Rent usually makes up a big portion of total costs in a traditional business. Online business cuts costs in this area, which should increase profits. Internet services cut a lot of middle processes, so that jobs such as receptionists are not needed any more. Employing less people means lower costs, which is beneficial to the business.

Increased efficiency in searching for trading partners, communications, negotiation and confirmation of transactions, transaction automation, along with reduction of inventories contribute to cost reductions (Wen 2010). Wen found that if establishing and maintaining e-commerce has a lower fixed cost, and/or the improvement in unit transaction efficiency through e-commerce has a higher degree, it is more likely that e-commerce will be adopted.

Tom's story

Since Tom's photo printing firm is located in the suburbs, not a lot of people need photos for printing every day. Before, when Tom had a traditional brick and mortar business, it was hard for Tom to advertise his firm. Tom tried every possible way to advertise his firm, and invested a lot of time and money. Back then, he printed out flyers and posted near the bus stops and malls. However, he actually never knew how many people actually read the flyers. The printing costs for flyers were expensive as well. There was also an additional cost of fuel since he needed to drive around to post flyers. Tom also posted an advertisement in the local newspaper, and he was surprised at the high price for such a small space in the newspaper. Tom spent a lot of money on advertising, but there was still only a small group of potential customers because the town itself is quite small.

With the help of the Internet, Tom has set up a website for his photo printing firm, so that theoretically, with Internet access, anybody from any part of the world can read information on this website. When customers search for photo printing service, they will be able to see his website on the list. Tom also creates a fan page of his photo printing firm on Facebook, which is the most popular social network website, especially among young people. There are five universities and colleges in the

Pioneer Valley. Creating a Facebook fan page definitely helps Tom reach out to the college students.

Benefits: 2. Advertise more efficiently

Traditional ways of advertising such as flyers or ads in the newspaper are costly. Advertising online can reach a much bigger audience than sending out flyers. Businesses can buy an area in the main web portals such as AOL and Yahoo, which have millions of visitors per day. The same amount of money used for online advertising can reach much more potential customers than traditional advertising.

Lim *et al.* (2010) in a survey on response to Internet advertising among Malaysian college students suggest that they have a positive attitude of Internet advertising and they can recall about half of the brand names which they have seen from the Internet. On a scale from 1(strongly dislike) to 5 (strongly like), the attitude towards Internet advertising has a mean of 3.52. In addition, the respondents found Internet advertisements to be useful (mean = 3.81), informative (mean = 3.74), intelligent (mean = 3.73), and knowledgeable (mean = 3.60).

There are ways to spread the word for free. One way is to send e-mails to customers. Most online business websites have a mailing list for users to sign up, and they send out deal alerts, sales and sometimes coupons regularly. Another way is taking advantage of online social network websites, such as Facebook. If a user of Facebook becomes a fan of a firm's fan page, his friends will be informed, so that his friends are likely to check out the firm because recommendations from friends appear more reliable than general advertisements.

Tom's story

With the help of technology, Tom finds customized products easier to process. Take customized calendars as an example. Previously, customers needed to bring their photos to the studio, and Tom would spend some time working with the customers discussing the order, the layout and the background design etc. Tom was often frustrated because the customers couldn't explain well what they wanted and the final product turned out to be not as expected.

Thanks to technology, customers can follow a simple guide and design their own products: upload photos, choose background, edit the layout and photo order, and visualize the final product. All the work is done with a couple of clicks by customers themselves, and it is easy and fun. Tom actually has a much lighter workload than before.

Benefits: 3. Customized products

Online business websites give the customers more freedom in designing their own products and services. Previously, employees are needed for individualized services; technology enables the customers to play around by themselves. The customers feel more in control, and they find the products they will get are unique, different from the mass production. Apple allows customers to engrave any words on their iPods and other products. Nike has a NikeiD site, which means Nike individualized design. Besides choosing color and size, customers can choose materials and colors for all 12 different parts of the shoes: tip and heel, toe box and tongue, swoosh and cupsole stitching, quarter, eyestay, underlay, strap, lining, lace, midsole and outsole. All together, there are over a thousand different combinations of the 12 parts with different materials and colors. Customers can also type in the text they want to show on the shoe straps. Customization service is wanted by business to attract more customers. In the traditional sales, customization services require many human efforts. Technical support from websites make the customization process less demanding for the business, and now the customization work is done by customers, usually with a good feeling because the customers feel in control.

Marino *et al.* (2002) introduced a tool kit called Servizi Telematici Adattativi, which supports creation of Web-based stores with user-adaptive, multilingual interaction with customers. The amount of information presented is designed to be appealing to customers' interests and receptivity. Customization gives the customers more freedom, but the customization process is carefully tailored so that customers don't feel overwhelmed.

Tom's story

A photo printing business basically needs paper and inks for printers. There aren't many raw materials needed, but it is still a hard task to estimate the needed amount to purchase. Tom once ran out of a color and the new order hadn't arrived, so he had to close the studio for a while. Another time Tom ordered a huge amount of paper, and he stored them in the basement. However, a storm hit the town and some papers got wet and couldn't be used. Tom has always wanted to know a fairly accurate amount to purchase of raw materials needed. Also, Tom wanted to know what customers thought about his services, but sometimes in face-to-face conversations, customers might not express their true feelings.

After transforming to an online business, Tom is able to collect data about customers' activities. For example, he has a clear record of the number of visitors to his website in a certain period of time, so he gets an idea of what might be a peak period. Also, the website keeps records of each order and feedback from customers, so that Tom can analyze the target group's consumption behavior and shopping habits, and he can also improve his services with references from customers' online feedback.

Benefits: 4. Collection of information on consumers' behaviors

Online business administrators have records of visitors, so that they have data to analyze consumers' preferences and shopping patterns. Collecting consumers' information is a key to business, because the more the business understands the consumers, the better they can modify their business plans to gain more profits. Traditionally, there are surveys and cold-calls to ask about customers' preferences and shopping habits, which are time consuming and not very efficient. By contrast using the internet, business owners can easily see which product is popular by how many times the product is viewed.

Tom's story

Although there are many benefits of online business, Tom still has three major concerns. First, the online market seems more competitive. Previously, there were only two photo printing firms in the Pioneer Valley. However, the online market is much bigger, which means that his customers could order from other photo printing firms far away and have the products shipped to them. The second concern is that it is harder to build a personal relationship with the customers. Tom used to talk to a lot of customers, and they kept coming back not only for the service but also for having a nice chat. However, facing the computer all day and processing all the orders, Tom actually doesn't really know who he is working for, and it is harder to communicate in e-mails than face-to-face conversations. He is concerned that losing a good personal relationship with customers reduces their loyalty. The third concern is shopping online actually presents issues with privacy and security. Tom himself is an e-commerce customer and he is familiar with the risks in online shopping. He wants to find some ways to increase customers' trust. Tom wishes there was more advice about garnering trust and consumers' loyalty, so that he can run a better e-business firm.

Solutions for consumer loyalty in e-commerce

You probably find these two stories familiar with your own experiences. Trust and loyalty are two important issues in e-commerce. Customers are concerned with which online business websites are trustworthy, while business owners are worried about keeping their customers. There are eight factors, the 7Cs—Data was collected from 1,211 online customer, which demonstrate that there are seven factors which impact e-loyalty: customization, contact interactivity, care, communication, cultivation, choice, and character (Srini S. Srinivasan *et. al* 2002).

Customization

Customization is the ability of the retailers to individualize their products, services and also transaction environment for customers. According to Srinivasan (2003), customization increases the chance that customers find products they wish to buy.

Contact interactivity

Engagement between an e-retailer and customers through websites is known as contact interactivity. Good contact interactivity makes the websites easy to navigate, product information easy to find, inquiries quickly answered.

Cultivation

E-retailers should provide relevant information and incentives to the customers so that they extend the breadth and depth of future purchases.

Care

Customers need to be paid attention to in both pre-purchase and post-purchase stages. Some examples of care are making sure there is no breakdown of services, and backup plans to reduce customers' loss if identity theft happens.

Community

An online social entity keeps existing and potential customers in a bonding relationship with each other. Many consumers regularly consult other consumers for advice and information on products and services they want to purchase. Consumers also exchange opinions of products and service. Online communities help the individual customers to identity with a larger group, so that they are likely to return because of the bonding.

Choice

Compared with traditional sales, online business websites usually offer a wider range of products and a bigger variety of goods and services. Customers don't like to deal with several vendors, so that if one retailer can satisfy all their needs, they are likely to return.

Character

With numerous websites, making your website memorable is important to e-retailers. If a website has a creative design, it helps the retailer to build a positive reputation and characterization in consumers' minds.

Conclusion

In this chapter, we have shown benefits and concerns in e-commerce from both perspectives through one story of a consumer and one story of an online business owner. Consumers benefit from a wider range of products, save considerable time on comparing prices, reduce additional cost such as transportation, and use time more efficiently. Business owners save costs on advertising, employment; they are able to provide customization services, and they can collect data on customers' shopping habits and preferences. However, the world of e-commerce is not a paradise; there are privacy and securities concerns. For business owners, it is crucial to maintain customer loyalty. Seven factors play an important role in e-loyalty: customization, contact interactivity, cultivation, care, community, choice and character. E-commerce plays a vital role in today's world of business. As technology develops fast in today's world, e-commerce's future is promising as long as the "jungles" (issues such as privacy, security, loyalty etc.) are not in its way.

REFERENCES

Anckar, Bill and Davide D'Incau, "Value Creation in Mobile Commerce: Findings from a Consumer Survey", *The Journal of Information Technology Theory and Application (JITTA)*, 4:1, 2002, 43-64

Anderson, Ben and Karina Tracey, "Digital Living: The Impact (or Otherwise) of the Internet on Everyday Life", *American Behavioral Scientist* (2001) 45:456

Bakos, Yannis, "The Emerging Landscape for Retail E-Commerce", *The Journal of Economic Perspectives*, Vol. 15, No. 1 Winter (2001): 69-80

Bichler, M., Kalagnanam, J., Katircioglu, K., King, A. J.,Lawrence, R. D., Lee, H. S., Lin, G. Y. and Lu, Y. "Application of Flexible Pricing in Business-to business Electronic Commerce", *IBM Systems Journal* 41.2 (2002): 287–302

Brown, Jeffrey R. and Austan Goolsbee, "Does the Internet Make Markets More Competitive? Evidence from the Life Insurance Industry" October (2000)

Brynjolfsson, Erik, and Michael D. Smith. "Frictionless Commerce? A Comparison of Internet and Conventional Retailers." *Management Science* 46.4 (2000): 563-85.

Chatterjee, Debabroto, Rajdeep Grewal and V. Sambamurthy, "Shaping up for E-Commerce: Institional Enablers of the Organizational Assimilation of Web Technologies", *MIS Quarterly*, Vol. 26, No. 2 June (2002): 65-89.

Choi, Soon-Yong and Andrew B. Whinston, "Benefits and requirements for interoperability in the electronic marketplace", *Technology in Society* 22, (2000): 33-44.

Clay, Karen, Ramayya Krishnan, Eric Wolff and Danny Fernandes, "Retail Strategies on the Web: Price and Non-price Competition in the Online Book Industry", *The Journal of Industrial Economics*, Vol. L, September (2002).

Earl, Peter E., and Tom Mandeville. "The Competitive Process in the Age of the Internet."Prometheus 27.3 (2009): 195-209.

Fogg, B.J., Marshall, J., Laraki, O., Osipovich, A., Varma, C., Fang, N., Paul, J., Rangnekar, A., Shon, J., Swani, P. and Treinen, M., "What makes websites credible? A report on a large quantitative study", *Proceedings of the SIGCHI Conference on Human Factors in Computing Systems*, Seattle, Washington, USA, March 31-April 4 (2001): 61-68

Foster, Ed. "Shipping and handling: The big surprise on your e-commerce shopping bill." *InfoWorld* 21.45 (1999): 101.

Gabbott, Mark, and Gillian Hogg. *Consumers and Services.* Chichester, Sussex: John Wiley & Sons. 1998.

Gregg, Dawn G., and Steven Walczak. "E-commerce Auction Agents and Online-auction Dynamics." *Electronic Markets* 13.3 (2003): 242-50.

IBM launches Japan E-business advertising. Computing Japan [serial on the Internet]. (1999, June).

Janek Uiboupin, et al. "Organizational and Sectoral Changes in Transition Banking: Estonian Experience." *TRAMES: A Journal of the Humanities & Social Sciences* 11.2 (2007): 155-172.

Lim, Yet-Mee, Ching-Seng Yap, and Teck-Chai Lau. "Response to Internet Advertising Among Malaysian Young Consumers." *Cross-Cultural Communication* 6.2 (2010): 93-99.

Lustsik, Olga, "E-Banking in Estonia: Reasons and Benefits of the Rapid Growth" (2003). University of Tartu Economics and Business Administration Working Paper No. 21.

Madden, Mary. "Internet Penetration and Impact". *Pew Internet & American Life Project* (2006).

Marino Segnan, et al. "Personalization in Business-To-Customer Interaction." *Communications of the ACM* 45.5 (2002): 52-53.

Moores, Trevor. "Do Consumers Understand the Role of Privacy Seals in E-Commerce?." *Communications of the ACM* 48.3 (2005): 86-91.

Morton, F. Scott. "Consumer Benefit from the Use of Internet." *Innovation Policy and the Economy Volume 6* (2006): 67-90.

Oxley, Joanne E. and Bernard Yeung, "E-Commerce Readiness: Institutional Environment and International Competitiveness", *Journal of International Business Studies*, Vol. 32, No. 4 4th Qtr., (2001): 705-723.

Petre, Marian, Shailey Minocha, and Dave Roberts. "Usability beyond the website: an empirically-grounded e-commerce evaluation instrument for the total customer experience." *Behaviour & Information Technology* 25.2 (2006): 189-203.

Rochet, Jean-Charles and Jean Tirole, "Platform Competition in Two-Sided Markets", November (2001).

Salam, A. F., H. R. Rao and C. C. Pegels, "Consumer-Perceived Risk in E-Commerce Transactions", *Communications of the ACM*, Vol. 46, No. 12ve, December (2003): 325-331.

Srini S. Srinivasan, Rolph Anderson, Kishore Ponnavolu. "Customer loyalty in e-commerce: an exploration of its antecedents and consequences." *Journal of Retailing* 78 (2002) 41-50.

Teo, Thompson S.H. and Jing Liu, "Consumer Trust in E-Commerce in the United States, Singapore and China", *Omega* 35, (2007): 22-38.

Wen, Mei. "E-commerce, productivity, and fluctuation." *Journal of Economic Behavior & Organization* 55.2 (2004): 187-206.

2

Evolving Distribution Channels: Importance and Applied Strategies

Diana Chihai

INTRODUCTION

For a business to be considered a success it should have the ability to see into the future, to understand the customer's needs, to understand how technology is evolving and if it should be used in its strategy. Time is flying fast. The business that is here and relevant today might not be here tomorrow. One of the major factors that can influence the outcome of a business is the distribution channel. The purpose of this chapter is to disclose information and generate some discussion about the traditional distribution channel as well as the impact and importance of e-commerce. In addition, the differences between choosing one channel instead of the other will be outlined. Lastly, some strategies that business could consider will be summarized.

As the Internet has grown, it has become an unavoidable fact of a firms' life. The fact that traditional distributors are at risk to secure their position in the market has become clear. What are the reasons for choosing the Internet instead of a conventional retail channel? What are the factors influencing the switch?

Isaac Asimov (1977), an American author best known for his science fiction novels, expressed a vision: "The year 2025 will see the "drive-in market," a kind of computerized convenience store. The customer will call the store by using his own computer, and make his grocery list. The order will automatically be picked off the shelves of a computerized ware- house, packed, and ready for pickup by car, or whatever mechanized vehicle we'll be driving in the next century." But as we see, we couldn't wait another 14 years, as the future he described is quite similar to our present. As an example, I will describe the way I did my recent shopping: I created a list of what I wanted, went online to purchase it and waited for somebody to pack it and deliver it to my door. Who would not embrace the opportunity to shop from the comfort of their living room? If many customers are like me – trying to save some time, love to compare prices and find "good deals" or customizing merchandise – businesses will need to be flexible enough so that they do not lose their customers.

It is important to understand what the Internet is and why it is so attractive. The phrase "it is a small world" has a lot of meaning when it comes to the Internet. This virtual world that is based on our real one, was created so everything will seem so much closer – a click away closer. It is a web that can bring together people from different parts of the world, or from the same street. It is a portal that can offer an emotional support, advice for your problem or create an identifiable community. It also can be an overwhelmingly powerful source of information. If this information is filtered, it can create a strong database for a user. The Internet must have operational effectiveness (speed, flexibility, efficiency) to be appealing.

Looking at the statistics below, which are from June 2010 by ITU (UN agency for information and communication technologies), it is easy to notice a tremendous growth of Internet users in the United States population. In comparison with the year 2005, where the percentage of the population using the Internet was 44.1, in 2010 this number grew by 33.2 percent. If the 77.3 percent of the population that uses the Internet could be identified and grouped accordingly, it could present valuable data for businesses in order to assist them in targeting a specific sales markets and potential customers.

Internet Usage and Population Growth

Year	Population	Users	% Pop.
2000	281,421,906	124,000,000	44.1 %
2005	299,093,237	203,824,428	68.1 %
2010	310,232,863	239,893,600	77.3 %

A networked society, connected over high-capacity networks, is a widely shared goal among both developed and developing countries. As more people are connected to the Internet, the better the chances are for businesses to find customers.

How is the product going to reach the consumer?

A distribution channel is a set of interdependent organizations that help make a product available for use or consumption by the consumer or business user (Kotler, 2009). Channels provide time, place, and ownership utility. They should not be restricted to their physical products alone. Distribution channels might be considered for moving a service from a producer to consumer of a certain industry. For example, hotels may sell their services directly or through travel agents, airlines, tourist boards, centralized reservation systems, etc.

Channel intermediaries are individuals or firms who help move a product from the producer to the consumer or business user. It could be a retailer or a wholesaler, an agent or a broker. They make products available at a certain place and time and in the quantities that the customers want. (Kotler, 2009)

Functions that distribution channels possess are:

- Breaking bulk – buying by wholesaler or retailer of a huge amount of products and selling it to customers in smaller amounts
- Assortment – providing a selection of different products in one location
- Transportation and storage of goods
- Facilitating function of making the purchase process easy for customers
- Offering credit to customers and accepting customer returns
- Providing repairs and maintenance services
- Taking the risk of a defective product
- Providing the marketing of products

But depending on a business strategy and its size there are different dimensions of the distribution channel. A simplified version of it is provided below:

- A favorite old fashion distribution that works great with a small business is *Producer – Beneficiary*. There is direct contact between the manufacturer and the consumer, so there are no intermediaries involved.

- A short channel distribution, which involves only one intermediary, is *Producer – Intermediary - Beneficiary*. For the consumer goods there is a retailer and for industrial goods there is a distributor. Small markets could apply this channel, where it is practical to reach the whole market having one intermediary.
- A long distribution channel, which include 2 or more intermediaries is *Producer – Intermediary × n – Beneficiary* (where n is the number of intermediary used). This channel is more appropriate for a large business that attracts more intermediaries in order to operate efficiently.

A major key for every successful business is creating and using an appropriate distribution strategy in order to maximize sales and profits. The distribution channel can give a product a distinctive position in the market. The choice of retailers and other intermediaries is strongly tied to the product itself. Most of all, if the company underestimates the importance of a distribution channel, there is significant chance both the customer and the customer's product preference will not be understood. Today's customers shop and buy very differently than before. The access customers possesses to high-quality information through the internet, combined with their heightened price sensitivity, has created a customer that is more sophisticated, better informed and often times, more hostile than customers of the past. Some companies such as FedEx, Dell Computer, and Charles Schwab have used creative distribution systems to gain a competitive advantage. For example Dell Computer constructed a channel direct to their customers. The clients customize their own computer and then Dell builds what they choose. This tactic uses less storage space, creates a faster business cycle for the supplier, and ends with a happier customer who takes pride in building his own computer.

In order to understand if a business is using the right distribution channel, some steps can be taken which will help the business either choose or change the old ways of conducting business. First of all, the company needs to chart its products to the end-user. Then they should try to determine why its customers prefer to use a certain channel. Next, the business should use a new channel, and compare it to the ones that were used before. The company needs to examine the competitors' strategies and compare it to the strategies it uses. Lastly, the business should conduct interviews with its distribution partners to identify areas needing improvement or liquidation.

According to InfoTrends, a research and strategic consulting firm for the digital imaging and document solutions industry, the most identifiable problems of establishing and maintaining a distribution strategy are:

- Unwillingness to establish different distribution channels for different products
- Concerns about erosion of distributor loyalty or inter-channel cannibalization
- Failure to periodically re-visit and update distribution strategies
- Lack of creativity and resistance to change

Considering e-commerce for a business

E-commerce presents business marketers with profound opportunities. It is a new channel that is not controlled by companies in any industry, so there is no barrier to entry. Its distribution cost is low. It enables fast distribution of information about products. It enables a relatively quick product rotation. It gives access to a new market segment.

The Internet is expanding at a high rate, but it is still considered a new technology in its early stage. As with any new technology, market signals can be unreliable and should be interpreted with caution. It might involve out of control experimentation, which is more often economically unsustainable by both companies and customers. Market behavior can be interpreted incorrectly if for example we use sales figures. Many companies have subsidized the purchase of their products and services in order to proclaim a position on the Internet and to attract a base of customers. Rather than concentrate on delivering the real value of the product, the firms have pursued indirect revenues from sources such as advertising and click-through fees from Internet commerce partners.

When considering the Internet as a possible distribution channel, it is important to assess its advantages and liabilities if other companies enter the market with the same line of activity and products. In order for a firm to obtain a competitive advantage in its industry, it should position itself strongly in a marketplace by innovating and preventing new products or services that could replace their own. Michael Porter (1985) argues that the most important competencies of a firm in order to reach a competitive advantage are by product differentiation, product cost and targeting the market.

Product differentiation is the position a company can acquire in the marketplace. It creates a physical or a psychological barrier for new firms to enter where there are well-established companies whose names are almost synonymous with the product itself.

In order for a company to obtain its product *cost efficiency*, it is vital for it to produce large quantities that enable prices to be competitive.

For *targeting the market* it is important to use an effective distribution channel to reach the clients that require the firm's products.

E-commerce can also introduce potentially notable challenges.

Some firms can make bad decisions that might erode the attractiveness of their industries and undermine their own competitive advantages. For example some firms have used Internet technology to shift the basis of competition away from quality, features and service and toward price. This shift makes it more difficult for anyone in their industries to turn a profit.

Internet brands have proven difficult to build. Regardless of huge advertising expenses, product discounts, and purchasing incentives, most dot-com brands have not approached the power of established brands. It is possible that direct human contact used in the traditional businesses makes virtual ones less tangible and desirable to customers.

Buyers can easily switch suppliers with just a few mouse clicks, and new web technologies promote switching. For example, companies like PayPal, the so-called e-wallet, have enabled customers to shop at different websites without having to enter personal information and credit card numbers. As the cost of switching to new suppliers is low, customers don't need to be loyal to a supplier. For example a company that uses a reverse auctions ("name your own price") model, such as Priceline.com, might lose customers' interest because the inconvenience of searching is sometimes greater than the savings provided.

The Internet limits the ability to learn about the suppliers and customers by the lack of face-to-face contact. Spontaneity and judgment that can result from an interaction with skilled personnel is missing in the process of gathering online knowledge. There is a risk involved because of the inability to physically inspect products, and the lack of personal contact places accountability at a distance if a problem arises.

In spite of the fact that digitization by firms has decreased distribution costs, it has also made the use of unauthorized duplication of copyrighted material and its transmission over the Internet easier. The unauthorized file sharing via Peer-to-Peer networks continues. Why would somebody want to pay for merchandise if it can be found for free? This could be a significant threat to the long-term profitability of the media industry and other businesses whose products are easily deliverable over the internet.

Does every company need to create a web page?

Having asked this question of many of my peers, I received a positive answer from all. Why is that so? One of the important factors related to the distribution channel is the value-added and the cost of each channel. Using e-commerce, a business could cut its costs and could introduce its products to a different range of customers. A research study by A.T. Kearney (Muhamad, 2003) showed that Web-based processes can save 10-30% from operating costs, cut cycle times up to 90%, and virtually eliminate the supply and demand mismatches that cause inventory buildups and stock outs. For example, according to Benjamin and Wigand (1995), the high quality shirts market could reduce the retail price by almost 62% if wholesalers and retailers could be eliminated from the traditional value chain.

For some businesses implementing the access of its product on the Internet is not only possible, it is necessary. Some products that can be digitized and delivered electronically, such as software, music, video or words, help a company's distribution channel to operate with no intermediaries. For buyers, the digital marketplace implies low transaction costs, easier access to price and product information, and the capacity to combine volume. For suppliers, it involves lower selling and transaction costs, access to wider markets, and the avoidance of oligopolistic distribution channels. New technologies innovation will undoubtedly make it easier for parties to search for and exchange products with one another.

Promoting web businesses

If a business is not using the Internet to operate as a sale tool, it can be used as a communication tool. It can help people locate the nearest available source for products and can potentially boost a company's sales.

Lets consider some unconventional channels of distribution on the web. These could be a medium to promote a business and increase website traffic.

1. Social networks such as Facebook or MySpace are the popular social networking sites, which could be of a great advantage to a company's distribution channels. Understanding its potential and its impact on Internet users, the firm could reach more people.
2. Social bookmarks such as Delicious, StumbleUpon or Digg enable users to share, organize and store web pages of companies they like or find useful.
3. Social media such as YouTube, Flickr are the video and photo-sharing network, which might help market a business and its products.
4. Blogs are a popular media as well. These provide up-to-date information and allow readers to engage in discussions via comments. Businesses can create loyal readers and interact with its customers.
5. Widgets and gadgets such as iGoogle gadgets or Yahoo widgets deliver a dynamic and updated content for news, photos and weather to strengthen the presence of a specific brand.
6. Browser extensions such as customized search engine and toolbars provide users with easy access to business websites.
7. Search engines have the power to drive targeted and qualified traffic to a website and improve visibility of a business.

Choosing the right strategy for a business

Eric K. Clemons, Wharton professor of operations and information management, suggests that before launching an e-commerce effort and bypassing its traditional distribution channels, a business should analyze which products are appropriate for electronic distribution, which consumer activities will be supported by which channel participants, and which segments or groups of consumers are likely to adopt electronic distribution. In order to prove his point he used as an example the British banks and its credit card industry with "one size fits all" approach to their credit cardholders. It resulted in extreme differences in profitability due to a cross subsidy. (Knowledge@Wharton, 2001)

V. Kasturi Rangan (Silverthorne, 2006), Harvard Business School marketing professor, argues that most channels are constructed from the supplier out, rather than from the customer in. So the product or service is designed first and it is only then that the supplier thinks about ways to get the product/service out to the customer. More information can be delivered on the Internet compared to what a human being could possibly remember and convey. Sales channels can successfully use the Internet as a complement to carry certain aspects of its selling job.

However, a company might need to use multiple distribution channels for different products. Kevin L. Webb mentioned that the advantages of having more distribution channels are:

- The multichannel distribution strategy allows manufacturers to better adapt to changing customer needs and shopping patterns.
- Firms that have broad product lines can benefit by creating different optimal channels for its wide selection.
- Firms with excess manufacturing capacity can profit from additional outlets when existing channels are full with supply.
- Supplier can focus on more precise target markets, thereby ameliorating competitiveness.

Some disadvantages of the company in having multiple channels:

- It places competing demands on company resources such as capital, personnel, and technology.
- Multiple distribution channels may compete with each other for the same customers in the marketplace, which might raise intermediary dissatisfaction and customer confusion.

How companies can use both traditional methods and the Internet to greatest strategic advantage

Unfortunately some people or organizations are not open to change, as they are skeptical of the new technology or perhaps because they lack the necessary capabilities or financial resources. It is hard to change. It implies a different thought process, imagination and flexibility. Some strong companies that didn't change their distribution strategy and no longer exist include WT Grant, Montgomery Ward, Venture, Ayr-Way,

Gold Circle, Hills, Super-X, Bambergers, B. Altman, Bonwit Teller and Wannamakers.

A successful company that has changed and added flexibility to its business is Ebay, an Internet store with an auction format. With more than 90 million active users globally, eBay is the world's largest online marketplace. While it started out as simply an auction site, it has expanded by acquiring innovative businesses, such as Shopping.com, StubHub, Rent.com, Bill Me Later, Half.com, and others.

However, it is easier for established firms to adopt and integrate Internet methods than for dot-coms to adopt and integrate traditional ones. A company that does not take the time to consider its vulnerabilities and opportunities related to e-commerce stands a good chance of being overshadowed by ones that do. Virtual activities do not eliminate the need for physical activities, but often magnify their importance. By using the Internet, a company can create a technological platform that reinforces its strategic functions. It can complement but not hurt the traditional way of competing. For example Walgreens drug store chain, which consists of 6,000 stores, provides on-line prescription ordering in addition to its traditional way. Customers who order over the Web, 90 % of them prefer to pick up their prescriptions at a store rather than have them shipped to their homes. Its extensive network of stores remains a powerful advantage. Web ordering increases the value of its physical locations, so complementing the existing competitive advantage. W.W. Grainger, a distributor of maintenance products and spare parts to companies found that its printed catalog bolsters its on-line operation. Many firms have the instinct to eliminate printed catalogs once their content is replicated on-line, but Grainger continues to publish it as it has found that each time a new one is distributed it boosts its online orders.

By integrating virtual and physical activities to compensate for the Internet's functioning limits such as the inability to try or touch a product, the firm can gain competitive advantages.

Future implications

Internet commerce has emerged quickly. It allows the user to connect straight to his purchasing needs in a rapid way. Businesses can no longer ignore this movement and will need to adapt, presenting merchandise in a virtual world.

Inspired by Isaac Asimov, in the next century e-commerce may well be dominated by monopolies that will try to control each individual's life. Having acquired key information about each human being from the internet, these giant enterprises will try to manipulate each decision individuals make online.

However, what is apparent is that in order to be a successful company, the established ones need to use the Internet and its technology to make traditional business activities better. They need to find and apply new combinations of virtual and physical activities that will help generate profit. The Internet presents many companies with the option of reducing or eliminating the role of intermediaries. In this way the business could cut its costs and introduce its products to a different range of customers.

REFERENCES

Akaah, I. P., Korgaonkar P. K. "A conjoint investigation of the relative importance of risk." *Journal of Advertising Research*. 28 (4), 1988, pp.38-44.

Asimov, Isaac. "The Supermarket 2077 A.D." *Progressive Grocer* 56, June (1977)

Benjamin, R. and Wigand, R. "Electronic markets and virtual value chains on the information superhighway." *Sloan Management Review*, Vol. 36 No. 2, pp. 62-72. (1995)

Dirk Van den Poel, Leunis Joseph. "Consumer Acceptance of the Internet as a Channel of Distribution." *Journal of Business Research* 45, 249–256 (1999).

Edelman, David C. *Branding in the Digital Age: You're Spending Your Money in All the Wrong Places.*

Foderaro, Lisa W. *"In a Digital Age, Students Still Cling to Paper Textbooks."* NY Times, October 19, 2010.

Goel, Sanjay and Miesing, Paul and Chandra, Uday. *The Impact of Illegal Peer-to-Peer File-Sharing on the Media Industry.* May 01, 2010.

Jantan, Muhamad and Ndubisi, Nelson Oly and Yean Ong Boon. "Viability of e-commerce as an alternative distribution channel." *Logistics Information Management* Volume 16, Number 6, pp. 427-439 (2003).

Koo, Bonwoo and Mantin Benny, and O'Connor Peter. *Online distribution of airline tickets: Should airlines adopt a single or a multi-channel approach?*

Kotler. *Marketing An Introduction.* Pearson Prentice Hall (2009).

Lam, Calvin K.M. and Tan Bernard C.Y. "The Internet is changing the music industry." *Communication of the ACM*, August 2001/Vol. 44, No. 8.

Levy, Efraim. "Old Economy Meets The Internet." *S&P Equity Analyst.*

Pitt, Leyland and Berthon, Pierre and Berthon, Jean-Paul. "Changing Channels: The

Impact of the Internet on Distribution Strategy.*" Business Horizons*, March-April 1999.

Peterson, Robert A. and Balasubramanian, Sridhar and Bronnenberg, Bart J. "Exploring the implications of the internet for consumer marketing." *Journal of the Academy of Marketing Science.* Volume 25, Number 4, 329-346.

Porter, Michael E. *Competitive Advantage: Creating and Sustaining Superior Performance.* NewYork (1985).

Shujaat, Komal. *Distribution Strategy.*< http://www.scribd.com/doc/18789011/Distribution-Strategy>.

Silverthorne Sean and Rangan, Kasturi V. *The Strategic Way to Go to Market* (2006).

Simpson, Penny M. and Barnett, William and Simpson Claude L. *Disintermediation: an exploratory study of changing channel structure in e- commerce b to c markets.*

Solá, Javier. *The Strategic Impact of the Internet in a Given Industry.*

Webb, Kevin L. *Managing channels of distribution in the age of electronic commerce.* 17 April 2001.

"Changing Channel Distribution Models in the Internet Age." Knowledge @ Wharton, June 06, 2001.

Scientific American, October 2010 volume 303, nr 4.

"Web enabling your sales and distribution channel." Stylusinc.< http://www.stylusinc.com/WebEnable/Ecommerce/DistributorNetwork.php>

http://www.census.gov/compendia/statab/cats/information_communications/internet_publishing_and_broadcasting_and_internet_usage.html

http://www.internetworldstats.com/am/us.htm

http://www.capv.com/public/home.html

http://www.consumeraffairs.com/travel/priceline_complaints.htm

http://eisabainyo.net/weblog/online-distribution-channels

3

Labor Markets and the Internet

Liz Tripp and Jess Azulay

As college students operating in a technology driven world, where an hour without internet access (even while sleeping) seems impossible to fathom, it can be hard to understand how labor markets existed and efficiently functioned before cyberspace permeated almost every aspect of American culture. How did people find out about any and every company they were interested in applying to without scouring endless newspapers and traveling to visit each one? How did potential applicants fire off resumes to twenty-five different potential employers, and simultaneously log their resumes in a database accessed by thousands or millions of potential employers to discover? How were companies able to post available jobs for instant viewing by millions of qualified (or, non-qualified) applicants? Better yet, how were companies able to create descriptions of their job openings so that lists of words entered into a search engine would trigger their job popping to the top of the list? How were employees able to communicate between one another, send documents instantly for collaboration? There are a hundred more questions that could be posed, all circling around to the same realization: cyberspace has dramatically altered the way that job seekers and job providers interact, the skills that are now necessary on the most basic level for employment, the efficiency with which companies and applicants can act, and the efficiency with which companies perform.

One of the most influential pieces of literature concerning cyberspace and the labor market is David Autor's article "Wiring the Labor Market." He sets up the main thrust of his argument about how the Internet is affecting the labor market in his opening paragraph: "Electronic commerce specifically, and the Internet more generally, promise to open new channels for improved worker-firm communications" (Autor 25-40).

This increase in society's dependence on technology and expectation of faster communication and happenings via the Internet is altering the way that labor markets are forming and interacting, as well as the skills that are becoming necessary to navigate the labor world. It is shifting the need for local labor, it is changing the way that applicants and employers are finding one another, and it is shaping the future industries and markets that are emerging, as well as increasing the efficiencies of the labor markets. Fundamental technological literacy is required for basic functions such as job applications, and real technological literacy is required for any sort of job that pays higher than minimum wage, and even some that pay minimum wage (Borghans, and Baster 85-98), (Henry 614-627).

One area where there is a very clear shift in labor market dynamics as a result of cyberspace's presence is applicant-employer relations. While there is a real lack of literature published (overall) regarding how the Internet is (or is not) changing labor market dynamics, there is a fair share of literature already published on how people use the Internet in searching for jobs, and how companies use cyberspace for the purpose of recruiting potential applicants. Throughout much of modern history, traditional methods (examples here taken from the CPS monthly survey) of recruiting have included private employment agencies, friends/ relatives, school/university employment centers; union/professional registers, placed or answered ads, and "other" active methods (Kuhn, and Skuterud 1-11). In highlighting just one of these methods, say, newspaper advertisements, it is clear to see that there are great inefficiencies in such methods. For a typical company to advertise for job openings in the pre-Internet recruitment age a company would have to develop an advertisement, mail or deliver it to a newspaper by a deadline, pay for ad space each week (or month, etc.), wait for the ad to begin to circulate, receive applications by mail or delivery over a period of time, processing all applications by hand, delivering decisions via mail or phone, and then waiting for replies via phone or mail. It seems a cumbersome process. And this is only for a single job posting. This time effect is simply multiplied when one considers a company hiring multiple positions, or that has to change the job description of a position posted, etc.

As such, Internet recruiting methods, or e-recruiting, has started to become quite commonplace, really emerging in the mid-1990s (Parry, and Tyson 257-274)). A 2002 study cites that over 90% of Fortune 500 companies use online recruiting (Feldman, and Klaas 175-192). By 2003 94% of Fortune 500 companies were using their websites for recruiting purposes, and researchers such as Farrukh Suvanakulov are making bold statements such as "Career web pages on corporate websites have also become a norm for most employers" (Suvankulov), confirming what most people see in their everyday job searches today: the Internet matters…a lot. Perhaps, however, it would be helpful to define online recruiting, or e-recruiting, before moving any further in this discussion.

As Nakamura, et al., define e-recruiting in 2008, e-recruiting services include three key components: advertising job ads on general jobsites, constructing and operating custom employment sections on corporate websites, and using searchable resume databanks (Nakamura, Shaw, Freeman, Nakamura, and Pyman). There are definite advantages for companies that can capitalize on e-recruiting, with the main advantages being: lower costs, critical time efficiency, increased user-friendliness, and access to vastly larger amounts of information. Freeman feels that "internet recruitment has the potential for making its biggest contribution to the labor market by producing better job matches" (Suvankulov). And, as with any great innovations and changes, there are downfalls as well, including, but not limited to: an adverse selection problem, which is related to companies receiving overwhelming numbers of applicants, the lack of human interaction, privacy concerns, and, as Linda Barber insightfully notes, unintended discrimination against minorities and low-income job seekers (Suvankulov).

One of the seemingly largest advantages of e-recruiting is the decreased recruiting costs that almost any firm can experience, although the positive effects of this are amplified among larger institutions due to increased returns to scale. For example, as Autor (2001) explains, a Monster.com thirty-day advertisement cost only 5% of what a Sunday New York Times advertisement cost. Not only that, but Monster.com was seeing 223% more traffic at this same time. When one really considers the tangible costs of producing a print ad versus publishing an ad online, it seems incredibly logical that the costs should not compare. Monster.com is currently advertising to employers that they can buy job postings for $210-$395 (monthly) that will be viewable by 17.9 million candidates ("Online Job Posting | Monster.com"). Careerbuilder.com is selling one month-long job postings for $419, with savings per job posting as employers post more jobs, and showing statistics of having over 23 million unique monthly viewers ("CareerBuilder.com Turns Dreams into Quality Job Applications"). Furthermore, many companies are also exploring and using the option of creating their own career websites. While they incur an initial cost of setting up the career website, the payoff becomes positive quickly as there are minimal maintenance costs and the reliance on finding information on the Internet is ever increasing. And, companies most often have internal technology teams that can perform these services, so they can receive services at a no-markup price. It is clear that cost-savings is a major advantage of e-recruiting.

Another efficiency of e-recruiting that is of an almost equal importance is the reduced time it takes to advertise positions. As they say, time is money, and in this case, time is cut drastically. As one can infer from the previous example of the lengthy time requirements for creating a newspaper advertisement, traditional methods of recruiting can have great time inefficiencies. Suvankulov (2010) cites a study in his dissertation that quite clearly shows the potential timesaving. For an average company with a forty-three day hiring cycle the study proposes that a seventeen-day decrease can be found through online recruiting: 6 days can be taken off for producing an online advertisement instead of a newspaper advertisement, 4 days can be saved through accepting online applications instead of paper applications, and using online screening and processing technologies can reduce the cycle by over a week. Especially when one considers a company that is in a time crunch for hiring a position, or a company that has high turnover rates or is constantly hiring, these timesavings can add up into very meaningful efficiency increases for a company. Efficiency increases lead to greater productivity, which leads to a higher GDP and income, according to the most basic economic models. And, you would be hard pressed to find someone to argue with higher income!

The two other main advantages, increased user-friendliness and access to information, go hand-in-hand, much like the first two advantages. When thinking about how user-friendliness is improved for companies, it is helpful to consider the process that companies must go through using traditional methods of recruiting, and then considering how the process is different in online recruiting.

Let's presume that a company wants to place a newspaper advertisement for its job openings. The advertisement must be sent to the newspaper, where it will then be printed after a certain period of time. However, what if an error occurs (either on behalf of the company or the newspaper), or if the job requirements change, or if the company is not getting the response that it expects and feels it should change the wording of its advertisement? In any of these cases the response by the company would be to resubmit the information to the newspaper, and wait for the cycle to begin again. It is a process largely out of their control, and does not have any aspect of instant gratification in it. Now, let's examine this same situation in the context of online advertisements. For any of the proposed changes to occur, a company simply logs onto their own career website or a job-board website, makes the appropriate changes, and is done. And, the power stays within the company to make changes or updates – it is not relying on a third party to execute such important tasks.

Right along with the improved user-friendliness is the vast amount of information that becomes available to potential employees with the use of cyberspace. Not only are print-ads expensive, as previously discussed, they are expensive for a small amount of space. Companies cannot really convey their mission statements, their benefits, their goals and expectations, or meaningful information about the jobs themselves (such as requirements, commitments, etc.) in a small print ad. Yet, when the box of online recruiting is opened, information galore is available. Employers can link their websites directly from job-board postings, and can post full job descriptions on their websites instead of just snippets of information intended to capture the attention of the correct applicants. Employers are not only able to offer more information to applicants, but they are also able to harvest endless information about who is viewing their job postings, what peer companies are offering in terms of jobs, salaries, benefits, etc., as well as access resume banks, etc. As anyone can attest that has performed a Google search, the Internet is home to extensive amounts of information. The more that employers know, the more efficient they can make their processes, as well as the more attractive they can make their positions, increasing applicant knowledge and, potentially, qualifications, and, again, increasing productivity as an end goal.

While most of the discussion on e recruiting thus far has been focused on advantages to the employers, these four main advantages apply to job seekers just the same. Reduced costs and time commitments are very applicable advantages for applicants. On a most basic level, the ability to apply online to jobs saves people the cost of printing and mailing applications. Depending on the volume of job applications one is sending, this cost can be significant. On a more general basis, applications can be instantly submitted to multiple companies with one click online, and the time it takes to find jobs dramatically decreases. One can perform an online search through a general search engine or a more specified website (such as Monster.com) and instantly find thousands of available jobs. The days of having to slowly peruse newspapers to find even one interesting job are no more, as you can filter results online by almost any qualification to find the jobs that you want. This leads right to the increased user-friendliness. It is not user-friendly to peruse ad section after ad section to not find any jobs of interest. It is user-friendly to log onto a job-board website that has already done the work of collecting tens of thousands job postings and click through by location, salary, necessary experience, work environment, etc. until you find a list of jobs that may fit your expectations. It is user-friendly to have the ability to upload your resume and CV one time, and then send it to as many employers as you wish without continuing to reprint or buy stamps, or having to continually re-upload documents. And finally, the applicants really benefit from the increased amount of available information. Since companies are able to make so much information available, applicants can really get an excellent feel for the companies they are perusing and make better decisions on where they want to spend their time and money pursuing jobs. Applicants need not visit every company they are interested in to see if they might be a good fit, but can narrow down the list to better spend their time on a select few that make really good sense. And, much like companies can utilize information gathering sites like salary.com, applicants can also learn to develop a better feel for what their salary range should be in their position as they can discover what the market is paying, across the board. More information leads to more informed applicants, which leads to better job selection and happier employees.

Like any new and flourishing system, there are potential drawbacks to job searching and matching via the Internet. One of the largest concerns for companies recruiting online is the problem of adverse selection, which is related to the predicament of targeting passive candidates. Since searching for and applying for jobs over the Internet is so easy for applicants, it has increased the numbers of applicants dramatically. However, many of these applicants are now not qualified for the positions. Furthermore, the overall pool of candidates is not necessarily increasing in quality, since now a lot of the people that would not have taken the time before to apply are applying (even the lazy can do it). Additionally, the passive candidates, or those that are currently employed – and therefore theoretically more valuable – are no more likely to apply. So, companies have to face the challenge of sorting through more applications, which are not necessarily better applications, in order to still find the top applicants. To help combat this problem, some companies offer screening devices such as online tests that must be completed to determine initial competency or using a software program that uses tagged words in resumes or CVs in order to sort out candidates. At any rate, excessive applications are a new problem encountered with this increased efficiency, and there is plenty of room for innovative ideas on how to curb this adverse selection problem.

Another concern for both employers and potential employees is the complete lack of human interaction when recruiting online. An advantage of having to call and speak with applicants, or see them in the flesh, is that companies are able to feel out the social skills of that individual, as well as see how the person may fit within the company. Additionally, the applicants are able to get a feel for the company's culture and expectations. Removing this personal aspect from the recruiting process can disadvantage both sides of the equation. On a related note, privacy concerns increase when information is transmitted in cyberspace. When the personal, human interaction still exists, people often feel more confident in the protection of their sensitive information. It is well known that the Internet is not particularly safe in terms of individuals' privacy matters, however, and this can be a concern when applying for jobs.

Discrimination can also be a concern with the advent of online recruiting, whether in terms of the "digital divide," or discrimination against minorities, or through any other channel. The digital divide refers to "the gap between people with effective access to digital and information technology, including the Internet, and those with very limited or no access" (Suvankulov). One can easily imagine that this divide then happens along a socioeconomic line quite often, as those without resources are those that will not have computers, computer access, or time for job searching over the Internet. And, the socioeconomic divide in the US is too often congruous with the racial divide. As such, this becomes a perpetuating problem that the Internet is only amplifying as it increases the efficiency of those that can use it, leaving those that cannot even farther behind.

While e-recruiting and job searching on the Internet can sound like wonderful new advantages that our society is still in the process of understanding and fully exploiting, there is still much space for improvement. Some companies have started to set some "best practices" for e-recruiting and interacting with applicants, while other companies have entered the market to capitalize on others' lacks of experience with e-recruiting and innovate brand new ways to utilize the Internet to its full capacity. Feldman and Klass conducted a study published in 2002 that analyzed experiences applicants had with online recruiting, and had several suggestions on how to improve the online recruiting experience for applicants. Since 2002, it appears that many of these suggestions have been enacted for most companies (such as allowing resumes to be uploaded in a uniform fashion and not having to continually change resume formats for uploading, etc.). However, the article also cites Cisco as an example of "one of the most user-friendly resume-building programs in the industry..." with features such as a button that one can click when their boss is coming to instantly display a fake screen with successful employee habits without losing the progress on their resume and a feature where applicants can connect with current employees in their department of interest. It is this kind of innovation that will continue to allow companies to excel in the e-recruiting world and change the way that employees and applicants view the job search process.

Another innovative approach that some companies are beginning to take is one that Jobs2Web is becoming a leader in. The company aims to help Human Resource departments advertise more effectively on the Internet through the use of their "Recruiting Marketing Platform." They advertise their core competencies to be: "automated job matching/alerts, email subscription management, recruiting dashboard and analytics, talent community, and passive candidate capture and source tagging of applicants" (http://www.jobs2web.com/solutions/). It is most interesting to see their advertisement of capturing the passive applicants as a recurring theme throughout criticisms of e-recruiting (Parry and Tyson

257-274). A company like Jobs2Web represents both a new market for labor, as they are creating a new type of company, as well as innovation for solving the problems found thus far with e recruiting. It would be quite interesting to look at their recruiting strategy!

Not only has the Internet changed the processes that occur before one begins a job, the dawn of the Internet age has changed the work place environment. Many jobs that were once restricted to the office may now be done from home and the physical interactions may now be conducted via the Internet. Bosses can email instructions and tasks and employees can submit paperwork electronically. This job flexibility allows for workers to make their own hours, and allows for a flexible working environment. It is no longer necessary to sit in an office from 9-5. With the Internet, one can work from home in pajamas or from a coffee shop down the street. For many new jobs, one does not even need to be in the same state as the brick and mortar location of the business. The only limitation is finding a place with a wireless signal. Having the flexibility to work anywhere has its advantages. A study conducted at the University of Iceland states the following advantages to job flexibility: You can chose when to start and end your day, where you work, you have increased autonomy, there is an enhanced employee productivity, a decrease in stress levels, improved work-family balance, and overall increases in job satisfaction. (Heijstra, Gudbjorb, and Rafnsdottir 159-159). Increased job satisfaction leads to workers who are dedicated to their jobs and work hard.

Many people prefer this job flexibility because they feel that it will improve their family relations. For parents, being able to work from home means that they can spend more time with their children. One can be home to prepare breakfast and school lunches, take the children to school, work while they are in school, pick them up from school and continue working after they have gone to bed. This reduces the cost of childcare needs. Reduced childcare costs is important as childcare is often a major factor in parents' decisions to find employment or to be a stay at home parent.

However, being accessible anywhere and at anytime can have negative impacts. Not having a personal connection to your workplace can lead to a sense of isolation. Information may not be transferred properly through email, whether through a misunderstanding of intent or technological difficulties on either end. Trying to coordinate tasks through email can be particularly stressful when you are working on a tight deadline and are not receiving the information you need from a colleague via email. Also, increased flexibility leads to the assumption that one is available at all hours of the day. This leads to an increase in the tasks one is expected to complete. An increased workload can cut into personal time and negatively impact work-family balance.

The same study at the University of Iceland examined the work-family balance amongst professors at the university. Those who participated found that the Internet greatly extended their working day. A few participants stated that checking their email was the first thing they did in the morning. One person stated that his working day ended when he fell asleep. Another participant appreciated being able to extend the working day beyond 9-5 and working on the weekends because the participant felt that she could concentrate with fewer distractions. Several participants reported anxiety if they were unable to check their emails. Staying on top of upwards of 70 emails a day allowed interviewees to feel like they were in control of their workload.

Along with having to check their inboxes for emails from students and their fellow academics, the academics were expected to prepare multimedia class lessons and extensive handouts. Several of those who participated in the survey expressed concerns that students were avoiding their course books and relying on professors to do the work for them. The academic's responsibilities extended beyond course work: "Participants work in the evening on things that they could not finish during the day, on their research that will help them to progress with their careers, on international projects, on emails from students and on contacts with co-workers in different time-zones." (Heijstra, Gudbjorb, and Rafnsdottir 161). While the participants identified the pluses and minuses of the Internet and their work lives, only a few felt that there was a positive correlation between the Internet and work-family balance. The study concluded that while increased job flexibility has it's benefits, it has become difficult to disengage from ones' work. This can increase work-family conflicts, the risk of burnout, and work related obligations.

We've seen how the Internet can both positively and negatively impact those with "traditional" 9-5 jobs, but how does the Internet affect those who are self-employed and therefore always make their own hours? The advent of the Internet has made self-employment easier than ever before. Not only do you have the flexibility to work wherever you want, depending on your business, but you can advertise and find clients around the world. When starting your own business, most of the tools you need can be found online: loans, advertising, information on trainings and tips for success, just to name a few. Once your business is established, advertising and communicating with your clients is much easier and cost efficient if done on through the Internet. People are starting to expect communications via email and as the world becomes more "eco-friendly", printed communications may become rare. Being technologically savvy is a great advantage for the success of one's business. Having a great website can make a huge difference when it comes to attracting clients and investors.

A young couple from San Francisco was asked to comment on the role the Internet has played in their lives. The woman is a self-employed yoga instructor and health counselor and the man works for a company that specializes in "dynamic personalization for e-commerce," (richrelevance). Like many around the world, the Internet is an important part of their daily lives.

She was able to learn about the certification classes necessary for her profession through the Internet. The resources provided online by the certification programs were very beneficial tools during her time of study. She describes her average workday as a bit erratic. A few days a week she teaches yoga across town, but generally starts working in the late morning. Most of her working hours are spent in her home office on her computer. Most of her time on the Internet is spent researching or writing articles and recommendations. She researches her clients' health related concerns, looking for both causes of their symptoms and finding the appropriate food based remedies upon which her business is based. Through her computer and her phone, she is constantly able to check her email. She says that she checks her email over ten times a day. Through two separate accounts she guesses that she receives between 30 and 40 emails daily. Aside from sending and receiving emails, the Internet plays an important role in her business.

The Internet has provided a space for her to advertise her business. She refers her clients, and potential clients, to her website and her social media pages which are regularly updated with information about the services she provides and her e-newsletter. Social networking sites have played a large role in increasing her client base. Through Facebook, Twitter, Linked in, and Yelp, she is able to keep her clients updated on upcoming programs she is offering and great healthy recipes. Her social media sites also allow for her clients to connect with each other and they make it easier spread the word about her business. The Internet has also provided a space for her to communicate. All of her monthly newsletters are sent via the Internet. She is able to share documents with clients and information with colleagues with a simple click of the mouse. While her business might be able to survive without the Internet, it would be much more difficult to succeed. The Internet has become such a crucial part of her life that she cannot imagine her life and business without it.

Her partner works for an Internet company that specializes in custom, personalized, e-Commerce. This company's major product is "personalized advertising on shopping media" (richrelevance). Their clients include Walmart.com, Overstock.com, Sears, Office Depot, 1-800 flowers.com and Disney Store, among other well-known brands. Personalized advertising is reflected in the section of the website that states "People who viewed this item also viewed" and "buy together with", though the wording of these sections is customized for each website. These sections specifically market similar items and are meant to show the shopper items they may also enjoy and increase the amount of items the shopper purchases while online.

Working for a company has created a more structured work environment for him. He arrives in the office around 8:30 each morning. He begins his day be checking his email. He then begins working on projects and reviews upcoming deadlines. He works for approximately three to four hours until lunch, and often takes lunch at his desk. After lunch, he remains at his desk, with occasional meetings, for six to eight hours. Upon leaving the office for the night, he works an additional one to two hours from home. Throughout the day he is consistently checking his email. It is a required form of communication for his company and he remarked that prompt responses are important. He guesses that he receives on average 100 emails a day, but there is a wide variance. Some days he has received as many as 300 messages.

The Internet plays a dominant role in his daily life. The ability for him to work remotely is very easy to do. The Internet has made video conferencing free and the quality of video conferencing has improved greatly. Instant messaging and emails have proven to be great communication tools, especially when one considers the expense of long-distance phone calls. There is also the added time saving of not having to wait on correspondences via the postal service. He also expressed the importance of the Internet in regards to resources and information. The Internet provides easy access to information and publicly available documents. There is also a greater access to discussion forums on technology, which directly relate to his job.

He also commented on the benefits and disadvantages of the Internet. Due to the Internet there is no concept of after business hours. It is expected that you will always be able to provide prompt responses. Being reachable at all times keeps you hooked to the Internet, checking to see if people have responded to your inquiries and responding to people's messages to you. Not only do you have access to your inbox, but you can also access your files from both a computer and your phone meaning you can conduct business at anytime, in almost anyplace.

Aside from the fact that the company's whole business model is based on the Internet, all of their clients also operate in the e-commerce space. The company provides services and software specifically for the Internet. He has found that the way he conducts business, project management, communication, and data management, all depend on the Internet. The company he works for would not be able to survive without the Internet. Not only has he been employed for the past seven year because of the Internet, but should he decide to pursue another job, the Internet has made professional networking much easier than it once was.

The Internet has created many new jobs. "The Internet-industry has been discussed as one of the most prominent forerunners of "new work", since it has emerged in the US constellation of the "roaring nineties" with its neo-liberal apotheosis of market hegemony, emphasis on shareholder- value and "new economy"-speak, particularly nourished by the new kind of economic activity and work centered around the World Wide Web," (Mayer-Ahuja and Wolf, 75). It was hoped that the jobs created by the Internet would create scores of new jobs and result in massive employment. Some places have not seen the boost in employment that was initially expected because companies were often able to adjust and can now provide maintenance and multi-media services themselves instead of looking to outside companies. "[There] is a "core" of specialized service providers, which were usually founded in the second half of the 1990s and are focusing on e-business, Web-Design, Hosting, e-learning or other Internet-related services as their main business," (Mayer-Ahuja and Wolf, 78). The Internet has definitely created a plethora of new jobs, "[as] Internet-Services are constituting a new blend of IT, telecommunications, advertising and media, however, companies need to assemble different competencies, thus employing programmers, designers, project managers and sometimes even content specialists," (Mayer-Ahuja and Wolf, 80). Mayer-Ahuja and Wolf have identified five task complexes that the Internet has created. Those five are customer contact, planning and organization functions, conception, design, and programming and technical implementation. All these tasks require knowledge of marketing, graphic skills, and a basic understanding of the Internet. Software development is another new industry created by the Internet. These new companies also present a new structural hierarchy in the work place. Internet based companies have seen an increase in both horizontal and vertical differentiation according to Mayer-Ahuja and Wolf. They conclude:

> "Moreover, the division of labor is currently increased, responsibility (for customer relations etc.) is centralized, and formal hierarchies are established in many companies, transferring authority and planning functions to project managers, heads of department or the management. This does not (necessarily) imply deskilling and micro-control of tasks, but nevertheless, the collective muddling–through of the late 1990s, which may have implied some potential for self-determined labor, is losing ground to an amazing extent. Finally, standardized working-hours seem to be emerging, which are usually associated with Fordist times, but accepted by employees in order to adapt to customers' office hours, to cooperate with colleagues and to match superiors' preferences," (Mayer-Ahuja and Wolf, 97).

The Internet has created several new industries and has had an impact on the work-environment.

Website design is one of the most important factors in many firms' public relations campaigns. Also, having a strong website can be a key factor in finding potential investors and employees. Computer programming and software design are two other computer-based industries that have benefited from the rise of the Internet. These two industries are integral to the development of the Internet. Often the challenges users experience with the Internet are the things start-ups are working on fixing. The Internet also allows for flexibility in these industries, because as long as you have a computer you can program. Since it is not necessary to be in the same location as your peers, collaborations can occur across continents. This increased flexibility leads to an increase in employment opportunities in existing firms as well as a place for new firms to rise to the challenge of fixing some of the setbacks of the Internet.

Making advertising easier and creating IT jobs is all well and good, but there are also several industries that are being threatened by the Internet thus leading to the demise of many jobs in these industries. For instance, with so much information readily available online, people find it easier, and more ecologically friendly to not get their news in print. Newspapers and printed forms of communication are becoming increasingly unpopular. Many papers around the world have been forced out of circulation because of a lack of subscriptions. This has led to increased unemployment among journalists and other workers dependent on the newspaper industry.

The Internet has also provided greater access to a global pool of potential employees. Now that the working day is no longer limited to 9-5, people have begun expecting 24-hour customer service. This means that companies need to provide services around the clock. While many companies have begun employing computerized systems, consumers complain about the impersonal nature of talking to machines. To rectify this many companies have begun to outsource their call centers. Now you can call a help line and talk to a person 24 hours a day.

Other jobs are being outsourced as well. Many jobs no longer require a physical presence in the workplace. Tasks can be completed from around the globe with the click of a few buttons. Physical communication is not necessary with the ability to have conference calls online and through programs like Skype that allow you to communicate and virtually share documents from anywhere in the world with Internet access. Chances are growing that you don't actually need to be present in your workplace to still be effective. The Internet allows for us to work wherever and whenever is most convenient. The amounts of resources available online, makes needing physical copies of things almost obsolete, and most computers can be programmed to perform the same basic tasks. Wall Street, once bustling with traders on the floor is relatively quiet now that traders can do the same jobs from a computer. Even classrooms are growing emptier as lecture notes are available online, professors can record their lectures and even telecast into a classroom, as long as there is a computer.

Companies can see the benefit of moving low-skilled jobs off-shore because the jobs are moved to low-wage economies. "It is precisely such differences in wages that have led some Western governments to give up the fight for low-skilled jobs enabling emerging economies to benefit from new export-oriented employment, at the same time that the developed economies are left to compete for the global supply of high-skilled, high-waged jobs," (Brown, Ashton, Lauder, and Tholen, 21). In the United States, Brown et al. cite that a majority of the fast-growing jobs that require advanced training are in IT related fields. This puts the US in direct competition with India. This competition is intensified by the fact that engineering a computer chip can be done for up to 10 times less the cost outside of the United States.

A T Kearny reports that a wider range of jobs will be outsourced in the near future. Traditionally, back office jobs, such as data entry and transaction processing, had been sent overseas. Now, any job that does not require physical interactions with customers will be fair game for relocation. Brown et al. state that "22 percent and 29 percent of all US jobs are impersonally delivered in that they can potentially be delivered electronically over long distance with little or no degradation in quality, and are therefore potentially offshorable," (Brown, Ashton, Lauder, and Tholen, 23). These jobs include call-center operators and scientists. Jobs like child-care workers, surgeons and janitors, are considered personally delivered, and are most likely safe from exportation. Few jobs are safe in a globalizing world, where technology has created new markets and made it easier to complete tasks from anywhere in the world.

In conclusion, since 2001, the Internet has become an increasing resource for those looking for jobs. Both those currently employed, but looking for a new job, and those currently unemployed use job sites like Careerbuilder.com, jobvertise.com and jobspider.com that allow you post your resume online. These sites also allow employers to post job openings online. E-recruiting can reduce the cost of hiring and can extend the reach of the recruitment efforts. The adverse selection process is present in the e-recruiting market. Many employers who post jobs online are looking for people who are currently employed. They are skeptical of hiring the unemployed because it is harder to verify why these people are unemployed. Employers may also assume that people are turning to job sites because they lack the social networks to find jobs other ways.

The Internet allows employers and employees to maintain connections around the globe. With e-mail, employees can send messages much faster than through the postal service. Programs like Skype allow employees call and exchange information with others, cameras in both computers enable people to make videoconference calls around the world, and through screen-sharing two computers can see the same things. Sites like Linked In allow people to connect to personal and professional networks. However, this can represent a negative as well as a postive for workers as employers often look at social networking sites such as Facebook and Myspace pages of potential employees. The contents of one's profile can influence employers' hiring decisions.

From changing the way that employees look for jobs to changing the way that companies expect their employees to work, and all the steps along the way, the Internet has provided a revolution within labor markets. It has increased efficiency in the job search process. It has made the standard workweek practically obsolete, and instant communication is becoming the norm through e-mail, instant messaging, and smart phones. Computer technology has dramatically changed work life, and the next few decades and beyond should prove crucial in understanding the ever-increasing implications of the Internet's role in labor markets and the workplace.

REFERENCES

Autor, David. "Wiring the Labor Market." *Journal of Economic Perspectives* 15.1 (2001): 25-40. Web. 27 Oct 2010.

Borghans, Lex, and Weel Bas ter. "Are computer skills the new basic skills? The returns to computer, writing and math skills in Britain." *Labour Economics* 11. (2004): 85-98. Web. 7 Nov 2010.

Brown, Phillip, David Ashton, Hugh Lauder, and Gerbrand Tholen. "Towards a High-Skilled, Low Waged Workforce?" Monograph No. 10, October 2008.

Feldman, Daniel, and Brian Klaas. "Internet job hunting: A field study of applicant experiences with on-line recruiting." *Human Resource Management, ProQuest Psychology Journals* 41.2 (2002): 175-192. Web. 8 Nov 2010.

Freedman, Matthew. "Job hopping, earnings dynamics, and industrial agglomeration in the software publishing industry." *Journal of Urban Economics* 64. (2008): 590-600. Web. 1 Nov 2010.

Heijstra, Thamar M, and Gudbjorb Linda Rafnsdottir. "The Internet and Academics' Workload and Work-Family Balance." *Internet and Higher Education* 13 (2010): 158-163.

Henry, Laurie. "The Critical Role of New Literacies while Reading on the Internet." *Reading Teacher* 59.7 (2006): 614-627. Web. 17 Nov 2010.

"Job Posting." *Online Job Posting | Monster.com*. Monster, 2010. Web. 14 Nov 2010. <http://hiring.monster.com/recruitment/Job-Postings.aspx?source=hp_jp_link>.

Kuhn, Peter, and Mikal Skuterud. "Internet Job Search and Unemployment Durations." *The American Economic Review* 94.1 (2004): 218-232.

Kuhn, Peter, and Mikal Skuterud. "Job search methods: Internet versus traditional." *Monthly Labor Review* 123.10 (2000): 1-11. Web. 10 Nov 2010.

Nakamura, Alice, Kathryn Shaw, Richard Freeman, Emi Nakamura, and Amanda Pyman. "Jobs Online." *Studies in Labor Market Intermediation*. David H. Autor: Chicago, IL, University of Chicago Press. 2009. Web. 3 Nov 2010.

Mayer-Ahuja, Nicole, and Harald Wolf. "Beyond the Hype. Working in the German Internet Industry." *Critical Sociology* 33:73 (2007): 73-99. Web. 5 December 2010.

Parry, Emma, and Shaun Tyson. "An Analysis of the Use and Success of Online Recruitment Methods in the UK." *Human Resource Management Journal* 18.3 (2008): 257-274. Web. 4 Nov 2010.

Rasmussen, Soley. "Social Computing: Inviting Multiple Ways of Evaluating Worth," *Working Papers on Information Systems* 10/7.

RichRelevance. 2010. RichRelevance, Inc. 1 Dec. 2010 < http://www.richrelevance. com/>

Suvankulov, Farrukh. "Job Search on the Internet, E-Recruitment, and Labor Market Outcomes." *The Pardee RAND Graduate School dissertation series*. James Dertouzos, Richard Neu, and Sebastian Negrusa: Santa Monica, CA, RAND Corporation. 2010. Web. 1 Nov 2010.

"The Career Builder Difference." *CareerBuilder.com Turns Dreams into Quality Job Applications*. CareerBuilder, n.d. Web. 17 Nov 2010. <http://www.careerbuilder.com/ JobPoster/landing.aspx?pagever=dreams>.

4

Internet Job Searching: Benefits and Concerns

Ye Li and Mengyun Tang

Introduction

Disparities that have existed in the labor market are mainly due to the process through which workers are matched with jobs; and the matching process depends on the availability of information, which is costly but crucial for both jobseekers and employers (Fountain, 2005). The emergence of Internet job searching services has changed the landscape of the job searching industry. As Christine Fountain (2005) points out in her paper *Finding a Job in the Internet Age*, the appearance of a large number of websites containing millions of jobs, not to mention online classified advertisements and job postings on corporate websites, indicates that the Internet is a new social space through which job information can flow. Information technology makes it easy and cost-efficient for employers to target a larger pool of potential applicants and allows jobseekers to find a larger number of vacant positions than traditional methods do.

In addition, besides just listing jobs, many of the job-searching websites provide a variety of other services for jobseekers to utilize, such as resume building tips and keyword searching. This has lead to a change in the job search strategies adopted by jobseekers. For example, as pointed out by Bonnie Easton (2010) in her article *Our World of Work*, "less than five years ago, a person filled out a paper application for a position advertised in the Sunday classifieds. Today, every job hunter needs a results-oriented, achievement-packed résumé listing a LinkedIn and Twitter account. He or she fills out an online application and may interview with prospective employers by webcam." The proliferation of these online resources invites one to ask, does online job searching truly approximate the "perfect information" and help workers and employers make faster and more successful matches?

This chapter will analyze the influence of online job search on the job market. We will first provide a detailed background review of the Internet job searching industry, including its development and major online sourcing websites. Then, we will discuss the benefits and problems of this relatively new method of job searching, from the perspectives of both jobseekers and employers. With these benefits and concerns in mind, we will then offer some suggestions to online jobseekers on how to make the Internet work for them in job searches.

Description of the Online Job Searching Industry

According to David Autor (2001), the first generation of online jobs was the job boards which were used much like the "wanted position" sections of the newspaper. By 2001, other e-recruiting services, such as career sections on corporate websites and resume databanks appeared. From then on, the use of Internet job searching has grown dramatically both in volume and varieties (Autor, 2001).

Generally, Internet job searching businesses provide the following services to corporations (A. Nakamura, Shaw, Freeman, E. Nakamura, Pyman, 2008):

- Establishing general job searching websites and managing job advertisements (monster.com, etc.) and related services
- Constructing and operating career sections for corporate websites, sometimes including the management of online application forms for job openings and associated database for these forms
- Collecting via searching websites and online application forms the qualified applicants for jobseekers and operating the searchable resume databanks.

On the other hand, jobseekers usually register for free to use the full features of these jobsites and establish an online profile. They may be required to upload their resume(s) sometimes. Registered jobseekers can search for jobs according to their industry (e.g. finance, healthcare, etc.) or position type (e.g. entry-level, internship, etc.). They can also take advantage of the job-alert services and choose the types of jobs they are interested in. When a new job posted meets the profile and preferences of the above-mentioned user, the website will send a "job-alert" email to him/her. This service is believed to be popular with students and employed users who are not actively looking for work at that time.

There are several leading commercial jobsites in the U.S. online job searching market, including Monster.com and CareerBuilder. Another big commercial jobsite, HotJobs, was acquired by Monster on August 24, 2010 (Whitney, 2010). These websites are collectively known as "the Big 3" (A. Nakamura et al., 2008). They charge corporations a fee for posting jobs or searching for candidates over the jobsites' resume banks (prices presented in Table 1). In addition to these commercial jobsites, there are also several non-profit providers. Despite the closure of America's Job Bank, Craigslist and JobCentral are best known by now as the non-profit Internet job searching sites, as a result of holding their prices down (A. Nakamura et al., 2008).

Table 1: Price comparison of different jobsites

Jobsite	Price of a single job listing	Price for resume search
Providers with profit purpose		
Monster	$210 - 395	$5200 (3 month)
CareerBuilder	$419	$6000(one year)
Providers with not for profit purpose		
Craigslist	$0 – 75 (depending on the location)	$0
JobCentral	$25	$0

Source: company websites (updated as of 11/20/2010)

We shall now take a closer look at "the Big 3" commercial jobsites:

Monster Worldwide: established in 1995 by the Telephone Marketing Programs Company. In 2000, Monster acquired the college and university e-recruiting market leader, JobTRAK, and renamed it MonsterTRAK. Employers can use this service to target specific schools for their posting jobs and pay to search over the resumes of students registered. MonsterTRAK provides recruiting services tailored to the needs of students and campus career offices, and has partnerships with leading educational institutions, such as Harvard, MIT and Princeton. For the experienced labor market, Monster has important sub-websites such as Military.com, targeting military personal reentering civilian workforce with technical skills and leadership experiences. Monster also built a vast network of local content and language Internet sites throughout Europe and Asia Pacific Region. This network helps US companies to look for foreign workers they need (A. Nakamura et al., 2008). Today, Monster is the largest job search engine in the world, with over a million job postings at any time, over 150 million resumes in the database (in 2008) and over 63 million jobseekers per month.

CareerBuilder: launched in 1996, was developed as a complement to the classified advertising activities of media giants: Tribune, Knight Ridder and Gannett. CareerBuilder has had an assured flow of job ads from the classified sections of affiliated newspapers. By the end of 2003, CareerBuilder also had achieved a global reach via partnerships in the United Kingdom, Ireland, Italy, Spain, France, Belgium, the Netherlands, Latin America, India, Australia, Malaysia, the Philippines, and Singapore (A. Nakamura et al., 2008).

HotJobs: launched in 1997, formerly owned by Yahoo!. On August 24, 2010, Monster acquired HotJobs for $225 million in cash, hoping to match up more working professionals with its business customers (Whitney, 2010).

There have been many studies that try to examine the effectiveness of these "Big 3" commercial jobsites. Rachilin Marbaix notes, in 2004, that according to a study by CareerXroads, a staffing consulting firm, among all new hires the year before through the Internet, only about 15 percent of those hires applied through the big job boards such as Monster, CareerBuilder, and HotJobs. Industry-focused niche sites were slightly more effective: 17.5 percent of new online hires were from sites like Medzilla.com, a pharmaceutical industry site, and IEEE.org, the electrical engineering association's website. In addition, the study showed the best place to find work on the Internet was the company's own website. Approximately 67.9 percent of Internet hires came through corporations' own career sites. Companies prefer choosing candidates from their own websites because doing so saves them money, brands them with candidates and builds better matches (McDermott, 2009). In his article *Job-search*

Upstarts Weathering Recession, Ed Frauenheim (2009) mentions that "for the first quarter of 2009, revenue from CareerBuilder.com's North America network – including its main job site and partner newspaper sites – fell 27 percent year-over-year to $141 million. Monster's North America careers revenue – which reflects all of the firm's career-related services in North America, including job postings – plummeted 35 percent, to $119 million. The third job board giant, Yahoo HotJobs, declined to provide information about its revenue for the first quarter of 2009." Perhaps this drop in revenue is a reflection of the ineffectiveness of these jobsites in helping employers achieve their recruiting goals. Ed Frauenheim (2009) also notes that jobsites like Indeed and SimplyHired have, on the contrary, experienced a growth in revenue. Indeed gets most of its revenue from pay-per-click advertising – principally through sponsored job ads, and both Indeed and SimplyHired allow jobseekers to see if they have any contacts from their social networks at firms showing up in job search results. Both sites also offer to help other websites publish job listings. SimplyHired now has a network of some 5,000 sites, which helps employers reach passive candidates (Frauenheim, 2009). A brief introduction to these jobsites is as follows:

Indeed.com: the user can create a free account to search and capture job listings collated from all the other major job boards, professional associations, newspapers, and the employment pages of major corporations. He can also search for employment by job title or browse by employment categories or cities and see hiring trends for specific jobs and join in discussions about them. Indeed.com also has sites for Canada, the U.K., France, Germany, Spain, and India (Goldsborough, 2000). To be more specific, Indeed.com indexes more than 500 websites, including Monster. com.

SimplyHired.com: in return for free registration, the user can use this job search engine to scour the web for classifieds in the U.S., the U.K., Australia, or India. SimplyHired has more than 5 million job listings drawn from online classifieds and company Web sites. It also offers statistics about salaries, city demographics, and hiring trends. One can search for known job titles or browse listings by industry, category, or location. A "Special Search" looks for jobs friendly to moms, seniors, and dog lovers, among other categories. The user can also use the site's widgets to track job announcements on iGoogle, blogs, MySpace, Facebook, and on mobile phones (Goldsborough, 2000). Besides, it also lets users filter their search by company type, such as Fortune 500, Working Mother's 100 best, dog-friendly, or gay-lesbian friendly.

More recently, Jena McGregor (2010) presents some findings about the external hires at the Fortune 500 companies – "For starters, only a small percentage of jobs are filled using the sites (online job boards), which claim over 95 of the Fortune 100 as customers… just about 13% of all external hires at the Fortune 500 employers are filled using boards (excluding LinkedIn)." As for the senior-level positions, the online job boards are not effective in helping seek talents (McGregor, 2010). The same author Ed Frauenheim (2009) also comments, in his other article *Logging off of Job Boards,* that "many organizations that once relied on general-purpose job boards are turning to alternative strategies, including social networking sites, search engine marketing and niche job sites. In a May study by research firm AIM Group, nearly 45 percent of recruiters surveyed said they used networking sites such as LinkedIn and Facebook with mixed or great results." The following are some good examples of industry-specific, location-specific or language-specific "niche" sites:

- *Medzilla.com*: the place to go for jobs in the pharmaceutical industry.
- *Malakye.com*: sports fanatics might find a dream job here.
- *IEEE.org*: the site for electrical engineers to look for jobs.
- *Dice.com*: this is the first stop for many IT professionals.
- *MediaBistro.com*: a niche site for publishing jobs. One can post resume, check *job* opportunities, obtain industry news, participate in forums and events for writers, editors, Web developers, etc.
- *CoolWorks.com*: offers postings for seasonal jobs nationwide at amusement parks, ski resorts, national parks and campgrounds.
- *Jobsinthemoney.com*: the place for financial jobseekers. With a solid job bank of open jobs in finance, this may be where you can find that next great accounting or banking position. The site also has useful financial news and career content, including a regular newsletter.
- *6FigureJobs.com*: this site is for senior executives looking for a compensation package of at least $100,000 hence the name. Many of the jobs are in sales and marketing, Internet and new media, and finance, and can be found mostly in the New York

area, on the West Coast, and in Texas.

- *PlanetRecruit.com*: this site may help jobseekers find that perfect IT job in London or become a business analyst in Paris. It lets you search by location first, rather than position. It lists jobs in eight categories and has more than 100,000 openings.
- *Saludos.com*: bilingual professionals in English and Spanish with at least a B.A. can post a resume and find a job.
- *LatPro.com*: a professional who is bilingual in English and Spanish or Portuguese can post their resume to find jobs with major companies.

As the social networking websites gain more and more popularity, more and more jobseekers turn to those sites to build professional contacts and identify potential employers. Irene McDermott (2009) comments, in her article *New Improved Internet Job Search*, that "the word on the street is overwhelming: It's not what you know, it's who you know. The big new story of job searching lies with the social networking sites, specifically the triumvirate of LinkedIn, Twitter, and Facebook. As new users flock to these sites, they are now reaching the critical mass that makes them useful as job resources." McDermott (2009) explains how Facebook and LinkedIn may be used to help jobseekers to be more effective in their job searching process:

Facebook.com: Facebook was launched in February 2004 and as of July 2010 has more than 500 million active users. It allows one to create a personal profile, add other users as friends and exchange messages. Users may also join common interest user groups and events created by individuals, organizations and institutions. According to McDermott (2009), Facebook is an ideal way to establish and maintain an effective business network—"If you needed a job, one of your newly found old friends could jump to help. These people are spread all over the country and one of them would know someone who is hiring and could get you an interview."

LinkedIn.com: officially founded in 2003, LinkedIn currently has over 85 million members in over 200 countries. Registered members can network with like-minded professionals and follow links to corporate websites. They can also invite everyone they know (who is already a member) to join their network, search through ready-made lists of classmates and colleagues and write recommendations for colleagues or subordinates. In

2005, LinkedIn launched its first premium service – *LinkedIn Jobs*, which helps members use their network to find employment opportunities. Many of the jobs listed on LinkedIn.com are exclusive. McDermott (2009) comments that "LinkedIn will tell you who knows who in your network that might give you an inside edge when you are looking for jobs." People can be introduced to a new contact through their contacts and expand their own network group. A person searching may happen to have a friend, who has a friend that works at the company that has a job opening. An insider's recommendation is always helpful.

The success of LinkedIn has been widely recognized among the professional world. Unlike the other social networking websites, LinkedIn focuses on the professional side of social networking. Jessi Hempel (2010), in her article *How LinkedIn Will Fire Up Your Career*, talks about how widely received LinkedIn is – more than 60 million members have logged on to create profiles, upload their employment histories, and build connections with people they know. Visitors to the site have jumped 31% from last year to 17.6 million in February. Being on LinkedIn puts you in the company of people with impressive credentials: the average member is a college-educated 43-year-old making $107,000; more than a quarter are senior executives. Every Fortune 500 company is represented. And recruiters rely on the site to find even the highest-caliber executives: Oracle found CFO Jeff Epstein via LinkedIn in 2008 (Hempel, 2010). In their article *Linking Up*, Madhu Unnikrishnan and Robert Wall (2010) also report that airlines like Southwest and Virgin Atlantic have been actively using LinkedIn to recruit personnel, while for carriers like JetBlue, Alaska Airlines and US Airways, LinkedIn is becoming an increasingly important recruitment tool (Unnikrishnan & Wall, 2010)

Hempel (2010) also discusses the reason why LinkedIn works well for professional matchmaking. Since most of its members already have jobs, in this environment, jobseekers can do their networking without looking as if they're shopping themselves around. This population is more valuable to recruiters as well. While online job boards like Monster.com focus on showcasing active job hunters, very often the most talented and sought-after recruits are those currently employed (Hempel, 2010). She comments that "the $8 billion recruiting industry is built on the fact that these passive candidates are hard to find. LinkedIn changes that. It's the equivalent of a little black book—highly detailed and exposed for everyone to see… as companies turn to the web to mine for prospective job candidates, it's no longer advantageous to refrain from broadcasting personal information." With this transparency, LinkedIn has successfully created a space for jobseekers and employers to build their professional network and exchange information.

Having examined the "Big 3" commercial jobsites, some of the "niche" sites and social networking websites and the effectiveness of each type of e-recruiting service providers, it can be seen that the niche websites and social networking sites are gradually gaining popularity among both jobseekers and hiring managers. Aggregate search engines that cover the major job search web sites, niche web sites, professional associations, company web sites, and employment agencies at the same time, like Indeed and SimplyHired, can possibly take away some of the market share of the "Big 3" commercial jobsites. With this overview of the e-recruiting industry, we shall now examine the benefits and problems of searching for jobs online.

Benefits of Internet Job Search

For Employers

As Fountain (2005) points out, for employers, the decision to hire is risky. With limited information with which to judge the productivity of a new worker, the employer may find it difficult and costly to make a right choice. Neoclassical economic theory would suggest that the more information an employer could gather about a potential worker before making a hiring decision, the more accurate the decisions would be. In cyberspace, a world where information can seem limitless and free, employers who can gather the most information about potential workers should be best able to identify the best matches (Fountain, 2005).

Compared to the traditional method of job searching, Internet job searching has several advantages for employers. First of all, as discussed by A. Nakamura et al. (2008), e-recruiting can help increase the scope and reduce the costs of hiring. Such services can help employers find and consider a much more widely located pool of candidates in the early phase of the recruiting process. For example, using the Monster's global websites, U.S. companies' foreign branches can find local workers they need; businesses looking for workers in other countries are also able to find workers in other countries to meet skill shortages or for outsourcing contract work. In other words, online job searching can allow businesses to search more widely and reach out to jobseekers in larger geographical areas.

Secondly, online recruiting services can bring down the variable and fixed costs of hiring. A job advertisement in the Sunday *New York Times*, circulation 1.7 million, costs $4500. By contrast, Monster.com, which has millions visitors worldwide, charges $395 for a 30 day advertisement – less than 10 percent of the newspaper (Autor, 2001). Furthermore, big businesses enjoy returns to scale in using online job searching services (A. Nakamura et al., 2008). The cost of advertising a job posting on a commercial jobsite like Monster is usually the same whether the employer is looking for one new employee of a given type, or 10 or 100 employees. Also, learning investments are required for employers to make good use of Internet job searching services and these costs can usually be spread over larger numbers of hires by large companies (A. Nakamura et al., 2008). Other fixed costs incurred by making custom employment pages for company websites and custom job application forms and their associate databases, can also be reduced when averaged by the large number of hires.

In addition, online job searching services indirectly promote search for employed workers (A. Nakamura et al., 2008). E-recruiting services can make it easier for recruiters to find and contact employed workers with suitable skills. Workers who passively look at job ads on jobsites like Monster.com typically must register to make full use of the jobsites, and by doing this, they will often make their e-mail and other contact information available to the employers who pay the large commercial e-recruiting firms to search over the resume databanks. Also, candidates that apply for jobs online are likely to disclose other kinds of information through the social networking websites such as Facebook, Twitter and LinkedIn. Hiring managers can Google a potential employee's information to have a better idea of the personality of the candidate, how he/she interacts with others and with what kind of people he/she interacts. This can help the hiring manager make a better and informed decision on whether or not to extend the mentioned candidate a job offer.

Moreover, e-recruiting services can help employers save time in screening applicants' credentials. The online resume banks often conduct key word searches, like "GPA" etc. Recruiters can filter the large pool of resumes and significantly cut down the number of resumes that they have to read. Online recruiting services can also match employers and jobseekers in a more active manner – rather than waiting on workers or firms to find one another, software or key word sourcing can often parse posted job listings and resumes to identify plausible matches and notify both parties (Autor, 2001). Also, through either a job board or other location online, employers can administer skills or personality tests at the point of application.

For Jobseekers

First of all, online jobsites and job searching tools reduce the time and costs for jobseekers to find out about job openings in their desired industry. As Autor (2001) points out in his paper *Wiring the Labor Market*, "they (online job boards) offer more information about more jobs in more locations than is conceivable for paper equivalents. They are easier to search. They are potentially more up-to-date, because ads are posted immediately and can be edited frequently." Jobsites like Monster. com and CareerBuilder.com also offer services like job-alert emails to make sure that jobseekers stay informed on the job openings that may interest them. With the ease to access information regarding job openings in a timely manner, jobseekers can send their resumes to many employers at the same time, hence potentially increasing their chances of getting selected for an interview. Another potential source of efficiency gains from delivering services remotely is that hours spent in unproductive commuting may be replaced by rapid on-line delivery (Autor, 2001). Interviews can be conducted online through Skype (with or without a webcam) or via phones, which makes communication easier for employers and jobseekers that are far away from each other.

Secondly, having learned about a position or a company, jobseekers can easily advertise their skills, apply for openings and communicate with potential employers through the Internet and the jobsites. These can done 24 hours a day, without the jobseekers ever having to leave their home or work desk. This allows for flexibility in one's allocation of time to job application. One can apply for jobs whenever he wants, as long as it is before the designated deadline of application. This flexibility can also enhance the labor market efficiency.

Thirdly, finding jobs online also naturally leads to finding out more about the job function, the company and the industry through the online information. Apart from learning about the existence of a job opening, jobseekers also have the opportunity to gather information about the characteristics of the job and the company's culture so as to become more knowledgeable about what they are getting into. Information exists not only in a job posting, but through company websites and other external sites that provide information about the industry or even the particular firm. For example, salary.com and glassdoor.com invite the current and former employees of a company to anonymously provide information on salaries, the corporate culture and their work life. Glassdoor.com also encourages its users to write reviews about their interview experience and to post comments on interview questions with about 32,000 firms (Easton, 2010). This information can help a jobseeker better prepare for interviews and enhance his chances of getting his desired job. If a job offer has been made, he can also use the information on salaries to negotiate for a higher pay and better terms on the benefit. In general, the jobseeker can be better informed about the outlook of the industry and be better prepared in his job search process.

Similarly, doing a more thorough research on the company or the potential employer may help the jobseeker decide if he really wants to work for the mentioned employer. In his article *An Aggressive Online Search Can Reveal a College's Secrets*, Stephen M. Winzenburg (2010) writes about his experience in search of a university faculty job. He notes that "it has become so common for hiring committees to use search engines to uncover information about applicants that the members of those committees should not be surprised that their own names are being Googled, in turn, by applicants. What can be discovered about a department or a faculty member is often embarrassing to an institution, and a real turnoff to jobseekers." He writes that a detailed search through the web might reveal that there has been discrimination in the department, that the position has been filled a number of times in the past few years, or that individual members of the department are themselves looking for a job.

This kind of information, that suggests the lack of internal organization of the potential employer or reveals the undesirable working conditions of the organization, should serve to caution the jobseeker to make an informed and more careful decision on whether or not this firm or institution is a good fit for him.

Problems of Internet Job Search

For Employers

With the proliferation of information online and the ease for the jobseekers to apply for a given position, companies may be overwhelmed by the large volume of applications as a result of their job postings online. Fountain (2005) argues that "the predicament of having too much information is well known; just as the job searcher must devote a substantial amount of time and effort to finding the handful of promising job leads from the Sunday classifieds, so must the employer invest in identifying the qualified applicants from the stack of applications. Finding the balance between casting a wide net and snaring qualified applicants may be particularly important in order for employers to hire a qualified candidate while minimizing recruiting costs." Excess and inappropriate applications can be a hindrance to recruiters' time and cost saving. Employers may not end up saving much time and money in recruiting due to the enormous volume of applications they have to read through, both from under- or over-qualified candidates, especially if they cannot filter the applications with functions like "key word search." There are web-based services like Pre-employ.com, Avert. com, and PreScreenAmerica.com that offer on-line background checks and pre-screening services (Autor, 2001). These screening services help employers to make sure if a student really goes to Harvard or if an applicant is really Microsoft-certified. These kind of services can save time for recruiters and double check the reliability of the information provided by applicants; but the subscription to these kind of services will also inevitably raise the cost of recruiting.

Another downside of online job seeking and recruitment is that it is better for entry- and mid-level jobs than executive positions. A. Nakamura et al. (2008) have raised the point about employers' fear of hiring "lemons" if they select from the pool of currently unemployed workers who have worked before. They argue that above the entry level, one might presume that problem workers could be reliably detected by checking references from past employers. However, employers sometimes ask unwanted workers to leave "voluntarily," offering these workers promises of good references if they comply. The use of e-recruiting can augment fears of hiring lemons because less of the information about individuals found using e-recruiting is rooted in personal acquaintance, a key traditional strategy for employers to detect workers with hidden flaws (A. Nakamura et al., 2008). In this case, employers might prefer candidates who are referred to them because some relatively reliable information can be gathered through personal contacts, reducing the need to conduct screens and thus lowering the cost of recruiting (Fountain, 2005). Employers also increasingly use the Internet to bypass the pool of self-identified jobseekers and target "passive candidates," currently employed individuals who might be enticed by a better opportunity (Autor, 2001). The potential problem of "hiring lemons" is not that relevant when recruiters try to fill entry-level positions, because the level of responsibilities that these potential employees are expected to take is relatively low. These positions normally do not require candidates to have previous work experience and a majority of the hiring firms usually provide training programs to orient these workers and to equip them with the knowledge, skills and resources they need to carry out the job duty.

Moreover, information online that is unreliable can damage a firm's reputation and discourage qualified candidates from applying for positions in the mentioned firm. It is often very difficult to separate fact from fiction in cyberspace. People who write reviews about their company's culture and work life are likely to provide a purely subjective and even biased view, which may hurt the company's chances of getting the application from their most desired potential candidate.

For Jobseekers

Likewise, for some social-network users, particularly the Facebook and MySpace crowd, an online profile can be more bane than benefit when it comes to landing a job. Scott Westcott (2009) reports, in his article *Search Me*, that a new survey by CareerBuilder.com found that more than one in five employers search social-networking sites to screen job candidates. The survey of more than 31,000 employers found that reliance on such sites to examine candidates is surging, and that one-third of hiring managers said they found information on social-networking sites that caused them to eliminate a candidate from consideration. He also points out that top areas of concerns include profiles that mention alcohol and drug use; inappropriate photos or information posted on a candidate's page; poor communication and writing skills; and criticism of co-workers or former employers. Some jobseekers therefore will have to make a choice between complete freedom of expression and the desire to project a positive image in order to impress a potential professional contact.

Another potential threat of using online job boards, and in fact any service online, lies in information security. In August 2007, virus writers set their sights on Monster.com using a Trojan in advertisements on the site as a means of installing malicious software on visitors' machines. In January 2009, Monster.com reported that their database was hacked and certain contact and account data were taken, including Monster.com user IDs and passwords, email addresses, names, phone numbers, and some basic demographic data. This leakage of the identifying information of Monster.com's users may lead to many undesirable consequences, including the users being flooded with unwanted advertisements and even identity theft.

Sarah Needleman (2009), in her article *It Isn't Always a Job Behind an Online Job Posting*, warns jobseekers on the practice of fraudulent online job postings in the U.S. The author mentions the case of Tom Greene who repeatedly received a marketing pitch from a career-marketing service, after accepting an invitation to interview for an executive position that did not exist. Needleman comments that the ads to most watch out for are those pretending to offer a job but are really trying to get the recipients to give up personal information, such as a bank account or Social Security number. They often mimic real postings, with some featuring company names and logos nearly identical to those of actual employers. The individuals behind these postings may even exchange multiple emails with job hunters to build up trust (Needleman, 2009). While many job websites review submissions to try and prevent inappropriate ads from getting published, fraudulent activity across the Internet continues to evolve and mutate.

Previously, we discussed the impact of e-recruiting services on unemployed labor. As A. Nakamura et al. points out, "in general, no one is paying commercial e-recruiting companies to help the unemployed find jobs." Most employers prefer not to hire those who are out of work for fear that there are hard to detect reasons why many of them are in this employment state (A. Nakamura et al., 2008). For jobseekers who have been employed before but are currently unemployed, online job search may not really help them land a new job, despite the amount of time and energy that they have invested to look for a job on the Internet.

In general, the free access to information online can be good or bad for both jobseekers and employers, depending on how this information is used to make judgments. Although there are concerns regarding the excess and inappropriate applications on the part of the employers and the information leakage and security risks on the part of the jobseekers, e-recruiting services have become an indispensable tool that facilitates the job-seeking or recruiting processes for both parties. With this in mind, we find it useful to offer some suggestions to jobseekers in order to help them become more efficient and effective in their job search process.

Suggestions to Jobseekers

First of all, when researching about the position and the company that you are applying for, it is also important to have accurate and reliable information regarding the particular industry that you are hoping to enter. One useful government site is the Occupational Outlook Handbook, published annually by the U.S. Department of Labor (www.bls.gov/oco). It provides overviews of hundreds of occupations, including job roles, qualifications, and salary information. This information, which is provided by government agencies, is generally more reliable than someone's personal website. Jobseekers should also check if the information on the website is up-to-date. In addition, jobseekers should be aware of the website's purpose. While many websites try to provide career-related information, some sites may be more interested in selling their publications or services, such as career development guidebooks or resume-editing services.

Another piece of general advice to all jobseekers is that they should not rely exclusively on the Internet in their job search. Traditional job-search tools, such as personnel agencies, newspaper classified ads should be used conjointly with the Internet to better their chance to getting employed. Job fairs, online niche communities (such as those listed in the background review section of this paper) and referrals may work even better than merely browsing through the major job boards.

In light of the possibility of falsified information on job openings, Needleman (2009) offers some tips for jobseekers – fraudulent job postings may lack details about the hiring company and position, whereas genuine job advertisements typically target applicants who have a specific amount of experience and pay salaries commensurate with their backgrounds. If you are unsure whether an advertisement is sincere, you can protect your identity when responding by providing a resume with a post-office box address instead of your home address. You might also list just your initials in the document and not your full name. Further, consider using a disposable email address to prevent spam from clogging up the one you normally use. If a business address or company name is provided, and that is a name you do not recognize, search for the employer's website to learn more about it. You also can check for any complaints filed against it with the Better Business Bureau at bbb.org and consult with people in your network (Needleman, 2009).

For jobseekers who are currently undergraduate or postgraduate students, as Scott Edwards (1999) recommends in his article *How to Use the Internet in Your Job Search*, one popular strategy that you should consider is giving priority to those recruiters who will be interviewing at your campus. This eliminates wasting time on the web prospecting and following up with recruiters who may be unwilling to come to your campus or fly you to their office. Check with your Career Planning and Placement Office for the schedule of recruiters visiting in the fall and spring, and then you can begin targeting these employers and recruiters with some online job search activities.

He also talks about the importance for jobseekers to make their resume more "noticeable" by the recruiters. According to him, resume databases are a useful technology that gives jobseekers additional exposure to recruiters. Many recruiters search resume databases in order to find candidates for their openings. Using keywords, just like job databases do, recruiters can search on job qualifications, special skills, G.P.A., or any other type of criteria and find candidates that match their needs. Jobseekers should try to maximize their exposure to recruiters and make their resume fit numerous queries; they need to supplement their resume with the keywords that a recruiter may search on. Jobseekers can do this by looking through online employment ads, for words used when employers advertise these positions, or by supplementing their resume with industry-specific terms that are in line with their experiences or qualifications (Edwards, 1999).

For jobseekers that already have a job but are still looking for better opportunities, posting resumes to an online job board may not be a good strategy, because many job boards have "auto application" features that route resumes into the general database after they have been reviewed. The human-relations professionals of your current firm may scan these resume databases and identify your name. Jason McLure (2004) recommends, in his article *Job Hunt at Work*, that since bosses not only have the tools but often the right to search your hard drive and e-mail, it would be more beneficial to store your resume at online storage spaces. Rather than making cold calls to prospective employers, jobseekers should try LinkedIn.com, which lets you build contacts through acquaintances. Finally, to erase the evidence that you have been surfing the help-wanted websites, you can also use software that will hide your domain while you go online and erase digital evidence like cookies and tracking bugs. While these suggestions require the jobseekers to be familiar with specific kinds of software and online tools, it can be concluded that there are feasible ways for the currently employed to find other opportunities confidentially.

For those jobseekers who are more tech-savvy, it is also recommendable that they assemble an e-portfolio that presents his/her background and past experience in a professional manner. It may contain graphics, writing samples, completed projects, or any other kind of online-accessible work. This measure takes advantage of the possibility that potential employers may conduct online research on their candidates. It is important to keep the portfolio professional; therefore, personal blogs and excessive personal photos may not be desirable.

Future Implications

According to the "2010 Job Board Future" survey, approximately 78% of jobseekers selected career sites as their top pick for job search methods; at the same time, over 78% of jobseekers said that they may rely on referrals to acquire a job. While traditional referring methods will not be excluded in the recruitment process, jobseekers will have new forms of networking based on Internet resources. According to the authors of the *Simply Hired Blog*, the development of online job recruitment will follow three important trends:

1. **Comprehensive and Transparent:** As more and more employers use online tools to post their openings and advertise their companies, jobseekers will have access to every available position, including hourly or local jobs rarely found online. Also, jobseekers will have relatively perfect information—everything from office culture to industry trends— to evaluate a job opportunity.

2. **Social and Personal:** Referral hiring will still be common in the hiring process. However, online social and professional networks will contribute more and more to the online recruitment and online networking processes. Websites such as LinkedIn, Facebook and Twitter will provide more network channels for jobseekers. Moreover, with advanced website designing tools, career websites will be more convenient to jobseekers and employers alike. Listings can be filtered by an individual's job and lifestyle criteria, producing highly personalized results. There will also be more detailed information for both recruiters and jobseekers in order to better fill a specific position.

3. **Advanced Technology:** For jobseekers, the traditionally manual processes, such as filling out application forms, will become automated. Also, new technologies of mobile services will create a new outlook for the online job searching. For example, the use of smartphones is rapidly growing; and this has lead to a variety of job board applications being made available through the phone, like the case for Monster.com, CareerBuilder and Adecco Jobs. Some organizations are using Skype to conduct interviews. Such new mobile usages will give jobseekers the most updated messages and facilitate the job searching process.

Therefore, the development of future online job searching is likely to focus on the efficiency and comprehensiveness of the exchange of information and the expansion of the different online channels to access this information.

In addition, the future online recruitment process should have more engagement and conversation between the employers and jobseekers. Both companies and jobseekers can have more "digital profiles" on a career website. On the one hand, employers can create videos to introduce the company and elaborate on what exactly they are looking for in potential candidates. On the other hand, jobseekers can also create "digital talking resumes" to explain their past experience and interest in the position in a creative way, showing more of their personality to the employers. Thus, in the future, the whole process of online recruitment should engage both prospective employers and jobseekers more than a simple job ad or paper resume.

Conclusion

In this paper we have examined the functioning and effectiveness of the major commercial job boards (Monster.com, CareerBuilder.com and HotJobs.com), the metasearch engines (Indeed.com and SimplyHired.com), the industry-, location- and language-specific niche jobsites and online social networking sites (Facebook.com and LinkedIn.com). There is no doubt that cyberspace has dramatically changed the way jobseekers look for jobs and recruiters get positions filled. Even though searching for jobs online can raise certain concerns for both employers and jobseekers,the   e-recruiting service industry will thrive and continue to be one of the most important ways in which recruitment takes place.

REFERENCES

Autor, D. (2001). Wiring the Labor Market. *The Journal of Economic Perspectives*, 15(1), 25-40.
Edwards, S. V. (1999). How to Use the Internet in Your Job Search. *Black Collegian* 30(1), 60-62.
Easton, B. (2010). Our World of Work. *Library Journal*, 135(2), 32-34.
Fountain, C. (2005). Finding a Job in the Internet Age. *Social Forces*, 83(3), 1235-1262.
Frauenheim, Ed. (2009). Logging off of job boards. *Workforce Management*, 88(7), 25-29.
Frauenheim, E. (2009). Job-search upstarts weathering recession. *Workforce Management*, 88(7), 27-27.
Goldsborough, R. (2000). Let the Internet Work for You in Job Searches. *Community College Week*, 13(4), 15-18.
Hempel, J. (2010). How Linked In Will Fire Up Your Career. *Fortune*, 161(5), 74-82.

Marbaix, J. R. (2004). Job Search. *U.S. News & World Report*, 136(8), 60-63.

McDermott, I.E. (2009). New improved Internet Job Search. *Searcher*, 17(4), 8-12.

McDermott, M. J. (2000). Fishing the Web's very deep job pool. *Christian Science Monitor*, 92(252), 15-15.

McGregor, J. (2010). Job Sites: Are They Worth It? *Fortune*, 161(8), 45-46.

McLure, J. (2004). Job Hunt at Work. *Newsweek*, 143(10), 60-60.

Nakamura, A.O., Shaw, K.L., Freeman, R.B., Nakamura, E., & Pyman, A. "Jobs Online," paper presented at the conference "Labor Market Intermediation," May 17-18, 2007. Sep 2008 draft.

Needleman, S. E. (2009). It Isn't Always a Job Behind an Online Job Posting. *Wall Street Journal Eastern Edition*, 253(38), B14.

Online Recruiting: Notable Websites. *Fortune Winter2001 Technology Guide*, 142(12), 224-226.

Rowh, M. (2005). The Great Online Job Hunt. Career World, 34(1), 22-25.

Unnikrishnan, M., & Wall, R. (2010). Linking Up. *Aviation Week & Space Technology*, 172(2), 44-44.

Simply Hired Blog. The Future of Job Search. [Web log comment]. Retrieved from <http://blog.simplyhired.com/2010/09/the-future-of-job-search.html.> [2010, September 28].

Westcott, S. (2009). Search Me. *Chronicle of Philanthropy*, 21(8), 42-42.

Winzenburg, S. M. (2010). An Aggressive Online Search Can Reveal a College's Secrets. *Chronicle of Higher Education*, 56(17), D10-D10.

5

The impact of online, campus-specific job search engines on student employment outcomes:
a comparative study of LyonNet (Mount Holyoke College) and E-access (Smith College) career services networks

Manuela I Mitkova and Zilin Cui

Introduction

As seniors at Mount Holyoke College, and students who are quite familiar with the process of job searching in a technological age, we decided to focus our attention on the first job search strategy most students use after graduation: the internet job search. A few years back, students took advantage of career sites such as Monster.com, and CareerBuilder. com. However, in more recent years, Mount Holyoke students have had the opportunity to use a more personalized tool for their job search: LyonNet, and that of our sister college, Smith College, called E Access.

LyonNet is a virtual career support site that provides a variety of services: employers of all fields and types can post opportunities such as internships, volunteer, as well as full time, paid opportunities. The students, besides directly applying for jobs, can also build a personal profile with their resume; upload their transcript and writing samples in some cases, which will conveniently generate more potential job matches for the applicants. In addition to the online opportunities search, LyonNet, the Career Development Center at Mount Holyoke College also provides the students with advice on resume/cover letter writing.

The online career service, LyonNet also introduces a more active role for the Career Development Center. For a student to be able to submit a job application, her resume needs to obtain approval from the CDC reviewing board, which also provides constructive feedback for the student to integrate into her future job search and resume building.

E-access, another online opportunities search engine, has the same purpose as LyonNet. The only differences are: first, it belonged to Smith College from its creation to 2009, and second, the employers who listed with E-access were not necessarily the same employers who listed with LyonNet.

These career websites offer many potential benefits to both hiring, and job seeking parties, by narrowing down the information gap between students and employers. The online, campus job database saves the students time, travel costs, and energy. They no longer have to browse through heavy portfolios, wonder if they are the most up to date resources, look through each company website to find openings, or travel to far away (Boston, New York, for example) places to attend recruiting fairs or information sessions. LyonNet provides a one-stop shop for the student's job search and offers additional support with search sites for resume and cover letter advice. For employers, LyonNet provides them with access to a pool of highly qualified applicants with a liberal arts education. Therefore, a lot of employers list with liberal arts schools like Mount Holyoke or Smith College because the applicants carry potentially transferable skills to a wide variety of positions.

This study is particularly relevant because LyonNet is one of the most used career search tools by Mount Holyoke students and E Access, Smith students. Many seniors start their post-graduation job search using these career tools. Also, in 2009, Mount Holyoke College and Smith College merged their career services. One of the main consequences is that job postings at one of the two colleges are accessible by students of both colleges. Also, career fairs and informational sessions have become cross advertised on both campuses, giving students more exposure to employers, interview opportunities and increased number of job postings. In addition, the employers who have listed with Smith College can now make their opportunities available to the pool of applicants at Mount Holyoke College, who are equally qualified. However, with the merger of these two career services, it is worth noting that there is also increased competition between Mount Holyoke and Smith colleges' students. In conclusion, the overall effects of the merger remain to be critically examined with data we have gathered from both Smith and Mount Holyoke colleges.

Literature Review

In their paper published in 2004, Peter Kuhn and Mikal Skuterud conducted a study on the impact of internet job search on unemployment duration based on data from the 1998 and 2000 Current Population Surveys (CPS). The study concludes that internet job search creates different types of self-selection by job seekers: observable factors seem to be selected positively while unobservable factors selected negatively. The study also concludes that internet job search does not seem to have a positive effect on reducing unemployment duration. However, the authors only presented speculative reasons, with no data backing up their claim, as to why this may be true, suggesting, amongst many factors, that people who rely on the internet as a job search tool tend to have poorer social networks.

Despite the authors' skepticism of internet job searching as an effective strategy to reduce unemployment durations, they recognized the fact that internet job searching may improve employment quality. Aside from the above mentioned study, the impact of internet usage for job search and employment attainment has not had many studies. In fact, to our knowledge, there haven't been any publications or working papers dedicated to examine the impact of campus-specific internet job search and applicants' employment outcomes. Thus, our study could contribute to one of the first academic studies to analyze the impacts of specific job search tools, adding to the larger body of studies that contribute to providing a platform of information on how college students could use the internet to their advantage in searching for employment opportunities.

In one of the few studies on the impact of internet technology on job searching, Stevenson (2008) indicates that the internet changes the very behavior of job seekers, reducing the cost to learn about employment openings and gather useful information on the characteristics of the job as well as qualities desirable to the position to be able to find "fits" and customize their application. The study also finds that internet use has broadened the variety of employment opportunities searched and ultimately obtained via the use of online tools. Also, the study has discovered that there is a positive correlation between income, education and the use of internet overall (Stevenson, 2008). In the case of Mount Holyoke and Smith colleges' students, the internet use is not limited by the income factor since both campuses enable wireless and wire connections at no costs beyond tuition, and students can have unlimited access to internet, which facilitates the wide usage of the internet and more specifically, its usage in job search. These highly educated students utilize the internet for a variety of tasks including planning for their future professional career. However, the study shows that internet job search has been more effective in helping the already employed to search for new jobs and increase the frequency of job change (Stevenson 2008). The study does not provide any information on how the internet job search may benefit those who are beginning to enter the labor force and have no prior professional experience to contextualize their job search.

Another study by Brown et. al. (2006) takes a more focused look at the usage of internet job search tools by college students, and analyzes the personality factors that influence the outcome of the search. Although it has been indicated that it is especially difficult to figure out what personal factors could influence the attainment of the first, post-graduation job (see Ontario Ministry of Training, College and Universities 2002), the authors focused on finding those crucial elements. The study justifies analyzing more qualitative factors (vis-a-vis Stevenson's approach on finding correlations between quantitative factors, such as the relationship between internet usage and education, income, etc) like the relationship between personality traits and internet job search tool usage and ends by pointing out that internet job searching is self-directed, which means that initiative taking and a proactive personality tend to influence job search behavior, and have an impact on results. The study argues that a proactive personality is conducive to self-efficacy, a robust and significant antecedent of behavior in many types of human activities (Holden, 1991; Stajkovic & Luthans, 1998), which influences job search efforts and income. By taking statistics of 497 undergraduate students from mid-western states, the study concludes that it is not the internet search by itself that leads to better employment opportunities, but students who actively use the internet as a job search tool are usually proactive students in the first place, and this personality trait influences their job search behavior, efforts and therefore results. Hence the impact of internet job search on employment obtainment is not just one way and straight forward; rather, it depends on many quantitative and qualitative conditions. This implies that many unobserved factors may have a significant impact on the job search outcome but due to the difficulty of measuring them, they become omitted variables: a type of problem that is beginning to be addressed by behavioral economics (such as Brown et. al. 2006).

As one of the first primary research study on campus specific internet job search tools, this study will offer benefits to both students and employers, by showing how effective the tool has been for the year observed. This will help them tailor their personal interests and maximize their potential gain. It will also provide a statistical basis for the career service officers of Mount Holyoke College, Smith College, and can serve as a case study model for other liberal arts colleges who work hard to help their students transition more smoothly into the professional field. Concrete, up-to-date statistics and trends could help career offices identify which services are most efficient and devote more resources to develop these strength areas and improve the overall service quality. To employers, this study could also be of help since campus specific sites offer them a pre-selected pool of applicants; and based on industry specific data and what type of jobs are most searched and obtained through these online services, they could refine their recruiting strategy by identifying and then focusing on key areas of high recruitment.

Hypothesis

We project the impact of LyonNet to result in the following aspects:

First, the number of employers' listings with both Smith and Mount Holyoke colleges is expected to be higher. Therefore, we expect the employer-student matching process will improve as a whole.

Second, LyonNet facilitates positive self-selection bias, which the employers recognize and consciously use as a pre-selection tool. This could potentially lead to more efficiency in matching and ultimately, hiring decisions.

Third, the use of LyonNet helps to decrease the information asymmetry between the employer and the students since LyoneNet is an internal network not available to all authorized employers and job seekers outside Mount Holyoke and Smith colleges' community. Thus, LyonNet narrows down the choices in both directions: students searching for employers, and employers looking to hire qualified student candidates.

Fourth, LyonNet attracts employers that value skills specially cultivated by the liberal arts education. These skills include writing, presentation, critical analysis, interdisciplinary thinking skills that are transferable and applicable to a wide variety of tasks and positions. This makes the liberal arts candidates more flexible and resilient in the job search market as compared to students who have gone through more career oriented college experience, such as finance majors or computer science majors. Employers who do not recognize the value of liberal arts education would not have an incentive to look for candidates at liberal arts colleges like Mount Holyoke and Smith College. Thus, LyonNet serves as a filter of employers for students as well.

Methodology

We will examine data in the following categories:

1. The number of employers that post on LyonNet
2. The specific industry each group of employers represents; the fields that employers come from, in order to analyze what sector of economy is emphasized the most in the online job search process
3. The number of information sessions held and number of students who attended, interviews scheduled, and job offers.
4. Work authorization criteria: Given the large percentage of international students at Mount Holyoke College and the fact that only a limited number of employers consider sponsoring work authorization, we also look at how work authorization status impacts student opportunities for international students on F1 (international students on student visas with only Optional Practical Training of one-year work authorization) , H1B (students with work authorization) and J1 (students working as teaching assistants at the College while taking classes) vs permanent residents and US citizens who benefit from these services offered by LyonNet. This impact will be analyzed through data on employers who consider accepting, for example, only US citizens, permanent residents vs. those open to sponsoring international candidates.
5. A specific focus on seniors looking for full time opportunities will be analyzed in our data. Also, given the fact that some seniors attend graduate programs directly after undergraduate education, this number of seniors will be deducted from the overall senior pool in order to isolate the impact of immediate graduate school plans on job applications.

6. For Smith College, the impact of E-Access will be analyzed. Furthermore, data to compare the impacts of separate online career services vis a vis joint career services will be analyzed.

Data

The data we collected was readily available on LyonNet. We also contacted the directors of the Career Development centers at Mount Holyoke and Smith colleges. The data was divided in two parts: first, we will review the data we have for Mount Holyoke College, and then we will do the same for Smith College.

The table below presents the total information that has been collected by LyonNet since its creation. The number of Registered Employers represents the number of all the employers who list and have listed with Mount Holyoke College in the past. The number of registered students represents not only the enrolled students, but also the registered, less than 5 years, alumnae who still use LyonNet to address their needs. The Job postings number shows how many postings we have had since the beginning of the last fiscal year: July 01, 2009. It is worth noting that some of the registered employers have provided Mount Holyoke College with new opportunities, perhaps during the same period, but those updates are deducted from the Job Posting number. The multi-school postings is the number of employers who have listed with the college, but have also listed with other liberal arts colleges.

LyonNet Data	
Registered Employers	6107
Registered Students	10552
Job postings	592
Multi-School Postings	29

In the next table, we look at all the job postings listed in LyonNet. We have provided the total number of jobs for 2010 fiscal year, and we have broken it down by category: full time, part time, etc.

All Job Postings MHC	
All jobs in database	957
Full time	586
Part time	171
Internship	365
Volunteer	47
Fellowship	58
Summer Jobs	33
Other	74

The table below shows a breakdown of the opportunities available to each student. Here, each employer has specified in their posting that the opportunity would be available to a certain class level, i. e. seniors only, juniors only, etc. Although this would be quite useful information to see what impact internet job searching has on the different class levels, we maintained our focus on the enrolled students, and later narrowed our analysis to Seniors and full-time opportunities matching.

Job Postings by Class Level	
Freshman	18
Sophomore	142
Junior	171
Senior	226
Recent Alum <5yrs	216
FP	58
Graduate student	125
Ada Comstock	75
Alum	151
SSW	81

The data below reviews the interview matching achieved for academic semester Fall 2010. We looked at the number of applicants who applied for each position, and then we looked at the number of interviews scheduled, given the number of open slots.

Interview matching achieved (Fall 2010) *		
Applicants	Slots open	Interviews
3	13	3
23	1	0
2	1	0
19	8	8
35	13	13
19	1	0

Since Mount Holyoke college has a very diverse student body, we thought it fundamental to look at the job authorization criteria provided by each employer. The following table lists the total number of job postings divided into 6 groups, according to the employers criteria.

Work Authorization Requirement (MHC)	
US Citizen Only	316
US Citizen Only or Permanent Resident	299
F-1 Student Visa	90
H1-B Visa	86
J-1 Visa	46
Other	70

In order to address the employers' work authorization criteria we matched it with the students work authorization status, and divided it into groups, by class level:

Students' Work Status	MHC	First Year	Sophomore	Junior	Senior
Active MHC US Citizen or Perm resident	101	0	22	19	36
Active MHC US Citizen only	1005	6	99	230	302
F-1	196	1	65	41	52
H1-B	32	0	1	5	10
J1	1	0	0	0	1
Other	1298	31	454	390	209

Smith College (E-access)

For the data of the online job database at Smith College, E-access, we were provided with the annual recruiting report for fiscal year 2010. We know that between July 2009 and July 2010, there were 1546 companies that posted 3368 opportunities. The chart below shows the division of those opportunities.

Full Time	1234
Fellowships	552
Internships	871

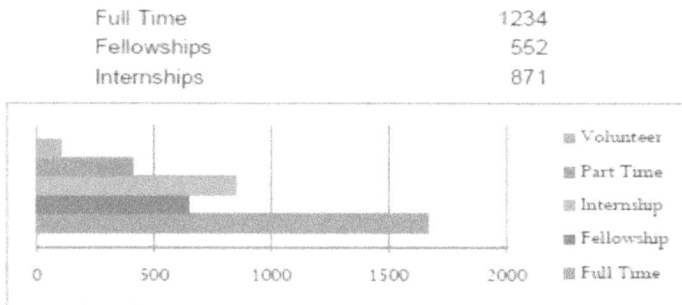

The following are the top career fields, with Education offering the highest, and Financial Services offering the least, number of opportunities.

Top Career Fields	
Education/ Academia	458
Science/Technology	349
Non-Profit/NGO	246
Social/ Human Services	184
Research	116
Financial Services	86

In addition, there were 4 on-campus career fairs, 3 off-campus career fairs, 3 virtual recruiting events, 27 informational sessions, and 47 on-campus recruiting employers, meaning they included a resume drop during their visit of the school (Annual Recruiting Report 2010, Smith College).

Discussions

Students make varying degrees of usage of the plethora of services offered by LyonNet and E Access. As a general trend, only a small percentage of students take full advantage of the many career support offered by these online platforms and only use the primary search function.

Also, it is observed that there is greater usage of LyonNet by international students with F1 visa status than other visa statuses (permanent residents, US citizens). Domestic students use LyonNet to an even lesser degree. Based on personal testimonies by both international students (with and without definite work authorization) and domestic students, the factor of other types of social networks is one of the differentiating factors that explains why domestics students continue to rely on traditional job search methods. Domestic students or international students with permanent residency tend to have the social network of families or friends who may be connected to employers or contacts which can provide information on job openings. In contrast, international students who are often times the only members of their families to rely on to facilitate their job search, which creates necessity, and therefore an incentive to rely on the internet as the primary job search tool due to a lack of alternative of established social network.

Survey

To complement and verify the quantitative component of our research, we will conduct qualitative surveys to gather opinions on the effectiveness and rankings of LyonNet services by random sampling. The questions asked will be as follows

1. Class year
2. Major
3. If looking for jobs? And if so, full time? Part time? Internship? Volunteer?
4. How often do you use LyonNet? How often do you use other generic career services? (times per week)
5. Do you still use non online based job search methods, such as career fair, newspaper advertising? And how is the relationship bewteen the usage of online job search methods and traditional search methods? What is the preferred method through which you hear about a specific opportunity
6. On a scale of 1 to 10, how do you rate LyonNet? Does your rating change after the merge (if you are aware)

The researchers conducted a randomized survey in Mount Holyoke College's main campus center, and were able to gather 86 opinions total. Out of the sample the researchers identified 36 seniors, out of which 27 shared that they were looking for jobs. According to the survey we were able to extract the following information.

Survey

*random sample of students

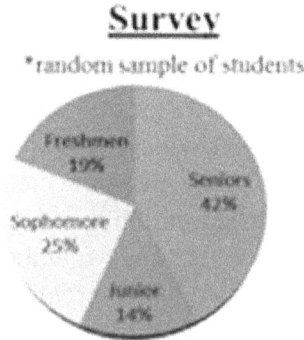

Out of 86 students surveyed, 42% were seniors, 14% - juniors, 25% - sophomores, 19% freshmen. We decided to focus on the students from the senior class. Out of the 36 seniors we surveyed, 27 looked for employment opportunities, i.e. full time, part time, internships, fellowships and summer jobs. Out of those 27 seniors 25 looked for full time, 6 looked for full time and other job opportunities, 2 looked for part time jobs, and 1 looked for fellowships.

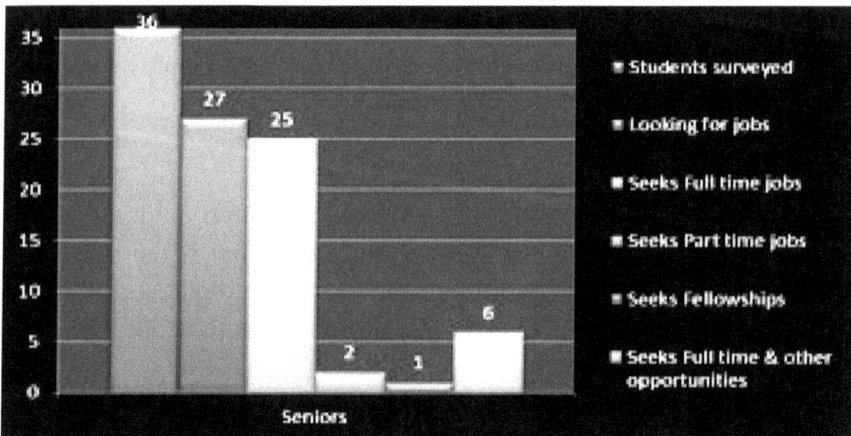

We asked the 27 seniors, who claimed they are looking for jobs, if they use the traditional job search method (including career fairs, networking events, informational session, job ads in newspapers, etc)in addition to the online method. Twelve of the students said that they rely entirely on the Internet to find jobs, and 15 responded that they seek additional resources via traditional methods to find a job.

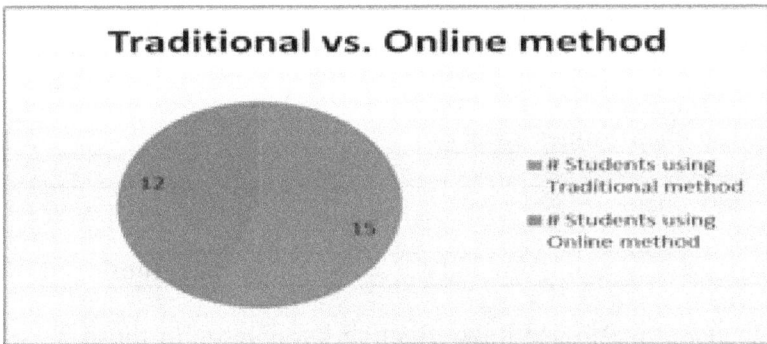

We then asked the same 27 students which of the two methods they find to be more effective. Twelve students said that the online method is more effective than the traditional; ten students voted for the traditional method versus the online; two students claimed that they find both methods to be equally effective; two other students shared that it depends on the job one seeks, and one student said that neither of the two is effective, when it comes down to job search.

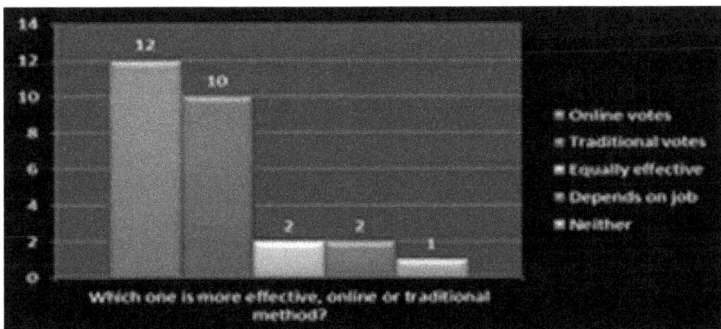

In addition, we wanted to see how many students use LyonNet, the college's job database that is particularly targeted to Mount Holyoke

college's students. We dound that nine students use LyonNet 1-2 times a week, two students use it more than twice a week, eight students use it very rarely, two students used it only once, and six students have never actually used the job database. This was a surprising finding, given that the employers who post in this database are specifically looking for students from Mount Holyoke college. We initially assumed that this would be the first, if not the only resource, students rely on, because the information gap between employers and job seekers is narrowed significantly.

LyonNet Usage	
1-2 times a week	9
More than 2 times a week	2
Rarely	8
Only once	2
Never	6
Total	**27**

We then wanted to see how effective LyonNet is to those 27 seniors, who look for jobs. Fifteen students gave LyonNet a rating of 7 or higher, meaning that they were satisfied with the opportunities LyonNet provided them with; 8 students ranked the database with 6 or less (* please note that some of these people did not, or rarely used LyonNet), and 4 people did not provide ranking.

LyonNet's Rating
*(10 - highest)

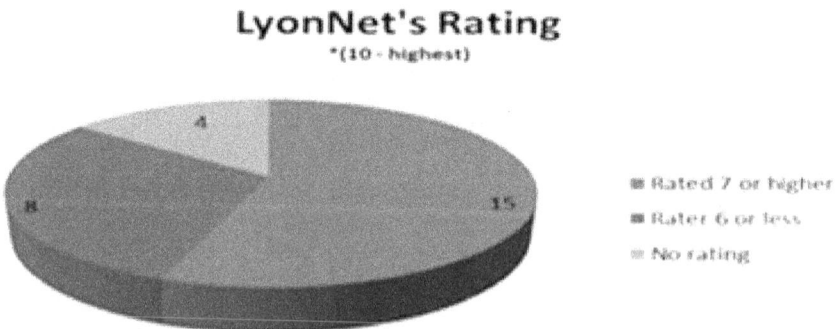

- Rated 7 or higher
- Rater 6 or less
- No rating

Due to the limited data we gathered from Mount Holyoke, we cannot yet draw conclusion about the selection effect of employer posting or students searching. However, based on the data obtained from E-access, we see that the three top job posting fields are Education or Academia,

Science and Technology, and Non-Profit & NGO. Not surprisingly, these are the fields that value critical thinking, and a wide variety of transferable skills, fostered by the liberal arts education.

While conducting the survey, we noticed that most of the students who prefer traditional job search methods, such as career fair, personal contact and "word of mouth", tend to be domestic students. Not surprisingly, the majority of the domestic students have a stronger social network, which they can rely on in addition to the online job search. Although Brown et al shares that personality traits may be an important factor when forming social networks he does not consider the citizenship status of the job seekers. Building a social network takes a long period of time to form, and in many cases, family connections play a fundamental role. This creates unfavorable conditions to the students who have spent less time in the country, and tend to have fewer family connections.

Conclusion and Implication for Future Research

In the future, more research on how employers specifically select candidates could be done in order to analyze the more concrete influences on employers in same fields but with different behaviors. For example, Apple recruits liberal arts students while EMC would only consider students with a sufficiently specialized background in one area, and would not choose to participate in posting nor recruiting at Mount Holyoke College. Often times, companies like EMC assume that liberal arts students do not have the specific financial understanding that would be required for a position at their firm. Instead EMC-kind employers would look for applicants that carry the technical skills and specific knowledge, rather than placing an emphasis on the learn-ability of the applicant.

Also, given the brevity of time of the merge, not enough data has been generated to derive conclusive interpretations of its full impact. It is the researchers' hope that future students interested in the theme of the impact of online, campus-specific career service websites continue with the research to broaden its length and depth.

REFERENCES

Holden, G. (1991). The relationship of self-efficacy appraisals to subsequent health related outcomes: A meta-analysis. *Social Work in Health Care, 16,* 53–93.
Stajkovic, A. D., & Luthans, F. (1998). Self-efficacy and work-related performance: A

meta-analysis. *Psychological Bulletin, 124,* 240–261.

Brown, Douglas, J, Richard T. Cober, Kevin Kane and Paul E. Levy. Proactive Personality and the Successful Job Search: A Field Investigation With College Graduates. Journal of Applied Psychology. 2006. Volume 91. No. 3. 717-726. American Psychological Association.

Stevenson, Betsey. The Internet and Job Search. NBER Working Paper Series. Working Paper 13886. Cambridge, MA. 2008. National Bureau of Economic Research <http://www.nber.org/papers/w13886>

Kuhn, Peter and Skuterud, Mikal. Internet Job Search and Unemployment Durations. American Economic Review. 2004. Vol 94. No. 1. Published by American Economics Association. <http://www.jstor.org/stable/3592776>

6

The Internet's Effects on Entrepreneurship

Ryan Conti and Kevin Cecala

With the rise of the internet, the business landscape has transformed into a place that the first moguls of entrepreneurship such as Andrew Carnegie and David Rockefeller would scarcely recognize. Not only has the internet transformed the way in which we interact with one another, but the advent of new technologies has made it possible for producers to market and distribute goods and services from anywhere in the world to anyone with remarkable ease. In his book, *The World is Flat*, Thomas Friedman describes a situation in which citizens of the world are becoming increasingly better connected as a result of ten "flatteners."[1] From the collapse of the Berlin Wall to open source coding to wireless data transmission, his work emphasizes the connectedness of the modern world. There are many advantages to this phenomenon and entrepreneurs have been able to take advantage of not only the far-reaching networks, but new types of industry that have resulted from this ever changing landscape. To take a line from Acs and Varga, "the entrepreneurial process is one of the entrepreneur recognizing and acting upon unexploited opportunity."[2]

International markets are among the hardest to penetrate using traditional business strategy. Arguably the most widely recognized brand in the world, McDonalds, operates in 117 countries on six continents.[3] Founded in 1948, the fast food restaurant has had impressive growth, reaching people all over the world. However, the global presence and brand recognition that McDonalds has achieved over 62 years can now be accomplished in much less time. Small and medium sized companies can improve their visibility and reach a larger customer base with drastically reduced global advertising costs.[4] "Internet removes many barriers to communication with customers and employees by eliminating the obstacles created by geography, time zones, and location, creating a "frictionless" business environment."[5] Companies can now instantly reach billions of people but more importantly they can now reach the right people easily. Previously advertisements were on billboards and in magazines where it was harder to target directly those customers with the highest propensity to purchase a company's product. Now advertising sites are amassing massive amounts of data on every user allowing them to target customers based on their preferences or location. For this reason, when you are reading an email about planning a vacation you will see ads for Travelocity and Orbitz pop up. This is beneficial to the advertiser in that they can reach a larger proportion of potential customers requiring them to buy fewer advertisements. However, it is also advantageous to the website allowing them to charge more per ad slot seeing as it is now more valuable to their clients. Because ads are reaching the right target audience, there is less waste thereby increasing everyone's profits.

As a result of this frictionless environment, small companies are able to have 24 hour support by hiring employees across the globe, transforming the world of business from 9 to 5 retail to nonstop global e-commerce. At any hour in the day you can go on Amazon.com and purchase anything you want. This increases impulse shopping but also increases time efficiency. You don't have to squeeze shopping into your schedule during the prime working hours of the day. Instead, you can just fit it into your schedule whenever you have time.

Cyberspace has created tremendous opportunities for billion dollar ideas to come to fruition almost overnight. Around the turn of the millennium, cyberspace became less of a specialized tool, transforming into a household commodity. As this was happening, many entrepreneurs recognized the potential of the internet. There was a mad dash among people to get into the sexy new environment emerging in front of them. "The Net's first big wave from 1996-2000, marked the height of the dot-com insanity and opportunities."[6] "If you had a good idea for a company, it would either go public at a fabulous price or be sold for a handsome profit," says Trevor Traina, who sold his first startup to Microsoft for about 100 million dollars in 1999.[7] According to Traina the only thing crazier than being able to sell his company for 100 million dollars was seeing others with bad ideas getting the same result. This kind of enormous growth and profitability obviously could not last and the dot.com bubble burst in 2000. However, the creation of a new type of marketplace remained, and online retailers like Amazon have thrived since then with the proliferation of cyberspace.

The largest boundary that E-commerce entrepreneurs first needed to overcome was the uncertainty that was inherent in peoples' activity due to the strange nature of this new invention.[8] Services like eBay (particularly with the addition of PayPal) and Amazon were instrumental in eroding peoples' trepidations about shopping on the internet. With the path cleared by internet giants, entrepreneurs were then able to enter this new marketplace filled with easy marketing, low costs, and no need for physical stores. For example, founded in 2001 with little more than a web address and $500 in startup capital, BizChair.com was founded by a 14 year old in his bedroom, but managed to amass revenue of $13.6 million in only four years, reaching $42 million in revenue by 2008.

The Internet changed everything for entrepreneurs by drastically reducing barriers to entry. Where once BizChair would have needed to compete with the Office Depot and Staples of the world, low advertising costs and wide access coupled with no physical inventory requirement brought the cost of starting and operating a business down to a level that was accessible to anyone with a good idea and the initiative to make it happen. For these new retailers, the only thing that was of great importance was the appearance of the virtual store, even if the company's conference table was a piece of plywood propped up on two sawhorses in a cluttered warehouse. With prudent planning, an entrepreneur is able to start a company such as Cold Fusion which offers discount snowboards and be the first result people see when they type "snowboard" into their favorite search engine. The cost of this great advantage? $50 to $70 for every thousand people who see the ad, said chief executive Niel McKinnel. He equates his great advantage to "owning Boardwalk and Park Place – we beat out companies with 200 times our revenues by registering the words first."[9]

Another effect of the internet is the easy access to information which makes it much easier to start a company. Using the internet, one can gather information about tax codes, legal regulations, advice about marketing techniques, and the ability to try and fail over and over without any significant consequences.[10] Low operating and investment costs allow entrepreneurs to deploy their idea with little risk while at the same time researching competitors and crafting a better business plan to foster greater success. Due to the rapid progression of technology, the individual is also given a rare opportunity to compete with corporate behemoths if they are able to offer a service or product that is a step ahead. Given the bureaucracy involved in major corporations, there is generally longer time of development for large companies because of the simple fact that they have something to lose. If the company rolls out a new product or service that is defective or behind the technological curve, they are damaged in the intangible field of their reputation. For the upcoming entrepreneur, low start-up and operating costs allow the deployment of new services with very little risk. In this way, they are able to gain competitive advantage by developing a novel business strategy before the competition.[11] However, the advantage for entrepreneurs is a potential danger for consumers due to the entry of "unfitted individuals."[12]

Perhaps the most significant development in internet entrepreneurship is the internet itself as a medium for business creation. Entrepreneurs have realized the power of creating collaborative websites and products that effectively serve as a medium for people to interact with each other, develop ideas, or spend their leisure time. Companies such as Facebook, Youtube, and Google have no place in the "real" world, but have served to define the internet experience as we know it. These companies create a virtual product and are able to make money selling advertisements to other companies seeking to widen exposure to users of these virtual services. Another extension of this is the creation of an entirely virtual economy, where people will spend money that they have earned in real life, usually in an online game. A notable example of this is the MMORPG, World of Warcraft, where users can buy virtual property and upgrades to their characters.[13]

In this vein, entrepreneurship has been revolutionized by the creation of an entirely new form of technology. The ease of sharing information and connecting with such a large audience enables people to collaborate and connect with each other in ways that don't just enhance previous forms of interaction, but create completely new ways of thinking about founding businesses. With the open source coding movement, people with little more than an idea about how they could enhance their experience in the world, whether physical or virtual, are able to create products with very little experience or time investment. This means that it is simply easier for people to develop ideas regardless of prior experience and without a significant investment outside of reading some basic online tutorials.

Case Study: badNYCapartments.com

BadNYCapartments.com started as a project between brothers Sam and Pat Bauch. They initially got the idea to start the website after a bad experience renting a duplex apartment in Queens, New York. During the first major rainstorm after they moved in, their basement flooded with over a foot of water, destroying furniture, electronics, and other items. They later found out that the previous tenant had broken her lease because of the same recurring flood problem, suggesting that it had existed for a long time. Stumbling upon an information asymmetry first-hand, they realized that the broker had every incentive not to inform them about the problem, for if they knew about the problem they would likely not have signed the lease. As such, they created the site as a place for New Yorkers to share bad experiences about apartment rentals to eliminate the asymmetry in the market. Co-founder and CEO Sam Bauch likened the apartment experience to buying a car, saying "not every '94 Dodge Neon is the same, and neither is every apartment unit." In this light, they set out to establish a company to eliminate the same adverse selection problem with apartments that Carfax does for cars.

Bad NYC Apartments gets their information largely from government data sources, and the largest current source is the Department of Buildings Database of Caller Complaints. Ultimately, they hope to expand their range of data and provide access to real estate brokerages that can access the content on the website on behalf of clients seeking to rent apartments in the city. In this way they can stay true to their original desire of being a renter protection service.

Once the team had decided there was not a company that provided the same service, they decided to set up a website and began to look for someone to build it for them given that neither had any programming experience. The first step was Vcoder.com, a collaborative website that allows you to post project ideas to the community which then will bid to complete the project described. The bids they received were higher than they were willing to pay at the time, so Sam began to try to figure out web development on his own. Again turning to the Internet for help, he was able to find several free open source coding websites which provided both tutorials and sample code which he was able to tinker with until he was satisfied with what he had developed. In this example is another major advantage provided in cyberspace. With no prior knowledge of coding or web design, this entrepreneur was able to use the wide range of free information available to learn enough to get a basic website up and running, all without a need for increased capital investment in the business. Though he now feels he has hit a ceiling with his ability to design the site using the current program, it has allowed the site to grow to the extent that enough interest has been expressed that he can be fairly certain to receive a positive return on his investment.

Due to the Internet, the start-up costs were extremely low for the company. They were able to purchase their domain for $10 per year and file as a corporation on the New York Department of State website for $200. Along with this registration, they received free advertising credits from Google Adwords and Facebook Ads; however they saw this as a relatively ineffective way to spread word about the website over cyberspace. Instead, they appealed to blogs and Internet content. They were able to get featured in the New York Times "Freakonomics" blog, as well as The Atlantic Online.[14] Here lies a significant form of press for a small company, courtesy of the internet. If a start-up can receive press on a major blog, word about the idea can reach thousands of people within hours of a post. This viral marketing has been a great way for entrepreneurs to spread their service to a very broad audience with no additional capital required for advertising.

Using the Internet has been invaluable in establishing the website, and Bauch credits its existence with storage and hosting of data, marketing, content management, and IT expertise. In an interview, he said of cyberspace; "writing a formal business plan, getting a bank loan, all of these things that previously stopped people from starting a business on a whim are, for better or worse, no longer required with Internet entrepreneurship."

However, there are aspects to the Internet that can take the unprepared entrepreneur by surprise. Due to the rapid spread of news of the site while it was still little more than a functional prototype, there was a great deal of criticism about the design of the website. The high-profile press the company received resulted in an increase in traffic from 3000 page views per month to 3000 page views per day. The site received such rapid and broad press at a preliminary stage in design that Bauch is worried that there might not be a "second chance to capitalize on the short attention span of the Internet audience." Herein lies a significant downside to starting a business in cyberspace—due to reasons that have been previously described, almost anyone can start a website. As a result, entrepreneurs are constantly in an uphill battle for their product or service to be perceived as legitimate. This is a serious issue for Internet entrepreneurs. The less recognized negative of having such easy access and start-up process is that there are new ideas flooding the Internet every day. Some of them stick immediately, while some are destined to fail. However, even if a company is able to grow their market share and become 'top dog' in whichever their field of expertise may be, there are dozens of other people trying to erode their market share, and in cyberspace, this can happen in a matter of days or weeks, not months or years as is the case with traditional business.

In order to start a company, one must have a "unique value proposition," says Bauch. Inventing a product is a great way to create a unique opportunity, but fabrication costs can be a significant and risky investment if there is no way of knowing whether or not the product will either be profitable or be able to capture a broad distribution network. By offering a virtual product that no one else does, a person can capture a monopoly in whichever new field they have expanded into originally, but without constant innovation and development, it is easy for a new contender to come in and capture users with a slightly modified version of the same basic design. Though not a competitor in a strict sense, shortly after running a story about Bad NYC Apartments, the New York CityRoom blog ran a story titled "Tell Us about Your Worst New York Apartment."[15] The low boundaries to entry not only mean that small companies can grow to compete with larger ones, but it also can work the other way around, in that a large company can focus a very small portion of its resources to very quickly and effectively expand into a new segment with a superior marketing network and resources, thus undermining the competitive advantage of the entrepreneur or small business.

Case Study of BizChair.com

At the tender age of 14, while sitting in his bedroom, Sean Belnick decided to start his own company. With only 500 dollars to his name

Belnick was able to begin operating an online office furniture business which was grossing $24 million dollars within 5 years.[16] Not your basic lemonade stand of old and today this is not as uncommon of a story as one might think. Due to the growth and development of cyberspace, the ability to start and operate your own business is an increasingly real possibility for anyone. What previously was a daunting and impossible task without large start-up capital now is seemingly all too easy. The internet has allowed entrepreneurs the ability to reach an infinitely greater market size while maintaining very low running costs. Everything from advertising to bill collection has become substantially easier.

While most kids at the age of 14 were playing with Pokémon cards, Belnick was selling them. Recognizing the popularity of the cards at school rather than seeing an opportunity to play, like all of his friends, he saw an opportunity to get paid. Using the internet to buy and sell cards Belnick made $4,000 dollars before he entered high school.[17] This venture only lasted with the popularity of the game and as the velocity at which cards were bought and sold on eBay began to fizzle, so did his profits.

In 2001, having learned from his previous experiences Belnick decided to embark on a new project, BizChair.com. His stepfather was an office chair salesman and tapping into his expertise, Belnick created a business plan and website. For only 500 dollars Belnick started his internet business which made $42 million in 2008. It is because of the internet that this company was able to grow so quickly, under the leadership of a teenager. Belnick says himself, "Basically there was very, very limited risk... I didn't have to buy tens of thousands of dollars worth of inventory to get started."[18] Just like merchants in days of old, he was just a middle man cataloging chairs sold by different manufacturers and marketing them to the world. By selling them for more than he would buy them for he made money on the margins. With his operating costs so low he did not need to significantly mark up the prices. Expenses were directly tied to his revenue stream so he incurred no expenses until he received an order. At that point the risk of buying a chair from a manufacturer and not selling is negligable and therefore you can never be left with stale merchandise sitting in a warehouse and eating up profits. This plan was even better than selling Pokémon cards, which can change value every day or go obsolete,since office chairs are not as volatile a product.

However, one major problem with this business plan is that given that it was so easy to start up in the first place there is nothing stopping a competitor from entering the market and driving the profits down. To stay ahead of the competition, BizChair.com offered two incentives: free shipping and a 60-day money-back guarantee. BizChair.com then expanded after about four months to include desks. Conference tables and school furniture were added, and now the site has medical equipment, chairs for churches, office furniture and accessories, among other items."[19] Belnick realizes that he needs to stay one step ahead of the competition or his company will become obsolete. He is constantly trying to expand the selection he offers. People want choices and the internet allows you to give them just that all in one location. With the development of search tools you do not overwhelm the customer by having extensive selections as you could in a store. A customer can instantly narrow down price, features, brands, colors, etc. to only see what they are truly interested in. Because there is not the need to warehouse every item and have it on hand there is no added cost to offering more choices. "We've focused on continually adding more vendors, more products," Belnick said recognizing his customer's diverse desires. When asked what he would do differently if given another chance Belnick replied, "Most likely it would be to expand our product selection faster than we did. We really stayed in the office chair market for a while before expanding into office furniture and home furniture as well as some other segments. If we had done that faster, we could have cemented a larger position as a market leader."[20]

With the internet there is an impersonal touch that can be felt by the customer. "One of the most important components is your customers. Ensuring that they are taken care of and that you go above and beyond the expectations shows them how much you care and will likely increase repeat business."[21] When Belnick was first starting up he had his mom install an 800 number line in his room so that he could encourage customers with questions and concerns to call in. This allowed him to provide them with that personal touch.

In 2007 when you typed 'office chair' into Google the top result was BizChair.com.[22] With the development of the internet, consumers have gotten lazy. They assume everything is supposed to be easy and they have become more trusting. By being the top search result on Google.com, the top search engine in the world and most visited site on the internet, a company can drastically increase site traffic. When it is the top site for a keyword on Google, it also instills a sense of reliability with customers who feel more confident that it is a legitimate business. This is especially important when your CEO is a teenager.

As a teenage entrepreneur it can be extremely difficult to garner respect from customers and fellow businessmen who may be much older and more experienced. It is understandable that a customer may not want to buy an expensive product from someone who hasn't even gone through puberty yet. This isn't like selling Girl Scout cookies or running your own lawn care service. Businesses may buy thousands of dollars worth of products and they need to feel confident that the product is going to arrive, be in working order, and that the company is not about to go bankrupt before it can provide necessary customer support. The internet, fortunately, prevents these prejudices from coming into play. When evaluating the strength and health of a company people do not look at the age of the owner and if he is wearing a nice suit. The face of the company is the company's website. Companies are judged based on the professionalism they display in their website, the products they offer and the reputation that precedes them. For this reason the playing field seems to be leveled by the internet. When previously you could be held back by gender, race and age, now it appears as though those that are the smartest and have the best ideas have the greatest ability to prosper. This, in the case of the office chair industry, happens to be a now 20 year old Emory College student.

The world of business has always been a constantly changing field. However, with the introduction of the internet the velocity at which change is occurring has increased exponentially. As a result of this development, in order to remain successful and in control of market share a company must constantly stay one step ahead. The best example of this is Apple. In Dec of 1997 APPL was trading for 3.25 a share. Then with the introduction of the IMac the company rebounded and continued to grow peaking in early 2000. However, without new innovation, sales fell and it looked like Apple was going to lose its market share and potentially disappear. However, today we can't imagine a world without Apple innovations and that is because, lead by Steve Jobs, they diversified and innovated. Despite having a strong hold on the personal computer market, they continue to innovate by continually creating fresh new products to boosts sales and grow. Now APPL is trading at over 300 dollars and with the introduction of the IPhone and IPad it seems as though there are no signs of them slowing down.[23]

What Apple shows us is that even a company with one great idea cannot survive in this day and age. Amazon is branching out and selling Kindle electronic readers. Google has its hands in just about everything these days from the droid telephone to email hosting.

The internet has broken down many of the barriers to entry that previously prevented competition from entering the market. As basic economics tells us, with greater competition we see increased efficiency and innovation while driving down prices. We have definitely seen this, but, as great as the internet is, there are some disadvantages as well. With this jump in legitimate profits made on the internet and more and more of the money floating in cyberspace we have seen a development in electronic theft. It has become increasing easier for theives to plunder the internet, posing new and constant problems for different industries. The banking industry for example has tried to cut costs and cater to customers changing needs. In providing instant access to funds from anywhere in the world over the internet, banks are also allowing easier access to hackers. Scammers can anonymously steal money without getting up from their seat. Similar to the Wild West when a con artist could go from town to town using the same scam every time; In the Wild Web scam artists can work the same scam with millions of people and by the time the public has caught on, it is too late.

Although the Internet has created many new industries it should also be said that it has really handicapped some others, the music industry being the most obvious example of this. With the spread of illegal music sharing the industry has lost billions of dollars in revenue. Peer-to-peer file sharing allows millions of people to possess a song for free, preventing artists from reaping the rewards of their talents.

We do not think there is a need to debate over whether the internet has been good or bad for our economy. It is important to realize that there have been some detrimental effects caused by the evolution of the internet, however, its overall effects on entrepreneurship and our economy has been overwhelmingly positive. Breaking down barriers to entry has allowed equal opportunities for everyone to compete and succeed within our society. Every facet of business has become more efficient and this ultimately limits waste, increasing profits and decreasing prices—a phenomenon rarely seen in traditional business.

ENDNOTES

1   Friedman, Thomas L. *The World Is Flat: a Brief History of the Twenty-first Century*. New York: Farrar, Straus and Giroux, 2005.
2   Acs, Zolan J., and Attila Varga. "Entrepreneurship, Agglomeration and Technological Change." IDEAS: Economics and Finance Research. Web. 18 Dec. 2010. <http://ideas.repec.org/a/kap/sbusec/v24y2005i3p323-334.html>.
3   Our History :: McDonalds.com." Home :: McDonalds.com. Web. <http://www.mcdonalds.com/us/en/our_story/our_history.html>.
4   Moen, Oystein, Iver Endreson, and Morten Gavlen. "Executive Insights: Use of the Internet in International Marketing: A Case Study of Small Computer Software Firms." Journal of International Marketing11.4 (2003): 129-49. Print.
5   Quelch, John A., and Lisa R. Klein. "The Internet and International Marketing - The Magazine - MIT Sloan Management Review." MIT Sloan Management Review (1996). The New Business of Innovation - MIT Sloan Management Review. Web. 18 Dec. 2010. <http://sloanreview.mit.edu/the-magazine/articles/1996/spring/3735/the-internet-and-international-marketing/>.
6   Swartz, Jon. Young Wealth. Bloomington, IN: RoofTop, 2006. Print.
7   Ibid..
8   Lim, Kai H., Choon Ling Sai, and Matthew KO Lee. "Is ECommerce Boundary-less? Effects of Individualism-collectivism and Uncertainty Avoidance on Internet Shopping." Journal of International Business Studies 35.6 (2004): 545-59. Print.
9   Hardy, Quentin. "Making the Sale --- Think Big: For Entrepreneurs, Size Isn't Nearly the Handicap in Cyberspace That It Is in the Real World." The Wall Street Journal [New York] 7 Dec. 1998, Eastern Edition ed. Print.
10 Fairlie, Robert W. "The Personal Computer and Entrepreneurship." Management Science 52.2 (2006): 187-203. Print.
11 Phan, Dien D. "E-business Development for Competitive Advantages: a Case Study - PDFCast.org." Upload PDF Documents - Broadcast - Share. Web. 18 Dec. 2010. <http://pdfcast.org/pdf/e-business-development-for-competitive-advantages-a-case-study>.
12 Colombo, Massimo G., and Marco Delmastro. "Technology-Based Entrepreneurs: Does Internet Make a Difference?" Small Business Economics 16.3 (2001): 177-90. 20 Jan. 2004. Web. 17 Nov. 2010.
13 Buley, Taylor. "What's Next For The Virtual Economy - Forbes.com." Forbes.com - Business News, Financial News, Stock Market Analysis, Technology & Global Headline News. 04 Jan. 2010. Web. <http://www.forbes.com/2010/01/04/virtual-economy-gaming-technology-breakthroughs-levchin.html>.
14 Dubner, Stephen J. "How to Avoid a Bad Apartment in New York City - NYTimes.com." Opinion - Freakonomics Blog - NYTimes.com. 29 Sept. 2010. Web. <http://freakonomics.blogs.nytimes.com/2010/09/29/how-to-avoid-a-bad-apartment-in-new-york-city/>.
15 Rosenblum, Constance. "Share Your Stories: Bad Apartments in New York - NYTimes.com."Metro - City Room Blog - NYTimes.com. 12 Nov. 2010. Web. <http://cityroom.blogs.nytimes.com/2010/11/12/tell-us-about-your-worst-new-york-

apartment/>.

16 "Interview With Sean Belnick – Making $50,000,000 A Year Selling Business Chairs | Young Entrepreneurs." Young Entrepreneurs | Making Money Online. 31 Jan. 2008. Web. 18 Dec. 2010. <http://www.retireat21.com/interview/interview-with-sean-belnick-making-millions-selling-business-chairs>.

17 Swartz, Jon. Young Wealth. Bloomington, IN: RoofTop, 2006. Print.

18 Johnston, Lori. "Young Entrepreneur Distinguishes Self in Office Furniture Business | Atlanta Business Chronicle." Business News | The Business Journals. Atlanta Business Chronicle, 10 Dec. 2007. Web. 18 Dec. 2010. <http://www.bizjournals.com/atlanta/stories/2007/12/10/smallb1.html>.

19 Johnston, Lori. "Young Entrepreneur Distinguishes Self in Office Furniture Business | Atlanta Business Chronicle." Business News | The Business Journals. Atlanta Business Chronicle, 10 Dec. 2007. Web. 18 Dec. 2010. <http://www.bizjournals.com/atlanta/stories/2007/12/10/smallb1.html>.

20 "Interview With Sean Belnick – Making $50,000,000 A Year Selling Business Chairs | Young Entrepreneurs." Young Entrepreneurs | Making Money Online. 31 Jan. 2008. Web. 18 Dec. 2010. <http://www.retireat21.com/interview/interview-with-sean-belnick-making-millions-selling-business-chairs>.

21 Swartz, Jon. Young Wealth. Bloomington, IN: RoofTop, 2006. Print.

22 Webber, Liz Jul. "The Chair Man of the Board - 30 Under 30 - Sean Belnick - BizChair.com." Small Business and Small Business Information for the Entrepreneur. Inc., 25 July 2007. Web. 18 Dec. 2010. <http://www.inc.com/30under30/2007/the-chair-man-of-the-board.html>.

23 "Apple Inc.: NASDAQ:AAPL Quotes & News - Google Finance." Google. 18 Dec. 2010. Web. 18 Dec. 2010. <http://www.google.com/finance?q=NASDAQ:AAPL>.

REFERENCES

Acs, Zolan J., and Attila Varga. "Entrepreneurship, Agglomeration and Technological Change." IDEAS: Economics and Finance Research. Web. 18 Dec. 2010. <http://ideas.repec.org/a/kap/sbusec/v24y2005i3p323-334.html>.

"Apple Inc.: NASDAQ:AAPL Quotes & News - Google Finance." Google. 18 Dec. 2010. Web. 18 Dec. 2010. <http://www.google.com/finance?q=NASDAQ:AAPL>.

Buley, Taylor. "What's Next For The Virtual Economy - Forbes.com." Forbes.com - Business News, Financial News, Stock Market Analysis, Technology & Global Headline News. 04 Jan. 2010. Web. <http://www.forbes.com/2010/01/04/virtual-economy-gaming-technology-breakthroughs-levchin.html>.

Colombo, Massimo G., and Marco Delmastro. "Technology-Based Entrepreneurs: Does Internet Make a Difference?" Small Business Economics 16.3 (2001): 177-90. 20 Jan. 2004. Web. 17 Nov. 2010.

Dubner, Stephen J. "How to Avoid a Bad Apartment in New York City - NYTimes.com." Opinion - Freakonomics Blog - NYTimes.com. 29 Sept. 2010. Web. <http://freakonomics.blogs.nytimes.com/2010/09/29/how-to-avoid-a-bad-apartment-in-new-york-city/>.

Fairlie, Robert W. "The Personal Computer and Entrepreneurship." Management Science

52.2 (2006): 187-203. Print.

Friedman, Thomas L. The World Is Flat: a Brief History of the Twenty-first Century. New York: Farrar, Straus and Giroux, 2005. Print.

Hardy, Quentin. "Making the Sale --- Think Big: For Entrepreneurs, Size Isn't Nearly the Handicap in Cyberspace That It Is in the Real World." The Wall Street Journal [New York] 7 Dec. 1998, Eastern Edition ed. Print.

"Interview With Sean Belnick – Making $50,000,000 A Year Selling Business Chairs | Young Entrepreneurs." Young Entrepreneurs | Making Money Online. 31 Jan. 2008. Web. 18 Dec. 2010. <http://www.retireat21.com/interview/interview-with-sean-belnick-making-millions-selling-business-chairs>.

Johnston, Lori. "Young Entrepreneur Distinguishes Self in Office Furniture Business | Atlanta Business Chronicle." Business News | The Business Journals. Atlanta Business Chronicle, 10 Dec. 2007. Web. 18 Dec. 2010. <http://www.bizjournals.com/atlanta/stories/2007/12/10/smallb1.html>.

Lim, Kai H., Choon Ling Sai, and Matthew KO Lee. "Is ECommerce Boundary-less? Effects of Individualism-collectivism and Uncertainty Avoidance on Internet Shopping." Journal of International Business Studies 35.6 (2004): 545-59. Print.

Ljungqvist, Alexander, and William J. Wilhelm. "IPO Pricing in the Dot-com Bubble." The Journal of Finance 58.2 (2003): 723-52. Print.

McGee, Matt. "Michael Jackson's Death: An Inside Look At How Google, Yahoo, & Bing Handled An Extraordinary Day In Search." Search Engine Land: Must Read News About Search Marketing & Search Engines. 27 June 2009. Web. 6 Nov. 2010. <http://searchengineland.com/michael-jackson-extraordinary-day-in-search-21641>.

Moen, Oystein, Iver Endreson, and Morten Gavlen. "Executive Insights: Use of the Internet in International Marketing: A Case Study of Small Computer Software Firms." Journal of International Marketing 11.4 (2003): 129-49. Print.

Noyes, Edward, and Ian MacInnes. "Small Business Electronic Commerce Implementation: A Case Study." Journal of Internet Commerce 5.1 (2006): 1-22. Print.

"Our History :: McDonalds.com." Home :: McDonalds.com. Web. <http://www.mcdonalds.com/us/en/our_story/our_history.html>.

Phan, Dien D. "E-business Development for Competitive Advantages: a Case Study - PDFCast.org." Upload PDF Documents - Broadcast - Share. Web. 18 Dec. 2010. <http://pdfcast.org/pdf/e-business-development-for-competitive-advantages-a-case-study>.

Quelch, John A., and Lisa R. Klein. "The Internet and International Marketing - The Magazine - MIT Sloan Management Review." MIT Sloan Management Review (1996). The New Business of Innovation - MIT Sloan Management Review. Web. 18 Dec. 2010. <http://sloanreview.mit.edu/the-magazine/articles/1996/spring/3735/the-internet-and-international-marketing/>.

Rosenblum, Constance. "Share Your Stories: Bad Apartments in New York - NYTimes.com." Metro - City Room Blog - NYTimes.com. 12 Nov. 2010. Web. <http://cityroom.blogs.nytimes.com/2010/11/12/tell-us-about-your-worst-new-york-apartment/>.

Schuman, Michael. "Internet Start-Ups Revolutionize Korean Economy --- Drawn by Fast Money, Young Entrepreneurs Abandon Conglomerates." The Wall Street Journal [New York] 28 Dec. 1999, Eastern Edition ed. Print.

Shane, Scott, and Daniel Cable. "Network Ties, Reputation, and the Financing of New Ventures." Management Science 48.3 (2002): 364-81. Print.

Swartz, Jon. Young Wealth. Bloomington, IN: RoofTop, 2006. Print.

Webber, Liz Jul. "The Chair Man of the Board - 30 Under 30 - Sean Belnick - BizChair. com." Small Business and Small Business Information for the Entrepreneur. Inc., 25 July 2007. Web. 18 Dec. 2010. <http://www.inc.com/30under30/2007/the-chair-man-of-the-board.html>.

7

The Value of the Open Source Revolution: Monetizing and Mainstreaming "Free"

Charlotte Wen

A Crash Course in Open Source

Once upon a time, a laser printer broke in an MIT laboratory.

It doesn't sound like an especially interesting story, or an especially notable beginning, but this one broken printer started a chain reaction of events that eventually led to the establishment of the Free Software Foundation (FSF) by MIT researcher and eminent programmer Richard Stallman in 1984. What happened was, the printer suffered from chronic paper jams, and when Stallman contacted Xerox for the source code of the software that powered the printer so that he could fiddle with it and hopefully fix the problem, he was flatly denied. The refusal ate away at Stallman, and he began to envision a world where software was free— where a program's source code was readily available to anyone who wanted to modify it, instead of locked up and guarded zealously.[1] The pursuit of a world with freer software became somewhat of a moral mission for him, and remains so to this day.

But what does Stallman and the rest of the Free Software Foundation mean by free? It's an important question. "Free" is the type of word that makes your average shopper quite happy, but makes investors, capitalists, and software vendors squirm uncomfortably in their seats. Make no mistake: it is now entirely possible to go your entire computing life without paying a cent for software, *legally*. A vast quantity of software on the internet is available legally free of charge, from operating systems to photo editing software to music players to office suites. But money has nothing to do with the "free" for which the FSF is named. The $0 price tag is simply an incidental and occasional side-effect for what Stallman terms as "free" software; it does not define it. What he means by free software is, software with the following qualities:

- the freedom to run the program for any purpose,
- to examine the source code of and make your own modifications and improvements to the program as necessary,
- to redistribute the software, either free of charge or carrying a fee,
- and to distribute those modifications and modified versions in order to allow the entire user community to benefit.[2]

Stallman's definition of free software differs only slightly from the topic of this chapter, which is open source software. Some types of open source software fall under the definition of free software as supplied by the FSF. Open source software is, after all, software for which source code is openly available for public viewing, modification, reproduction, and redistribution in the public domain.[3] Familiar examples include internet browser Mozilla Firefox, web server Apache, operating system Linux, databases MySQL and PostgreSQL, content management systems Drupal and Wordpress, and office suite OpenOffice.org. But whereas free software must be defined under the General Public License (GPL), open source software bundles are sometimes released under more restrictive licenses.

So, what's a license?

Software Licensing

When you purchase software, you are not purchasing the program, but the license to use the program. For instance, if you buy a copy of Windows 7, you haven't purchased the actual program or its source code. Both of those still belong to Microsoft. What you've purchased is the right to install the operating system a couple times. So here, we've identified several components to the sale and purchase of a software bundle under a *proprietary* license: the software itself, which still belongs to the vendor, and the license, or right to use it, which now belongs to you. There is only one thing that you as a user can do with proprietary software, and that is, run it. The purchase of proprietary software does not come with the right to view its source code, as it is protected by a litany of increasingly convoluted copyright and software ownership laws. In fact, taking Microsoft as an example once again, it is not only impossible for anyone outside of Microsoft to view and modify the source code, but it's also impossible for some people *within* Microsoft to view and modify the source code.[4] There are a ton of licenses under which a software vendor can release a program, and many are very restrictive. Open source licenses, however, are far less restrictive than proprietary licenses.

Let's say you download an open source program on the internet. But first, let's differentiate between free-of-charge software and open source software. A huge number of proprietary programs are available for download free of charge—for instance, Apple iTunes, Google Chrome, Opera, the list goes on. None of those are open source by any stretch of the imagination, but you do not have to pay in order to obtain a license to use the program. One telltale difference between free-of-charge proprietary software and open source software is the presence of an option to download or view the source code. Most people only pay attention to the single file that allows them to install a copy of the program on their machine, but all open source projects have their code available for download as well. Open source programs, too, are protected by licenses, but they are radically different from most proprietary licenses. The definition of what qualifies as an open source license is several paragraphs long, but the most salient points for the purposes of this chapter are: (a) that the licenser must not require royalties be paid when other people are redistributing their software as part of a bundle, and (b) there is no requirement that open source software must be made available free of charge, nor is there any requirement that derivative works remain free of charge. These two conditions, primarily the second – that it is possible to incorporate open source software into a proprietary program without paying royalties to the original program – are crucial to the commercialization of open source.[5] It is also the point at which definitions of open source and Stallman's definition of free software diverge, but this will become more important to the discussion later on.[6]

So again, why open source?

So why is the discussion of open source software *itself* important? The reasons are too many to number, but it really boils down to this: the open source software movement is part of a larger technological and social trend toward intellectual freedom. It also produces software that is a heck of a lot cheaper and often much higher in quality than the bundled-up, clunky, CPU-guzzling programs churned out by proprietary software giants. As such, it is the software trend that will define the future. By no means does this mean that the era of monopolistic software giants is over. But the open source movement is pushing for a fundamental change in our understanding of intellectual property, and rather than making futile attempts to adapt, abridge, or otherwise hinder the phenomenon to suit existing conceptions of software development, availability, and pricing, businesses, entrepreneurs, and developers alike must learn to adjust to the incoming wave.

Open source is so many things: it is a free exchange of ideas, a wealth of untapped knowledge, cutting-edge progression, a tool of anarchists, and it is unstoppable. But it is also not entirely infallible, especially if a company is attempting to monetize it, and there are problems with the model that must be addressed going forward.

Open Source: A New World Order

The situation with open source bears a superficial degree of resemblance to the multimedia filesharing debate that rose to prominence with the Napster lawsuits of the early 2000s. The situations are not 100% comparable, but the basic question is the same. A consumer is given products A and B. Product A is free, B is not, and the differences in quality between A and B are either insignificant or negligible. What rational human being would choose B? And knowing that, what should beneficiaries of sales of A do?

The MPAA and RIAA reacted to the perceived threat by trying to stomp it down. Ten years later, they are still fighting what appears to be a losing battle. Once consumers are given something for free, it is utterly irrational to construct a business or legal strategy around convincing them to start paying for it again. A better course of action would have been to innovate some way to make the situation work for them – not engage in a legal version of endless Whack-A-Mole with torrent indexing websites and individual users. In short, instead of making this new technology work for them, they chose to go against it—a fatal mistake, since resistance to technological advancements is futile. Just ask shoemakers and blacksmiths. So too, must proprietary software companies also confront the rising popularity and power of the open source revolution – especially as there is no legal recourse to "stop" the rise of open source software.

Open source is thus the future, not only because it comes at a much lower price than proprietary software packages (the suggested retail price for a copy of Microsoft Office 2007 for Home and Student is $149.99; OpenOffice.org's equally functional office suite is available for download online free of charge or on CD-ROM for negligible processing and shipping fees), but also because, as the internet becomes more accessible and easier to use, the computer-literate community will only grow, not shrink.[7] With more research tools and information at their disposal, the number of people who will consent to buying overpriced software on simple blind faith will decrease. Why should consumers continue to pay for subpar, clunky proprietary programs when free or much cheaper programs that are more extensively developed and supported are cheaply available?

The trend is already making itself apparent. Whereas the rise and fall of profits earned by proprietary software companies fluctuates with the economy, open source companies instead display a "largely unreported continuity of vitality."[8] Not only do open source businesses retain steady profits regardless of overall economic conditions, but they also have the unique ability to thrive, rather than wilt, during economic downturns. Why is this? The answer is fairly simple: the price tag on open source software is far more inviting than its proprietary counterparts. In 2001, after the dot-com bubble burst, financial services company E*Trade was forced to slash its operating tech budget by a third. To accomplish this, technology chief Lee Thompson moved away from proprietary software and tapped into the wealth of the open source community. By the end of 2002, E*Trade was saving $13 million a year thanks to the combination of open source software adoption and cheaper hardware.[9] Indeed, E*Trade's 33.3% reduction in budget is even *modest* compared to statistics projected by open source service provider Synaq, whose CEO suggested that businesses that choose open source alternatives over proprietary software can expect 50 to 60% reductions in their tech budgets after three years.[10] To make matters worse for proprietary software giants, the economy is once again in recession. At the end of 2008, 40% of corporate representatives questioned by research group ChangeWave said their companies were aiming to spend less on software in the coming 90 days.[11] But this is where things get a little sticky. Where does all that extra money go?

Opponents of the open source movement would like you to believe that it is not only "the ultimate in disruptive technology," but also that the missing cash flows (estimated at about $60 billion yearly) drop into a hole and disappear, but that is hardly the case.[12] It is true that the low cost of open source software shrinks the size of the software market, but that just means that those funds are redirected into other sectors.[13] While this is obviously not an ideal situation for software companies, who want to keep as much cash circulating in the software market as possible, there is a certain inevitability to the momentum being enjoyed by the open source movement that cannot be denied. The question isn't whether or not software companies *want* to deal with the reality of open source, it's *how* they'll deal with it.

Some might argue the case that migrating to open source is only an attractive option when money is tight and budgets must be slashed, and thus, open source is seasonal or temporal. Open source software and proprietary software are complementary, and demand for open source software indeed rises when money is tight, but this does not necessarily imply that the open source option is inferior. A trend of "open sourced" companies switching back to pricier proprietary software after profits took a turn for the better has yet to be observed. In a survey done of European enterprises, companies did not, in fact, cite low cost as a reason for open source adoption—rather, they considered the top benefit to be the "flexibility allowed by the open-source licence," coupled with the customizability of open source software.[14]

Quality-wise, Herter finds that, under the open software regime, product quality tends to be higher than under a proprietary regime.[15] For one, open source programmers only work on projects in which they have a personal interest, resulting in code "with a lot of heart behind it."[16] Moreover, since source code is viewable to the public and fully attributed to each individual contributor (this is an unspoken rule within the open source community; open source project contributions are an integral part of programmers' resumes), there is weightier pressure to produce solid code than in a proprietary setting, where sloppy implementation is invisible to the public.[17] In short, stable open source releases are often the combined work of a variety of programmers, as opposed to a salaried and not necessarily varied team being forced to work on a deadline and within the constraints of convoluted software protection laws.[18] The open source community also provides a uniquely eager testing base that is "orders of magnitude" more effective than a traditional beta-test program, resulting in a much more streamlined product.[19]

Which in turn brings up another problem: how to monetize open source software.

The Value of Open Source

Open source is valuable. This much is unmistakable, even if its value sometimes manifests in untraditional ways.[20] For instance, it is completely and totally impossible to write a program, distribute it freely, source code and all, and expect to see profits in the next quarter, not if you don't do anything else. It is not a typical business model – some argue that it isn't even a business model at all, just a distribution strategy within a wider business model.[21] But open source is brimming in value, and also brimming in commercial potential. There is nothing in open source licensing that precludes the possibility of monetization and commercialization, for software vendors and business owners alike.

Beneficiaries of open source can be divided loosely into two groups: one, the broader cyberspace community, and two, for-profit companies intent on monetizing open source. This can include both open source software vendors as well as third-party companies seeking a cut of the pie.

The Community

The question of how the open source software movement can benefit the "community" as a whole necessitates a definition of community, so for the purposes of this section, the word "community" refers to anyone and everyone in cyberspace, with a special emphasis on consumers of software. Here, the value of open source is fairly obvious. Since the vast majority of open source software is free, using it instead of paying for costly proprietary software is an easy way to save money.

It would also be remiss not to mention the substantial value that open source adds to the intellectual community; even though it only constitutes a subset of the wider community of cyberspace, it is the one that sits most neatly on its cutting edge. The free exchange of ideas, information, and code that the open source movement fosters is crucial to intellectual development. Eric Raymond envisioned the open source development model as a bazaar – a buzzing hub of free-floating ideas, exchanged openly by all sorts of different people.

Consider the Sourceforge website, a massive web-based repository-cum-archive of open source projects and software. Sourceforge provides a platform for the development and distribution of new open source projects, resulting in a thriving database and community of over 260,000 projects and 2.7 million developers.[22] The most popular software on the site gets tens of thousands of downloads per day. But of course, not all the projects on display are as successful. The vast majority never see more than 100 downloads, and over half have gotten lost in cyberspace, or so to speak, and have fallen inactive.[23] In 2007, the *Harvard Business Review*, in a list of new breakthroughs for the year 2007, published an article by technology writer and consultant Clay Shirky that praised the open source development community for its ability to fail, spectacularly, frequently, and with almost total impunity.[24] Typically, in the course of praising something, one does not point out the tendency of that thing to fail, and not surprisingly, some members of the open source community immediately rallied up in arms against Shirky's bold assertion.[25]

But Shirky was pointing out a unique quality of the open source developmental model that makes it utterly invaluable to the pursuit of intellectual progress: the incredibly low cost of failure. His use of "ready, fire, aim" to describe open source is an accurate summation of the open source process, which for many developers is simply: come up with an insane idea, start hacking away at it willy-nilly and, if you're lucky, the project will hit critical mass and start making sense, at which point (a) parameters for its development can be defined more clearly, and (b) the programmer has gained a further understanding of his craft. Shirky's point, while littered with words like "failure," is in fact a celebration of the open source community, and how it is able to foster and encourage individual innovation like few other environments can. In a traditional business setting – even in firms "committed" to experimentation and development – the cost for failure is high, and the potential risk of any new project is weighed carefully. There are no such barriers in open source.[26]

Critics of Shirky's repeated connection of open source with "failure" actually patched a major hole in his argument by bringing up an aspect of the open source movement that Shirky failed to address: the groupthink factor. Individual innovation is well and good, but open source development is a *collective* of individuals – as such, there is no traditional end of the road for an open source project. In an angry rebuttal to the *HBR* article, Chris Holt writes that open source is in fact a success, because it allows for a huge amount of code to lay out into the open "to stimulate possibility, dialog, collaboration [...] occasionally some useful code will get picked up. It's about sharing and working together and providing alternatives."[27] Charlie Lowe adds to this by noting that open source succeeds "not only because the cost of failure to experiment and innovate is low, but also because the return is higher on both success and failure."[28] In this way, open source software development is uniquely invincible – if a proprietary project is stalled, it never sees the light of day, which is more or less tantamount to project death. The unused code is relegated to a junk heap, and the project is written off as a loss on the company books. But if an open source software project is stalled, it simply becomes inactive until another developer decides to either pick up the slack, or stick a hand into the cookie jar. It might also languish until the end of time, but it will do so out in the open, where any interested party can examine and learn from it at their leisure.

Thus, the cost of failure is reduced within open source developmental model, compared to the traditional intellectual or business setting. It is not *zero*, because there is still some element of time wasted, but it is still not as big of a deal. Typically, project managers and academics must select their projects with care, doing speculative research and weighing the risks of every option. Time is money, and the cost of failure is substantial. In corporate settings, most pitched ideas are left in the dust, never even getting the chance to blossom. Academics must choose their projects carefully as well – the "publish or perish" environment leaves little wiggle room for rounding errors. Conversely, the open source setting is far more conducive to meandering for truth, which is death within a corporate or cutthroat academic setting but is perfect for the collaborative and curious ecosystem that open source creates.

Open source is also a playground. Its value to the community of software developers who are not seeking to benefit financially from the code is also unmistakable. If a programmer makes a living out of producing boring code for a closed source software team, or doing some other menial IT-related job, open source development can be a hobby. All developers of open source projects choose to contribute to projects of their own free will.[29] There is no metaphorical whip on the horse's back, enforcing deadlines and delegating tasks to people who may not have any interest at all in finishing those tasks.[30] These developers contribute to open source projects because they are interested in the project or invested intellectually in the outcome, not because they are being paid.[31] There is a huge degree of personal satisfaction and accomplishment associated with contributing to an open source project.

In a lot of ways, open source is more of an ideology than a business model, and that's why it can be rather difficult to implement truly successful monetization strategies that remain true to the core of open source belief while keeping companies solvent.

For-Profit Companies

For-profit companies face a multitude of challenges when dealing with open source, for many of the reasons outlined above. The biggest challenge is, of course, that revenue streams cannot come as a result of the software itself. First, the fact that the source is available publicly means that very few people are willing to pay for it. Second, and more importantly, since an open source project usually includes code from so many different contributors, there are a litany of legal issues surrounding its commercial redistribution. As a result, open source business models must be indirect. Monetization of open source software *necessarily* occurs at the periphery rather than the core. One web technology company calls it the open source "Product Halo" effect, and others simply call it complementary.[32] Whatever the name for it, there are several strategies for-profit companies can adapt to indirectly profit off open source software.

Note, of course, that there is no "one size fits all" open source business model, reason being that all open source software is different. You cannot market an operating system the same way as a content management system or an office suite. But there are an array of general business strategies that can be used. Key to all of them is the development of a strong relationship with the community, because without that, there is no consumer *or* developer base.[33] The success of an open source project is hugely contingent on the robustness and fortitude of the community that surrounds it. So it should be assumed, for each of these models, that a strong community is a necessary prerequisite, and the establishment or assurance of one should take precedence above any monetization strategy.

The Major Complementary Monetization Strategies

Firstly, a business can engage in **support services**. This hinges on a thorough understanding of the software, and thus is an ideal monetization strategy for developers and project leaders themselves. Support services can broadly be categorized into a handful of groups: product distribution, consulting, training, custom development, and support.[34] Distribution will not yield much revenue – proprietary companies sell licenses and open source companies sell packaging, as far as distribution is concerned. Consulting, training, and support can be said to be a type of insurance policy and become especially important with corporate clients, while custom development is a key service to offer to firms who do not have the resources to develop code themselves, even if the software is open source.[35]

Support services tend not to sell to the individual user level because of the prevalence and wide availability of open source support forums, but firms are willing to pay for (a) the guaranteed support response, (b) the assurance that they are being helped by someone who is intimately familiar with the software, and (c) the private channel of communication.[36] In addition, companies tend to be uncomfortable with the idea of open source unless they can secure this support contract.[37] What is important to note here is that what is being sold is not software or code – it's experience and labor. Developers are marketing themselves at the same time that they are marketing their product, which is a marked difference from the proprietary model. While the support model is applicable to most types of software, this model is especially useful for highly integrated software systems targeted toward the business and corporate setting, such as enterprise operating systems, ERP (enterprise resource planning) programs, and CRM (customer relationship management) programs.

A working example is Oracle's Solaris enterprise OS. In 2004, Sun Microsystems, suffering from a brain drain, made the decision to make Solaris open source. The transformation wasn't immediate – the commercial version of Solaris was released in late 2004 and it wasn't until the second quarter of 2005 that Sun managed to clear every legal hurdle for the open source program – but it was a huge, and to some, surprising, shift.[38] Instead of having users pay for the combined package of a license to use Solaris and support post-sale, Sun switched to a pure support and service model. And according to Sun's former Open Source Chief Simon Phipps, the move generated seven million additional registrations by "removing the barrier" of having to pay upfront on a leap of faith.[39]

Under the **accessorizing** model, a third-party company sells open source accessories. These are physical products which, while not directly related to the software itself, are built on its product halo. Accessories can range from stuffed Linux penguins, T-shirts, and other useless, just-for-fun doodads to more heavyweight and serious products like user manuals and reference volumes. An exemplar of success in this model is the *Linux Journal*, a magazine published exclusively for the general Linux community.[40] There is also the O'Reilly Publishing Group, which publishes a line of high quality open source reference materials and has actually managed both to raise its reputation significantly within its target market – the open source community –and create brand loyalty by hiring some of the community's most respected software developers.[41]

Another option is known as the **loss-leader** strategy. A business might offer free-of-charge open source software to stimulate interest for related proprietary, paid programs.[42] But more broadly, under this model an open source program can also be used to save a "spot" for proprietary software, which is what happened with Netscape Navigator after Internet Explorer started eating away at its market share. Netscape open-sourced its own browser, creating the open source Mozilla project, which successfully stole market share back from Microsoft. Furthermore, the community of developers that began work on Mozilla also indirectly helped to improve Netscape's proprietary Navigator browser. While the model was not a complete success – Navigator is hardly relevant – Mozilla Firefox has become a real contender in the browser war.[43]

The **widget frosting** model applies only to companies selling hardware that requires a software package (e.g. a driver). The choice to go open-source here is obvious: the influx of developers into your community will not only generate more buzz about the hardware you are marketing, but will eliminate the overhead costs of software development.[44]

These strategies and models are all well and good, and they certainly have been successfully implemented by a variety of companies (one overwhelming success story is JBoss), but the fact remains that support services are not guaranteed to generate as much revenue as enjoyed by proprietary software companies. Some argue differently – some people who are actually in the business of open source support services, such as Sun Microsystems' Open Source Chief and Steven Noels, Managing Partner at a small Apache consulting, insist that the value is in the "intellectual property that sits behind a particular implementation," and not the code itself.[45] This is absolutely true. Programs are not valuable for their code—this is particularly true in the case of people who are not adamant believers in the free and open source movement. Usability and function have always trumped raw code; open source hasn't changed any of this. Open source software does tend to be a lot more useful and functional than similar proprietary software, but the question that was asked, but isn't being answered is: we know that functionality is the most important feature of any program. But is it easier to make money from selling software – the right to use the code – or is it easier to make money off the support model? One look at the comparative net worths of Red Hat and Microsoft and Apple will answer that question.

The Case for Hybrid Licensure

The last method differs significantly from the others, though it is perhaps the most commercially viable strategy. We can all agree that a wholly proprietary model is not ideal – it is too highly restrictive, and large corporations – which are where software companies get most of their money – are increasingly turning to open source solutions in order to save money and get better software, period. The proprietary model, with its shady back programming alleys and general reliance on the ignorance of its user base to survive, is an excellent cash cow, but is not invincible against the rise of free and open source software. But is a wholly open source model ideal? For the consumer, certainly. But open source companies simply cannot generate the same magnitude of cash flows as closed proprietary companies (at least not without Herculean effort, as the CEO of Red Hat will tell you).[46] As software becomes more and more free, monetizing it becomes more difficult. Programming for open source is no day job – it's fairly thankless work, and often, open source developers have "real" jobs, whereas writing for open source is only a hobby.[47]

The biggest hurdle to jump with open source is incentivizing programmers to contribute to open source projects. This can take some doing, given that there is almost no monetary reward and interest only goes so far – paying the bills often takes precedence over hobbyist pursuits. Some voices within the open source movement have thus suggested a marriage of the proprietary and open models—leading to the lovechild known as **hybrid, or dual, licensing**, also known by some (affectionately) as "having your cake, and eating it too."[48] (Note that this strategy is considered by some to be in contradiction with the philosophy of the open source movement, but more on that later.) Hybrid licensing is one of the more pragmatic ways to generate cash flows under the open source model, and can be executed in a variety of ways. However, a major caveat of this strategy is that it is rife with potential code ownership issues—the proprietary and open source versions of the codebase must be very carefully partitioned.[49]

(1) Fifty-Fifty Split

The crudest possible dual-license model would involve releasing *both* proprietary and open source versions of the software, and bears a distant resemblance to the support services strategy outlined above. The open source version can be downloaded by casual users, while the proprietary version comes in the traditional packaging, with traditional support services and, of course, the traditional price tag. One wonders, perhaps, how this could possibly generate any money, but those seeking the security and comfort of the proprietary software model (open source can at times seem like the charted unknown) may just bite. The proprietary version will also appeal to firms.

(2) The "Professional" Version

A slightly more complex implementation occurs when a program comes in two versions: the community version (which uses an open source license), and the proprietary "enhanced" version. This is comparable to the "try this free" trial version model used by some proprietary software to attract potential customers, except the community version is fully functional and does not expire. The caveat is, the community version is usually targeted towards the low end of the market – individuals and small workgroups – and is missing functionalities that would be essential to a larger firm.[50] And for larger firms, buying the professional (enhanced and proprietary) version of open source software is *still* much cheaper than going the full mile and paying licensing fees for a proprietary product. This model, then, takes advantage of the open source collaborative community while also generating cash flows from licensing, instead of simply using the support services model.

SugarCRM (a client relationship management software) is an excellent example of a dual-license success story under this model. The open source version of Sugar, which uses a Mozilla license, is quite powerful and boasts a bustling community of developers, but the professional version is where Sugar generates the majority of its revenue. Sugar has effectively structured a business model around "holding back things relevant to larger enterprises."[51] In this case, the community version lacks a functionality that is absolutely integral for use at the corporate level, which essentially forces interested corporate customers to opt for the professional version.

(3) Dual License

The dual licensing model implemented by MySQL combines the above two approaches. The MySQL codebase literally has two licenses: GPL, and a commercial version. By the definition of GPL, any software developer seeking to implement MySQL in their project must also license their derivative software under the GPL. But if that developer wants to write a proprietary program using MySQL, the GPL ceases to be a viable option. In this case, the developer must use the commercial license, and in doing so must pay a fee to MySQL.[52] Additionally, like SugarCRM, MySQL offers both a fully-functional open source community edition, as well as several grades of commercial MySQL packages that include both support services and extra features.

The "problem" with hybrid licensing is that it sits on the cusp of the open and proprietary models and is in a lot of ways philosophically inconsistent with the free and open source movement. As such, there are a lot of critics of dual licensing within the open source community. Hybrid projects like SugarCRM, MySQL, and TrollTech are periodically dismissed by open source bloggers as exploiting the good open source name without being "true" open source. In some ways, they are not. The hybrid licensing strategy adopted by MySQL can only be used by software vendors that own the rights to all of their code, so development for MySQL is necessarily limited to in-house programmers only. Outside contributions are allowed, but only after a considerably long vetting process and resolution of copyright issues. Can a project really be considered a part of the open source movement if it is literally only *open source* and not open development as well? Community, both on a development and user level, is integral to the survival and success of an open source project. Without the collaborative development that is so central to the idea of open source, how can a project sustain itself? This is not that significant of a problem for MySQL, which is basically the biggest database name in all of cyberspace and enjoys users of such magnitude as WordPress, Google, and NASA—but other projects seeking to emulate the model must thoroughly evaluate whether they are suited for it.

The license strategies described above integrate open and commercial licenses on a fairly superficial level. Is there a way to create a truer hybrid license case than that of MySQL, that allows open source development to coexist with the proprietary model? Sprewell, the creator of a new subscription program for open source, has proposed the concept of the "Time-limited Hybrid Source" model. The starting point would be a codebase under an open source license that allows for proprietary derivative code. Independent developers could then produce proprietary patches and add-ons for this open source codebase and sell them to consumers. These patches would be under a special license and only remain proprietary for a short period of time—enough for the developer to "recoup their investment," as it were.[53] This period would be determined by the type of software – for instance, swiftly-evolving software like internet browsers and media players might have a turnover period of 18 months, whereas slow-moving software could stay closed for as long as five years. At the end of the waiting period, the code would be released to the public. Under this model, at any given time, a majority of the codebase, including software patches and add-ons, would be open source.

The time-limited hybrid source model is unlikely to be adopted by companies that have already adopted a successful business strategy, but it does attempt to reconcile the lingering philosophical differences between the dual-license model and the free and open software movement. It also gives developers a monetary incentive to code, and tries to bridge the gap between proprietary and open source software. Instead of having two very similar codebases, one open source and one proprietary, Sprewell's model would ideally be able to fuse them into one, so that closed development and open development can occur simultaneously, *within the same code structure*. The problem again rises of free-of-charge open source add-ons edging out similar proprietary add-ons, but this is simply the nature of market competition – totally unavoidable.

The most ideal long-term armistice agreement between proprietary and open source software is perhaps this middle-of-the-road marriage, where one combines the best of both worlds: the cash flows from proprietary software, and the open development and spirit of collaboration inherent in open source. Not every open source company can be JBoss—and not every closed software developer has legal muscles to flex, like Microsoft and IBM. The model isn't perfect—software companies would prefer a fully proprietary system, and those who firmly believe in free and open source software would prefer everything be licensed under the GPL. But from a business standpoint, there is a strong need for compromise.

The Future of Open Source: Challenges Going Forward

Patents and the Legal Status of Code

One of the biggest obstacles to the development of open source software is patent enforcement by the huge corporate giants who own them.[54] The proprietary Goliaths aren't blind—competitors of open source software can see clear as day what open source means for their product, and they "cannot justify, in the classic model of profit and loss, any significant investment in a commoditized piece of technology, which they know perfectly well" is being distributed for free.[55] The earlier comparison made between the unfolding situation with open source and the RIAA-filesharing dispute is once again salient here. While the RIAA has entirety of copyright law on their side, patent enforcement is the only legal means by which a software giant can accuse an open source developer of breaking the law, as open source licenses are perfectly legal.

Steve Balmer, CEO of Microsoft, has made an annual tradition of accusing Linux of patent infringement. A ludicrous notion (Whom could you sue? Linux was developed by thousands of programmers around the world, based in GNU), to be sure. But in 2009, Microsoft finally filed suit – against TomTom, a company specializing in GPS navigation software using the Linux kernel, in 2009. TomTom fired a countersuit right back, claiming Microsoft had infringed on *their* patents as well. Crushingly, TomTom lost. Not only did it have to pay Microsoft a sum in damages, but Microsoft also gained access to the patents leveled against them in a countersuit.[56] Another large-scale real-life example transpired in early 2010, when software giant IBM threatened to sue open source company TurboHercules for extensive patent infringement.[57] To rub salt on the wound, among the list of patents were two that IBM had originally pledged to the open source community when they committed "not to assert any of [these] 500 U.S. patents [...] against the development, use or distribution of Open Source Software."[58] Critics who had dismissed IBM's initial offering of the patents as a simpering platitude (IBM controls over 40,000 patents; 500, in comparison, is less than pocket change—more like lint fuzz) claimed that IBM had finally shown its true colors. TurboHercules is just one tiny open source company, and software patents a tool used by giants like IBM to protect their monopolies on the market. The gaping difference between the staying power of a company like IBM, and a reputable *but ultimately much smaller* open source company is, well, gaping.

Should companies like IBM and Microsoft continue in their trend of threatening to or actually enforcing their patents, the open source movement could conceivably suffer a huge setback. Some parties might even take advantage of open source development and register patents before new ideas have time to get off the ground.

Governance and Management

Open source is frequently conflated with anarchy. It's an easy logical leap to make. Open source does not operate within a tightly-wound bureaucracy, and the visualization of developers from all over the world making modifications and contributing ideas to one project doesn't seem like it'd be terribly neat. Governance and management, however, are crucial to the success of any open source project.[59] Absent proper management, or management principles, open source companies can and do fail—one life-sized example of this is Compiere, an open source ERP company. Compiere enjoyed brand-name recognition and a considerable amount of success until schisms and lapses in communication between the partners led to (a) poor coordination of consumer relations strategy, (b) a forked-off, modified version of Compiere: Adempiere.[60] Project management is always important, but management is perhaps even more crucial to open source because of the natural tendency of the open source system toward chaos. A poorly-managed traditional company will eventually fail – a poorly-managed open source project or company will fail even faster.

In the most favorable open source project situation, there would, first of all, be a leader whose vision contributors both respected and supported. Sometimes it is possible to commit to a project or a cause on ideology alone, but it often helps if there is a talking head encouraging developers to stay. There would also ideally be a set of clearly-defined tasks that could be claimed and coded by interested parties. The role of an emergent leader within an open source project would be to rally developers to the cause, to define these moduled tasks, and to uphold and enforce an overarching "idea" in order to keep the project on track.[61] A well-organized project would have safeguards in place (contingency planning is an important tool of leadership), a good amount of trust among developers in the community, transparency of leadership and harmonious interaction, and a fostering of fair exchange.[62] Only in this type of environment can truly good code be produced. Furthermore, individual open source projects require more cohesive management to stay buoyed in the face of what is still a market dominated by proprietary and closed giants like Microsoft, Apple, and, increasingly, Google.

The movement to monetize open source necessarily calls for an emphasis on stronger, more emphatic leadership. In order for the movement to really take prominence, it needs an icon—and preferably one that isn't a penguin or an unshaven, embarrassingly unapologetic nerd. Open source needs to cease to be synonymous with Linux and do-it-yourself software. A strong release of an open source program can be every bit as user-friendly as its established proprietary counterparts, but unless open source can shake its mainstream association with geeks living in basements and the tech-savvy coding elite, it will forever remain the quiet kid in the back of the classroom whom everyone is surprised to find is actually pretty smart, but ignores anyway because she has a funny haircut. Open source needs its own Steve Jobs, or Steve-Jobs like oligopoly, both to rebrand its image and to act as a spokesperson. Who knows? This could also be a huge step in solving the problem of the open source movement being bullied by patent enforcements by trigger-happy software monopolies.

So let's go forward.

The open source movement is the future: this much is clear. Open source is becoming the medium of choice for corporations and private users alike, not only because it keeps costs down, but also because the nature of open source leads to higher-quality, more coherent, and more customizable software. Companies are increasingly turning to open source software, and some of cyberspace's most beloved technologies are beginning to go open source. As such, strategies for open source monetization must be developed in view of this trend; it would be a terrible mistake both to lose out on the opportunity to monetize cutting edge technological trends, and to let the software market become a no-holds barred, free-for-all download party. There must necessarily be incentive for software engineers to put effort into program development in order for solid software to be produced, and the incentive cannot be purely intellectual (software engineers need to eat too). In other words, monetizing open source is key, even if it must be done at the partial expense of the ideology that fuels the free and open software movement as defined by Richard Stallman and his myriad compatriots.

Whether the open source movement will eventually fuse with the existing proprietary model to create a community that is at once open, collaborative, and profitable remains to be seen. However, what is clear is that the open source movement is in dire need of stronger, more charismatic leadership as it prepares to take its rightful place as a *mainstream* and major player in the software market. Too long has it been the shunned but brilliant weird cousin – the time for the most superficial of makeovers is nigh.

FOOTNOTES

1   Scott Weber. *The Success of Open Source* (Harvard University Press).
2   Free Software Foundation. "The Free Software Definition." *The GNU Project* (Accessed 14 December 2010) <http://www.gnu.org/philosophy/free-sw.html>.
3   Open Source Initiative. "The Open Source Definition" (Accessed 14 December 2010). <http://opensource.org/docs/osd>
4   Josh Lerner and Jean Tirole. "The Simple Economics of Open Source" 26.
5   *Ibid.*
6   Richard Stallman. "Why Open Source Misses the Point of Free Software." *Free Software Foundation* (Version 2010 October 1) < http://www.gnu.org/philosophy/open-source-misses-the-point.html>.
7   MSRP for Microsoft Office 2007 from official Windows store, as of December 2010.
8   Matt Asay. "Open source a savvy bet, even in tough times." *The Register* (17 September 2010) < http://www.theregister.co.uk/2010/09/17/open_source_good_when_bad/ >.
9   Rachael King. "Cost-Conscious Companies Turn to Open Source Software." *BusinessWeek* (1 December 2008) < http://www.businessweek.com/technology/content/nov2008/tc20081130_069698.htm>.
10 Alastair Otter. "Economic downturn to boost open source." *Tectonic* (5 May 2009) <http://www.tectonic.co.za/2009/05/economic-downturn-to-boost-open-source/>.
11 *Ibid.*
12 Standish Group. "Free Open Source Software is Costing Vendors $60 Billion, New Standish Group International Study Finds." *Standish Newsroom* < http://standishgroup.com/newsroom/open_source.php >.
13 Glyn Moody. "Why No Billion-Dollar Open Source Companies?" *Open Enterprise* (11 June 2010) < http://blogs.computerworlduk.com/open-enterprise/2010/06/why-no-billiondollar-open-source-companies/index.htm>.
14 Matthew Broersma. "Companies buy open source because it's better, not cheaper." *TechWorld*. 21 April 2005. < http://news.techworld.com/operating-systems/3535/companies-buy-open-source-because-its-better-not-cheaper/>.
15 Joachim Henkel. "The Jukebox Mode of Innovation – a Model of commercial Open Source Development." *DRUID Working Papers* (2006) 1.
16 Satheesh Babu Vattekkat. "Why is Open Source REALLY better?" (25 April 2004) < http://vsbabu.org/mt/archives/2002/04/25/why_is_open_source_really_

better.html >.

17 Josh Lerner and Jean Tirole. *op. cit.*22.

18 See: Red Hat,

19 Fred Holahan. "Community Monetization is Fool's Gold." *Open Source Advisory* ()
<http://opensourceadvisory.com/wordpress/?p=860>

20 Bollier, David. "The Commons as a New Sector of Value-Creation." *On the
Commons* (22 April 2008) < http://onthecommons.org/commons-new-sector-
value-creation>

21 Anthony Ha. "Benchmark entrepreneur talks making money from open
source." *VentureBeat* (25 March 2008) < http://venturebeat.com/2008/03/25/
benchmark-entrepreneur-talks-making-money-from-open-source/>.

22 Sourceforge. "About." *Sourceforge.net.* < http://sourceforge.net/about>

23 Clay Shirky. "The HBR List: Breakthrough Ideas of 2007: In Defense of 'Ready,
Fire, Aim.'" *Harvard Business Review* (February 2007) 52.

24 Clay Shirky, *op. cit.*

25 Chris Holt. "The massive failure of FOSS." *Free Software Magazine* (21 February
2007) < http://www.freesoftwaremagazine.com/columns/massive_failure_
foss/>.

26 Clay Shirky, *op. cit.*

27 Christ Holt, *op. cit.*

28 Charlie Lowe. "Open Source as Massive Failure? How Are We Measuring
Success?" *Cyberdash* (22 February 2007) < http://www.cyberdash.com/open-
source-failure-success>.

29 Scott Weber, *op. cit.* 62.

30 Ted Neward. "Monetization of Open Source" (Parts 1-3). *OnOpenSource.* 5
September 2007. InformIt. 10 December 2010 <http://www.informit.com/
podcasts/channel.aspx?c=1977eb71-4a34-42dd-a7d0-7952a08c527e>

31 Josh Lerner and Jean Tirole, *op. cit.* 22.

32 eXtropia. "What is the Open Source Business Model?" eXtropia: the open web
technology company < http://www.extropia.com/tutorials/misc/opensourcebiz.
html>.

33 Jürgen Bitzer, Philipp J. H. Schröder. *The economics of open source software
development* (Emerald Group Publishing, 2006) 128.

34 Frank Hecker. "Setting up shop: The business of open source software." *IEEE
Software* (Jan/Feb 1999).

35 Stephen O'Grady. "Beyond Support/Service: Making More Money from
Open Source." *Tecosystems* (20 August 2007) < http://redmonk.com/
sogrady/2007/08/20/more_money/ >.

36 Jorg Janke. "Open Source Business Models (for Compiere)." *Compiere from the
Source* (26 July 2010) < http://www.compieresource.com/2010/07/open-
source-business-models.html >.

37 "Open source monetization – still a far cry?" *CIOL Interviews* (6 August 2010)
< http://www.ciol.com/News/News/Interviews/Open-source-monetization-
%E2%80%93-still-a-far-cry/139796/0/>.

38 Stephen Shankland. "Sun to release first OpenSolaris tidbit Tuesday." *CNet News*

(24 January 2005) < http://news.cnet.com/Sun-to-release-first-OpenSolaris-scrap-Tuesday/2100-7344_3-5548394.html>.

39 Ted Neward, *op. cit.*

40 Open Source Initiative. "Open Source Case for Business." *Open Source Initiative* (2010) <http://www.opensource.org/advocacy/case_for_business.php>

41 Eric Raymond. *The Magic Cauldron*, op. cit. and Moreno Muffato, *op. cit.* 129.

42 Kirk St. Amant. *Handbook of research on open source software: technological, economical, and social perspectives* (IGI Global: 2007) 547.

43 Moreno Muffato. *Open Source: A Multidisciplinary Approach* (Imperial College Press: 2006) 130.

44 Eric Raymond. *The Magic Cauldron* 9.

45 Jonathan Bennett. "Making an Open Source Living, Part 1." *Builder AU* (6 December 2004) < http://www.builderau.com.au/news/soa/Making-an-open-source-living-part-1/0,339028227,339168482,00.htm>.

46 Glyn Moody. "Why No Billion-Dollar Open Source Companies?" (11 June 2010) < http://blogs.computerworlduk.com/open-enterprise/2010/06/why-no-billiondollar-open-source-companies/index.htm>.

47 Marc Fleury. "White: How I learned to stop worrying and love the business of open source software." *The "Blue, White, Red Technology Trilogy* (2003) < http://www.jboss.com/pdf/white.pdf>.

48 Philip H. Albert. "Dual Licensing: Having Your Cake and Eating it Too." *Linux News* (16 November 2004) < http://www.linuxinsider.com/story/38172.html?wlc=1292900761>.

49 *Ibid.*

50 Karl Fogel. "Dual Licensing Schemes." *How to Run a Successful Open Source Project* (2010) < http://producingoss.com/en/dual-licensing.html>.

51 Dan Farber. "Commercial open source, a misnomer?" *ZDNet Blog: Between the Lines* (11 June 2010) < http://www.zdnet.com/blog/btl/commercial-open-source-a-misnomer/1787>.

52 Elena Blanco. "Dual Licensing." *OSS Watch* (6 September 2010) < http://www.oss-watch.ac.uk/resources/duallicence2.xml>

53 Sprewell. "Towards a Real Business Model for Open-Source Software." *Phoronix* (29 April 2010) < http://www.phoronix.com/scan.php?page=article&item=sprewell_licensing&num=1>.

54 Ted Neward, *op. cit.*

55 Marc Fleury, *op. cit.* 6.

56 Ina Fried. "Microsoft, TomTom settle patent dispute." *Beyond Binary* (30 March 2009) < http://news.cnet.com/8301-13860_3-10206988-56.html >.

57 Ryan Paul. "IBM breaks OSS patent promise, targets mainframe emulator." *Ars Technica* (6 April 2010) < http://arstechnica.com/open-source/news/2010/04/ibm-breaks-oss-patent-promise-targets-mainframe-emulator.ars >.

58 Florian Mueller. "IBM breaks the taboo and betrays its promise to the FOSS Community." *FOSS Patents* (6 April 2010) < http://fosspatents.blogspot.com/2010/04/ibm-breaks-taboo-and-betrays-its.html>. See also, IBM's Statement of Non-Assertion of Named Patents Against OSS < http://www.ibm.

com/ibm/licensing/patents/pledgedpatents.pdf >
59 Josh Lerner and Jean Tirole, *op. cit.* 29.
60 Janke, Jorg. "Open Source Business Models (for Compiere)." *Compiere from the Source.* 26 July 2010. < http://www.compieresource.com/2010/07/open-source-business-models.html >.
61 Josh Lerner and Jean Tirole, *op. cit.* 29.
62 Lorraine Morgan, Joseph Feller, and Patrick Finnegan. "Value Creation and Capture with Open Source Software: A Theoretical Model for Understanding the Role of Value Networks." 18th European Conference on Information Systems (2010) 21.

REFERENCES

Albert, Philip H. "Dual Licensing: Having Your Cake and Eating it Too." *Linux News.* 16 November 2004. Accessed 18 December 2010. < http://www.linuxinsider.com/story/38172.html?wlc=1292900761>.

Asay, Matt. "Bad economy may lead to good IPOs in open source." *CNet Blogs: The Open Road.* 11 December 2009. Accessed 20 November 2010. < http://news.cnet.com/8301-13505_3-10413254-16.html>

--. "On the record with Jim Whitehurst, Red Hat's new CEO: 'I must have a mission.'" *CNet Blogs: The Open Road.* 4 January 2008. Accessed 19 November 2010. <http://news.cnet.com/8301-13505_3-9839996-16.html>

--. "Open source: a savvy bet, even in tough times." *The Register.* 17 September 2010. Accessed 19 November 2010. <http://www.theregister.co.uk/2010/09/17/open_source_good_when_bad/>

Bitzer, Jürgen and Philipp J. H. Schröder. *The economics of open source software development.* Emerald Group Publishing, 2006.

Blanco, Elena. "Dual Licensing." *OSS Watch.* 6 September 2010. Accessed 15 December 2010.<http://www.oss-watch.ac.uk/resources/duallicence2.xml>

Blaustein, Julie. "The Value of Open Source Software: The Creation of Value Leading to Market Transference." *COSPA Knowledge Base: Economic Models,* 2003.

Bollier, David. "The Commons as a New Sector of Value-Creation." *On the Commons.* 22 April 2008. Accessed 19 November 2010. < http://onthecommons.org/commons-new-sector-value-creation>

Cohen, Stuart. "Open Source: The Model is Broken." *Bloomberg Businessweek.* 1 December 2008. Accessed 12 December 2010. <http://www.businessweek.com/technology/content/nov2008/tc20081130_276152.htm>

Exist. "Exist Global Demonstrates Open Source Value Creation at the Aboitiz Tech Forum."

eXtropia. "What is the Open Source Business Model?" eXtropia: the open web technology company. n.d. Accessed 17 December 2010 < http://www.extropia.com/tutorials/misc/opensourcebiz.html>

Farber, Dan. "Commercial open source, a misnomer?" *ZDNet Blog: Between the Lines.*

29 August 2005. Accessed 15 December 2010. < http://www.zdnet.com/blog/btl/
commercial-open-source-a-misnomer/1787>.

Fogel, Karl. "Dual Licensing Schemes." How to Run a Successful Open Source Project.
n.d. Accessed 20 December 2010 <http://producingoss.com/en/dual-licensing.html>.

Fink, Martin. *The business and economics of Linux.*

Free Software Foundation. "The Free Software Definition." The GNU Project. n.d.
Accessed 14 December 2010. <http://www.gnu.org/philosophy/free-sw.html>.

Fried, Ina. "Microsoft, TomTom settle patent dispute." *Beyond Binary*. 30 March 2009.
Accessed 19 December 2010 < http://news.cnet.com/8301-13860_3-10206988-56.
html >.

Ha, Anthony. "Benchmark entrepreneur talks making money from open source."
VentureBeat. 25 March 2008. Accessed 18 December 2010. <http://venturebeat.
com/2008/03/25/benchmark-entrepreneur-talks-making-money-from-open-source/>.

Hecker, Frank. "Setting Up Shop: The Business of Open Source Software." *IEEE
Software*. Jan/Feb 1999. pp45-51.

Holahan, Fred. "Community Monetization is Fool's Gold." Open Source Advisory. n.d.
Accessed 18 December 2010. <http://opensourceadvisory.com/wordpress/?p=860>

Henkel, Joachim. "The Jukebox Mode of Innovation – a Model of Commercial Open
Source Development." *DRUID Working Papers*, 2006.

Holt, Chris. "The massive failure of FOSS." *Free Software Magazine*. 21 February 2007.
Accessed 18 December 2010. < http://www.freesoftwaremagazine.com/columns/
massive_failure_foss/>.

Janke, Jorg. "Open Source Business Models (for Compiere)." *Compiere from the Source*.
26
July 2010. Accessed 17 December 2010. < http://www.compieresource.com/2010/07/
open-source-business-models.html >.

Rachael King. "Cost-Conscious Companies Turn to Open Source Software."
BloomsbergBusinessWeek.1 December 2008. Accessed 17 December 2010. < http://
www.businessweek.com/technology/content/nov2008/tc20081130_069698.htm>.

Lerner, Josh and Jean Tirole. "The Simple Economics of Open Source." *Journal of
Industrial
Economics*. Vol 50, no. 2. (June 2002). 197-234.

Lowe, Charlie. "Open Source as Massive Failure? How Are We Measuring Success?"
Cyberdash. 22 February 2007. Accessed 17 December 2010.
<http://www.cyberdash.com/open-source-failure-success>.

Morgan, Lorraine, Joseph Feller, and Patrick Finnegan. "Value Creation and Capture with
Open Source Software: A Theoretical Model for Understanding the Role of Value
Networks." *18th European Conference on Information Systems*. 2010.

Muffato, Moreno. *Open Source: A Multidisciplinary Approach*. Imperial College Press,
2006.

Mueller, Florian. "IBM breaks the taboo and betrays its promise to the FOSS
Community." *FOSS Patents*. 6 April 2010. Accessed 20 December 2010 < http://
fosspatents.blogspot.com/2010/04/ibm-breaks-taboo-and-betrays-its.html>.

Neward, Ted. "Monetization of Open Source" (Parts 1-3). *OnOpenSource*. 5 September
2007. InformIt. Accessed 10 December 2010 <http://www.informit.com/podcasts/

channel.aspx?c=1977eb71-4a34-42dd-a7d0-7952a08c527e>

O'Grady, Stephen. "Beyond Support/Service: Making More Money from Open Source." *Tecosystems*. 20 August 2007. Accessed 12 December 2010. <http://redmonk.com/sogrady/2007/08/20/more_money/>

Otter, Alastair. "Economic downturn to boost open source." Tectonic. 5 May 2009. Accessed 20 November 2010. <http://www.tectonic.co.za/2009/05/economic-downturn-to-boost-open-source/>.

Paul, Ryan. "IBM breaks OSS patent promise, targets mainframe emulator." *Ars Technica*. 6
April 2010. Accessed 16 December 2010. < http://arstechnica.com/open-source/news/2010/04/ibm-breaks-oss-patent-promise-targets-mainframe-emulator.ars >.

Raymond, Eric Steven. *The Cathedral and the Bazaar*. Version 3.0. August 2002. Accessed
17 December 2010. <http://catb.org/~esr/writings/homesteading/cathedral-bazaar/index.html>

--. *The Magic Cauldron*. June 1999. Accessed 19 December 2010.
< http://www.catb.org/~esr/writings/magic-cauldron/magic-cauldron.html>

Shankland, Stephen. "Sun to release first OpenSolaris tidbit Tuesday." *CNet News*. 24
January 2005. Accessed 19 December 2010. < http://news.cnet.com/Sun-to-release-first-OpenSolaris-scrap-Tuesday/2100-7344_3-5548394.html>.

Shirky, Clay. "The HBR List: Breakthrough Ideas of 2007: In Defense of 'Ready, Fire, Aim.'" *Harvard Business Review*. February 2007.

Sprewell. "Towards a Real Business Model for Open-Source Software." *Phoronix*. 29 April 2010. Accessed 18 December 2010. <http://www.phoronix.com/scan.php?page=article&item=sprewell_licensing&num=1>.

Stallman, Richard. "Why Open Source Misses the Point of Free Software." *Free Software Foundation*. 1 October 2010. < http://www.gnu.org/philosophy/open-source-misses-the-point.html>.

St. Amant, Kirk. *Handbook of research on open source software: technological, economical, and social perspectives*. IGI Global, 2007.

Standish Group. "Free Open Source Software is Costing Vendors $60 Billion, New Standish
Group International Study Finds." Standish Newsroom. n.d. Accessed 17 November 2010. < http://standishgroup.com/newsroom/open_source.php>

Vattekkat, Satheesh Babu. "Why is Open Source REALLY better?" 25 April 2004. Accessed
19 December 2010. <http://vsbabu.org/mt/archives/2002/04/25/why_is_open_source_really_better.html >.

Weber, Scott. The Success of Open Source. Cambridge, MA: Harvard University Press, 2005.

8

e-419

Essi Haffar

"The Internet is the Viagra of Big Business"
~Jack Welch (Former Chairman and CEO of General Electric)

The benefits of the internet to businesses cannot be underestimated. It is now almost unheard of for businesses whether small or large not to have a website and a domain with personalized email addresses, and of course, with PayPal to facilitate payments and money transfers. Cyberspace provides great opportunities for businesses to grow and flourish and is a great convenience for consumers because it allows for the display of a wider variety of products and services. Also, consumers never have to leave the house.

The internet first and foremost assists in the process of globalization and as such gives businesses a wider reach of customers and a greater potential to expand. It facilitates business literally around the world and products and services can be advertised to internet users across the globe. In addition, online transactions prevent the necessity of a brick and mortar building and imply more and faster transactions. Businesses will earn more revenue because the internet homogenizes time, makes location irrelevant and targets the traffic online which will result in exponential growth in revenue for the businesses. The internet lowers the cost of running a business. Fewer employees are needed to run it since the physical presence of workers in the work building is not necessarily needed anymore and the cost of printing flyers and catalogues for advertising is also lowered. The main problems with internet use for businesses are viruses, spam and security but safeguards can be adopted to limit the risks these pose. It is in the interest of any adaptable, forward-thinking business to adopt the internet as a means of operation. And the 419 business is doing just that.

What is 419?

Nigeria's Economic and Financial Crimes Commission (EFCC) defines 419 or advance fee fraud as "specialized fraud committed using fake claims, identities, positions and in most cases, enticing but not existent proposals." 419 has often been attributed to Nigerian fraudsters. It gets its name in fact from Chapter 38 of the Nigerian penal code which pertains to fraud:

419. Any person who by any false pretense, and with intent to defraud, obtains from any other person anything capable of being stolen, or induces any other person to deliver to any person anything capable of being stolen, is guilty of a felony, and is liable to imprisonment for three years.

If the thing is of the value of one thousand naira or upwards, he is liable to imprisonment for seven years.

It is immaterial that the thing is obtained or its delivery is induced through the medium of a contract induced by the false pretense.

The offender cannot be arrested without warrant unless found committing the offence.

419 is fraud where the fraudster sends letters, faxes and now emails to victims with the promise of monetary return for the usage of the victim's bank account to store money that was illegally obtained. It is typically associated with West Africa, particularly Nigeria. Advance fee fraud is a lucrative business grossing millions of dollars annually. In the past twenty years, 419 has generated approximately $5 billion dollars. Songs have also been made about this type of fraud boasting about the proceeds of 419: "the flashy cars, fanciful houses, beautiful women, five-star hotels,"among others. This type of fraud with its mass emailing system, now seems a part of the everyday internet experience.

419 is believed to have been started in Nigeria in the 1980s. However, some believe it dates back even further to the 1970s before the use of the internet. Because Nigeria has a reputation for being a country with enormous wealth due to its huge oil reserves, and also a reputation

for being corrupt, fraudsters sent letters and facsimiles to unsuspecting foreign victims telling them of grandiose plans to dupe the government and asking them to hide enormous sums of money in their accounts from which they would receive a share. These letters and faxes were supposedly government documents to add to the authenticity of the scam. When the victim agreed, the scammers would then begin introducing fees such as duties and taxes that needed to be paid in order to further the process of the money transfer. The victim would then pay the fees knowing that remuneration would far outweigh any amount of fees paid. After the initial fee had been paid, the scammer would then bring up a series of ongoing sets of fees that the victim was expected to pay. This could go on for a long time until the victim realized it was a scam or he or she no longer had the ability to pay the fees. Since the onset of cyberspace, the scams have gotten more sophisticated as the internet has presented a utopia of possibility for the different forms that 419 can take. The scams have expanded to include fake lottery tickets, stories narrating how a victim has inherited money from a recently deceased wealthy person, sick people who are requesting financial assistance and Nigerian or Ghanaian ladies who are seeking foreign men to marry.

419ers can also prey on established websites. In doing this they target social networking sites and job recruiting sites. The scammers can use websites that provide vital services such as job postings and apartment postings, such as Craigslist, to post fake advertisements and lure their victims in that way. In the same way, websites such as Facebook and other social networking sites provide avenues other than email that 419ers can use to con. They can send Facebook messages and create a profile to authenticate the plot.

The internet has created a haven for 419ers, as the scammers are called. They are able to create fake websites to reinforce the genuineness of their scams. In 419's primitive stage, the scammers were limited to letters, faxes and phone calls. They had only a set phone number and fax numbers and addresses that they could send to. Responses were also very limited. The internet now has given them a global reach and enabled them to send out hundreds of thousands if not millions of mass emails to anyone who possesses an email address, greatly broadening their market. In addition, this method is very cheap. No postage stamps, envelopes or paper is required in the process. All the scammers need now is computer access which they can obtain for a minimal fee at an internet café. The process is also expedited. Emails take less than a minute to reach their destinations and the process of transferring money has sped up greatly as well. All in all, the internet has increased the productivity of the 419ers and they are able to maximize their profits. Money transfers nowadays can take many forms; from bank to bank transfers at the click of a mouse to other money transfer systems such as Western Union and MoneyGram. The latter are a favorite of the scammers. They enable money to be sent easily from practically any country in the world to the country of the 419er. The scammer can also empty out a victim's account depending on the amount of information obtained from the victim.

The internet has become an added and improved mechanism to the workings of 419. The ready availability of the internet across the globe particularly in the developing world has increased the ability of a large number of people to engage in these scams. The email frauds are now occurring from various places all around the world. Though this type of fraud originated in Nigeria, it is erroneous to believe that it is not a fast growing activity spreading rapidly across the world. Today, 419 is synonymous with Nigeria. I remember a friend recounting the story of his Nigerian friend in college. As first year students, they were randomly assigned room numbers and his young Nigerian friend was assigned to room 419. As a Ghanaian who was well aware of the 419 schemes, this tickled him. However, 419 has been "internationalized" (Igwe 2007), moving beyond its traditional meaning and restriction to Nigeria and now encompasses this type of fraud all over the world.

It is easy to disassociate from these scams until it comes closer to home. A friend of mine had just found a new job in Washington DC and was apartment searching on Craigslist when she came upon this ad:

washington, DC craigslist > housing > apts/housing for rent
$800 / 1br - 1325 18th Street Northwest #302, Washington DC 20036
    (Washington DC)
Translation: One bedroom apartment for $800 a month. Address 1325 18th Street #302 Northwest, Washington DC 20036.

The following email correspondence ensued:

From: Yvette Reid* <yverei@gmail.com>

To: williamsfpresty@yahoo.com
Date: Wednesday, September 1, 2010, 9:50 PM
Subject: $800 / 1br - 1325 18th Street Northwest #302, Washington
  DC 20036 (Washington DC)

Hi,

I am interested in your post. I recently moved into the area and work
  close by at Women Today*. Please let me know if it will be possible
  to view the building and let me know of any other details you may
  have. I will be available to see the place sometime this week or
  next.

I look forward to hearing from you,

Y. Reid
(*Name, contact information and work place of victim have been
  changed to protect her identity.)

From: Williams f Presty <williamsfpresty@yahoo.com>
To: Yvette Reid <yverei@gmail.com>
Date: Thu, Sep 2, 2010 at 2:22 AM
  Subject: Re: $800 / 1br - 1325 18th Street Northwest #302, Wash-
  ington DC 20036 (Washington DC)

Thanks for your inquiry, I am Dr. Williams F Presety owner of the
property that is placed for rent,the property was initially put up for
sale before my family talked me into renting it out OK,it is spacious,
you can move in as soon as the deposit is paid, I resided in the
house with my family before getting a new job with the World Health
Organization as a consultant Epidemiologist and now resides in Africa , the house is in perfect state and it goes for the price as listed
per month including the utilities, and i will prefer a tenant that will
take absolute care of the house as his/her own,the deposit is $800
and you are not paying deposit for pets if any.

All i need from you is to maintain the house as its your OK.

Do provide the information's below:

KINDLY CONFIRM YOUR INTEREST BY FILLING THE FORM BE-
  LOW..
TENANT RENT APPLICATION FORM

FIRST NAME:
LAST NAME:_____
PROFESSION:
PHONE (_____
(CELL)PHONE (_____
(WORK)PHONE (_____ (HOME)
KIDS--
  HOW MANY_____
  PRESENT ADDRESS:___

  CITY:_____

  STATE_____
  ZIPCODE:_____
  HOW LONG?-- IF RENTING WHY ARE YOU LEAVING?
  IF THIS PROPERTY IS BEING GIVEN TO YOU,HOW LONG DO
  YOU INTEND
  STAYING

  WHEN DO YOU INTEND MOVING IN?IF YOU HAVE A PET,
  NAME OF PET:_____
HABITS .

I look forward to read your reply with all the details.

  Regards

  Dr. Williams F Presty
TEL. 0112347090787196

From: Yvette Reid <yverei@gmail.com>
To: "Williams f Presty" <williamsfpresty@yahoo.com>
Date: Thursday, September 2, 2010, 1:34 PM
Subject: Re: $800 / 1br - 1325 18th Street Northwest #302, Washing-

ton DC 20036 (Washington DC)

Hello Dr. Presety,

Thank you for your email.
 Below are the answers to your questions:

TENANT RENT APPLICATION FORM

FIRST NAME: Yvette
LAST NAME:___Reid_____
PROFESSION: Accountant
PHONE (_____
(CELL)PHONE (___413-XXX-XXXX_____
(WORK)PHONE (_____ (HOME)
KIDS-- None
HOW MANY_____
PRESENT ADDRESS:___

CITY:____Washington___

 STATE____DC_____

ZIPCODE:_____
HOW LONG?-- IF RENTING WHY ARE YOU LEAVING?
IF THIS PROPERTY IS BEING GIVEN TO YOU,HOW LONG DO
YOU INTEND
STAYING

WHEN DO YOU INTEND MOVING IN? I intend to move in on the 18th
of September, 2010.

IF YOU HAVE A PET: No pet.

From: Williams f Presty <williamsfpresty@yahoo.com>
To: Yvette Reid <yverei@gmail.com>
Date: Thu, Sep 2, 2010 at 2:21 PM
   Subject: Re: $800 / 1br - 1325 18th Street Northwest #302, Washington DC 20036 (Washington DC)

Hello Yvette Ried,
Thanks for sending in your application, the interior is in a very perfect condition and you will love upon getting the keys, i do have the keys with me and it will be sent to you by courier service, I can assure you that you are renting the best with all brand new appliances,large rooms and space you will love it ok.
Having read the details you sent in and taking time out to review all the applications submitted, i found yours very satisfactory, so be informed that i have considered you as my new tenant, do feel free in my house as it is now your new home,we will have the best of landlord / tenant relationship.
So all you should do now is to send the deposit of $800 which is all that is required for your move in and your rent starts from the date of move in OK, the deposit is to enable me send the keys to you via courier service and once the payment details is received which should include senders name,address and amount paid the keys will be sent to our present address.
The deposit should be sent through western union money transfer or money gram in my name and address below and the keys and signed lease agreement will be sent to you via courier service and you will receive it at your stated address within 48 hrs of receiving the payment information, i look forward to your reply.you can call me once you receive this email.

                      PAYMENT INFORMATION
NAME: Dr. Williams F Prestly
ADDRESS: 5 Martins Street Surulere
               Lagos .
               Nigeria.
TEXT QUS.: COLOR
TEXT ANS.: BLUE
PHONE: TEL. 0112347090787196

From: Yvette Reid <yverei@gmail.com>
To: Williams f Presty <williamsfpresty@yahoo.com>
  Date: Thu, Sep 2, 2010 at 3:48 PM
  Subject: Re: $800 / 1br - 1325 18th Street Northwest #302, Wash-
  ington DC 20036 (Washington DC)

Hi Dr. Presty,

Thank you so much for your email. I am very excited about the opportunity to live in your place especially since it is so close to my work
  place.

The price is a little steep for me. I was wondering if you would be willing to take $750 instead? Also, are all utilities included? Since I am
  from out of town, can you please tell me what metro the apartment
  is close to, the grocery stores, restaurants, etc?

When will I physically be able to view the apartment?

Thank you and I look forward to hearing from you.

P.S is your last name Presty or Prestly? You keep changing the spell-
  ing and I want to make sure I wire the money to the right person and
  with no confusion.

Best,
  Yvette

From: Williams f Presty <u>williamsfpresty@yahoo.com</u>>
  To: Yvette Reid <yverei@gmail.com>
Date: Thu, Sep 2, 2010 at 4:14 PM
  Subject: Re: $800 / 1br - 1325 18th Street Northwest #302, Washington DC 20036 (Washington DC)

Sorry for the typo ok am Presty,i can come down to $750 for you right and it includes the utilities too,it is very close to metro and there are grocery stores and restaurant around. as i told you that i have the keys here with me and it will not be possible to see the inside,so you go ahead and send the deposit.

(Correspondence finally ends here.)

419 can take the form of bank fraud, credit card fraud and internet trade fraud. However its main differentiating factor is the fact that the stories are bizarre and the responses are completely voluntary. Perhaps the worst part about 419 scams is how obvious they are, almost to the point of being obnoxious. The scams are often very transparent and it seems that only a combination of stupidity and greed could get someone to agree to the elaborate ruses often put forth by the fraudsters. Although the scams were initially perpetuated by Nigerians, this no longer seems to be the case. It is for this reason that the government of Nigeria cites the greed of foreigners as the principal reason for the success of 419 scammers.

There are both positive and negative aspects of 419 fraud and it is difficult to determine the extent of damage to victims because most do not report that they have been duped. This is either due to the fact that they are embarrassed to have fed into the scam or because they do not want to admit that in effect they were knowing accessories to illegal activity. The cost of 419 to individuals and businesses is very high. Individuals and companies lose hundreds of thousands of dollars to these scam artists. Besides the money already lost in the scheme, businesses also have to pay the cost of placing safeguards and security programs within their websites to prevent 419ers from breaching security controls. They also have to pay companies or more employees to specialize in creating theis software. 419 has created an additional security cost for businesses.

However, in contrast, huge sums of money are being pumped into the Nigerian economy and into the economies of many other developing countries, bridging the income disparity between the developed and the developing worlds. Within these developing countries, some of the money obtained from 419 is going into the hands of the lower income population who engage in these activities. This is one reason why a 419 scam artist referred to himself as the "Robin Hood of the Africans," paying back the Westerners for slavery and colonialism. To date, most 419 cases can be traced back to Nigeria. According to the World Bank, Nigeria's Gross Domestic Product (GDP) per capita in 2009 was estimated at US$1118. Nigeria's total literacy rate is approximated at 60% and the United Nations Development Program (UNDP) estimates that 15.9 out of every 1000 Nigerians use the internet. 419 has created an avenue through which creativity is enhanced and shows the intellect present in Nigeria. This creativity now needs to be nurtured and tailored into legal and productive processes which will benefit humanity as a whole.

Chidi Igwe in his book, *Taking back Nigeria from 419*, attempts to determine the causes of 419. He cites "colonial masters, the Nigerian post independence state, the oil boom of 1971-1978, the telecommunication era, and the increasing interest in Modern European languages" as the combination which brought about and allowed for the progression of 419. I believe that more than anything, it is inequality which forced people into the position where they are willing to con and make a livelihood out of it. Many of the efforts to stop 419 scams from being successful are targeted at protecting the gullible. Education about the presence of these scams is definitely a good attempt to stop their success. However, there are only so many spam blockers and security features that can be installed. The internet is an ever-expanding space and with the invention of nano-technology, will soon be much faster and with the capacity to store much more information. There are also many recent attempts to introduce the internet into more rural communities and promote its widespread usage.

419 scams become very elaborate when victims fall prey to them. They involve crossing national and state borders to exchange money and can become very dangerous. There are stories of people being kidnapped and held for ransom. In worst cases, some are even murdered. Perhaps the most dangerous thing the internet has been able to do to increase the

viability of the advance fee fraud is it has allowed 419ers to develop relatively sophisticated networks with members in different countries. 419 is organized crime and the scammers are able to conduct their operations like a legitimate business.

There are many global attempts to stop 419 scams and promote internet safety. The Nigerian government has taken up some of the responsibility of stopping 419 scams that occur within its borders. The government set up the Economic and Financial Crimes Commission (EFCC) in 2004 through the Establishment Act. The commission "investigates, prosecutes and penalizes" offenders. It enforces the Advance Fee Fraud and Other Fraud Related Offences Act of 1995. Imprisonment of offenders is also expected to serve as a deterrent to would be 419ers. The EFCC teamed up with Microsoft and formed a coalition of young Nigerian musicians who collaborated to sing "Maga don need pay", a catchy anti-419 song to dissuade Nigerian youth from engaging in the activity. Education and awareness being so important, the United States Federal Bureau of Investigation (FBI) has a section about 419 under its Common Fraud Schemes describing the 419 fraud and providing tips on how to avoid being a victim. In addition, businesses are adopting extra security measures to ensure the safety of their customers. One such measure is that companies do not allow credit card payments for certain transactions. Some companies do not even allow their websites or certain portions of their website to be viewed in certain countries. Ip addresses from Ghana or Nigeria are typically banned from making credit card payments online.

These are good solutions to dealing with the problem of 419. However they do not tackle the main reason behind the fraud: the lack of income and inadequate standards of living. 419 can only be completely eradicated when there is a more equal distribution of wealth in a country and in the world. 419 tactics will catch on as more and more people have access to the internet. In addition, it will only begin to get more creative and craftier when the old methods are finally being recognized.

The internet is seen as being an advancement in society and it definitely has played a role in increasing collaboration and networking among businesses and individuals. It has increased the number of transactions that occur within an economy. Companies that do not change to suit these cyberspace times will be put out of business as culture and tastes change. For these reasons, 419 has gone cyber and the internet has transformed the ways 419 is being carried out. 419 is a business and the internet has created the necessary environment for it to thrive. The internet can only get more expansive and will be coupled with a consequent increase in 419 activity.

REFERENCES

CIA World Factbook. <https://www.cia.gov/library/publications/the-world-factbook/geos/gh.html>.

Economic and Financial Crimes Commission. 20 December 2010 <http://www.efccnigeria.org/>.

History of Nigerian Spam. 20 December 2010 <nigerianspam.com>.

Igwe, Chidi Nnamdi. *Taking Back Nigeria from 419: What to Do about the Worldwide E-Mail Scam—Advance Fee Fraud.* iUniverse-Indigo , 2007.

International Development Human Indicators. 20 December 2010 <http://hdrstats.undp.org/en/indicators/default.html>.

Investigation, Federal Bureau of. *FBI - Common Fraud Schemes.* 20 December 2010 <http://www.fbi.gov/scams-safety/fraud>.

Nigeria - The 419 Coalition. 20 December 2010 <http://home.rmci.net/alphae/419coal/>.

nigeria-law.org. Criminal Code Act Part VI to the end. <http://www.nigeria-law.org/Criminal%20Code%20Act-Part%20VI%20%20to%20the%20end.htm>.

9

Impact of Cyberspace on Afghanistan's Social and Economic Structures

Getti Farhadi & Tahmina Qahir

Cyberspace, as a means of Information and Communication Technology (ICT) in the modern world, offers facilities to enhance economic development of a country. Thus, in order to improve the economic state of a developing country with rapid growth, it is crucial to encourage usage of cyberspace technologies as a customary activity among the citizens. As suggested by R. Ronkin in his article, *Global Cyberspace,[1]* national governments in developing countries need to "…formulate realistic plans to use cyberspace for development." (Ronkin, 4.2) For instance, they can facilitate professional training regarding proper usage of modern ICTs to the citizens, especially the younger generations. He further asserted that the donor countries and aid organizations should smooth the progress of introducing and bringing cyberspace to a developing country by investing in ICT's infrastructure needs, importing new technologies, and administering professional training requirements in the country. In this chapter, we review positive impacts of cyberspace on social and economic development of a central Asian developing country, Afghanistan. We argue that modern technology not only added to Afghanistan's economy but it also facilitated Afghan people with easy communication to exchange ideas, share information, provide social support, and conduct businesses.

To understand the impacts of cyberspace in depth on the social and economic structure of Afghanistan, exposure to some background is crucial. In this chapter we will provide a geographical and historical background of Afghanistan in the region. We will briefly explain the impacts of the rivalry of the two super powers, the Soviet Union and the United States, during the 20th century, and the consequences of their intervention on development and infrastructure of Afghanistan. We will then provide a brief economic overview of the country, discussing how the US invasion of Afghanistan in 2001 resulted in a revolution in the globalization and spread of modern technology, including cyberspace, in the country. We will further demonstrate the role of cyberspace in the country's economy, and how it helped boost the economy.

Geographic and Historical Background

Afghanistan, recognized as a developing country, is a landlocked and mountainous country, located approximately in the center of Asia. It has borders with Pakistan in the south and east, Iran in the south and west, Turkmenistan, Uzbekistan and Tajikistan in the north, and China in the far northeast. Afghanistan provides an important geographical location, connecting South and Central Asia and the Middle East. It is an intersection between the East and the West, thus it has been a focal point of trade and migration since the mid-nineteenth century. It is the strategic geographic location of the country that has created the element of instability in both its politics and economy in different eras. As in the late 19th century, Afghanistan became the country of interest to the two major powers of the time, the British Indian Empire and the Soviet Union. In 1919 the country gained its independence from the British Empire and became a sovereign country. In 1979, the Soviets invaded Afghanistan, to introduce a Communist regime in the country. It resulted in an uprising of a "local resistance group," the Mujahedeen, against the Soviets and their puppet government in the country. This was an opportunity for the United States, which was another hegemonic power of the time, to intervene in the battlefield and it supported the Mujahedeen. The US's sole objective at that time was to stop the spread of communism. The US sent financial aid and arsenals, supporting the Mujahedeen against the Soviets. Afghanistan became a battlefield between the US and the Soviet war.[2] This led to a decade long war between the USSR and the US-backed Mujahedeen, until in 1989 the USSR withdrew from Afghanistan.

After the collapse of Soviet–backed government in Afghanistan, Mujahedeen took over the state power. As a result, ethnic strife was created among different fractions. Since, various ethnic groups[3] remained in the country with the US aid massive arsenals. This led to multiphase bloody civil wars over power, in the country. During these civil wars, the infrastructure and economy of Afghanistan were vastly damaged. More importantly, Afghanistan lost its military force, universities, institutions, and media. As a result, Mujahedeen's administration faced failure and the power was slipping out of their hands. This gave birth to a new regional group—the Taliban.[4] In 1996, Taliban gained full control over the state power.[5] Under the Taliban regime, Afghanistan remained a shattered economy, directed by the state. Consequently, the economy of the country was caught in its devastating position, with no improvements in the systems and infrastructures of the country. After five years of Taliban rule, the United State's invasion of Afghanistan, under the mission of "War on Terrorism," put an end to the Taliban's regime in the country. With the fall of Taliban's administration, the economy of the country, too, entered a new phase, which to some extent relieved Afghanistan from its devastating economic condition.

Economic Overview

Afghanistan has experienced different economic systems throughout its history. After the invasion of the Soviet Union in 1979, the civil war destroyed much of Afghanistan's infrastructure and disturbed its economic activities. As a result, Taliban took power and the economy of Afghanistan shifted from a traditional, agriculture–based economy to a centrally planned economy directed by the state. During this period there were five different currencies in circulation in the country, i.e. the official notes of Afghanistan called the Afghani and two other types of currency printed by rival warlords. The US Dollar and Pakistani currency, the Rupee, were also predominantly used in the market places.[6] The over circulation of money in the country, resulted in the Afghani's loss of value.

The country remained in a devastated economic condition until late 2001, when the United States invaded Afghanistan. After the fall of the Taliban regime, the economic system of the country was once again replaced with a free market economy. As a result, the country opened its markets to all foreign investors, attracting a dramatic number of non-governmental organizations (NGOs) and companies such as telecommunication companies, internet providers, and private banks.

They brought modern technology to Afghanistan, directing the country towards globalization. Consequently, cyberspace was introduced in the country with its different features, becoming a major source of revenue to the country, while directing it towards modernization.

Globalization and Cyberspace

Globalization, a process driven by international trade and investment, aided by modern technology, was accelerated in Afghanistan after the collapse of the Taliban regime. The war had left the country with a destroyed infrastructure, roads and communication system. The trade system was very slow, the communication system was very poor, and thus the population of the country physically remained cut-off from the rest of the world. Until 2002, the communication system in Afghanistan consisted of 20,000 working analog land lines for a population of 27 million. Typically, the few telephone services that were in place had not been maintained for twenty years. Many Afghan families did not own a home phone, and to make local calls they had to attend *public call centers*, waiting for hours in the line. Making international calls were only possible with expensive satellite phones and a very limited private system, and it took hours to set up an international call. Therefore, people would often travel to the neighboring country, Pakistan, in order to make international calls.[7]

Modern technology, including a computerized financial management system, and information technology or cyberspace such as telecommunication, internet facilities, medias, and e-banking, were a revolutionary change that gradually took place in Afghanistan, beginning in 2002. This was made possible through extensive investments by foreign investors, companies and private banks. Emergence of these new systems was aimed to enhance the economy and infrastructure of the country, by developing a system of global integration in Afghanistan, within the government and the private sectors. Cyberspace, at this time, became a customary tool for interaction, connecting Afghanistan with international countries. Consequently, a vast amount of international aid flowed into Afghanistan, in order to help reconstruct the infrastructure of the country. As a result, transportation highways and roads were reconstructed to facilitate trade in Afghanistan. This immensely helped the economy of the country, opening the market for more investors to enter. Today, technology in Afghanistan is considered a fundamental key to development.

Telecommunication

Telecommunication is the first and foremost step that helps a rural country towards development. It narrows distances between the nations and connects a developing country or a rural community with international and developed communities. As the authors of *Rural Telephone Companies* [8] state in their essay,

> Telecommunications technologies have considerable potential for encouraging development in rural communities by helping them — through access to the information highway — overcome the barrier posed by their geographic location (Korsching, El-Ghamrini, and Peter, 23)

Consequently, telecommunication facilitates business and trade in a rural or developing country, adding to the country's revenues and overall GDP. Nonetheless, telecommunication plays an important role in the social aspects of a developing country, too, by enhancing the lives of its citizens both through local and international connections.

Afghanistan' telecommunication system, which was based on analogue phone lines, was vastly damaged during the devastating civil wars. The system received no improvements, at the time of Taliban's administration either. Hence, people in order to make international calls were traveling to the neighboring countries, Pakistan and Iran. There were few analog phone lines that were functioning locally, to which ordinary Afghan citizens had little or almost no access. The new telecommunication system was first introduced in Afghanistan after the fall of the Taliban, through private companies, replacing analog telephone systems in the country with digital phone lines. Several privately owned wireless communications companies entered the market such as, Afghan Wireless Communication Company (AWCC), Roshan, Areeba, Etisalat, Afghan Telecom, and Wasel Telecom. These companies not only facilitated the Afghan population with an easy communication system but also provided a vast number of job opportunities for the young generation of the country. Consequently, the need for education in modern technology rose in the country, in order for the new generation to meet the criteria of these new job opportunities. Although, a number of Afghan repatriates from the neighboring countries, Pakistan and Iran, came with the primary knowledge of operating new technologies, their number was not sufficient to meet the increasing demands of these companies. As a result, in a short period of time, several private institutions were launched inside Afghanistan, offering special education in English and computer languages.

Afghan Wireless Communication Company was the first mobile service company in Afghanistan, established in early 2002 by an Afghan-American investor, Ehsan Bayat.[9] AWCC was founded by Telephone System International (TSI)[10] and the Ministry of Communication (MoC), as a joint business enterprise, in which the MoC held only 20% of shares. In April of 2002, AWCC became a member of the Global System for Mobile Communication (GSM) that was first launched with four stations, in order to better facilitate local and international calls in the country with reasonable prices. In November, GSM network was promoted to 13 base stations, covering areas around the ministries buildings and markets in most parts of the country. In August 2002, the focus was on the provinces, connecting Herat first, and then Mazar-e-Sharif in September, and Kandahar in November. Today, the company covers more area than it had initially planned to reach.[11]

AWCC was also the first internet provider company, launching its first internet café in Kabul, in July, bringing Herat on line in early August. Meeting such a tremendous success in a very short period of time, encouraged AWCC to continue sending out its commercial services to more provinces. Subsequently, the company upgraded "switches" in the capital city, in order to maintain the high capacity of the system. It also unified with the government-owned landline system, to enhance its public network with international connectivity. With such a rapid expansion of services in the first nine months of hosting Afghanistan telecommunication system, AWCC obtained more than 25,000 subscribers with 30,000 calls in an hour. As a result AWCC offered employment opportunities to the people, hiring 300 national workers in different positions. The company and its initial investor, the TSI, immensely benefited from the huge progress of AWCC, while it also improved the lives of many Afghans in the country.

Besides facilitating the communication system among people, AWCC was also a direct contributor to the economy of the country, as a large sum of the money spent on AWCC by subscribers was directed to the government.[12]

Today, AWCC covers almost over 2500 km in all 34 provinces of Afghanistan. It has regional offices with branches located in Herat, Mazar-i-Sharif, Kunduz, Jalalabad, Kandahar, Farah and Khost provinces. The company further facilitates its wireless telecommunication service through provision of easy conference calling, per second billing, and an excellent connectivity on the highways and at difficult security situations in the country. The company does not only provide services locally, but it also provides worldwide telecommunication services, with international roaming. The postpaid connection of AWCC provides accessibility across 102 countries with 340 networks.[13]

Roshan is the second successful wireless telecommunication provider that began its operation in 2003 in Afghanistan. According to Samir Satchu[14], Roshan's largest *shareholder* or investor is Aga Khan Fund for Economic Development (AKFED), which is part of Aga Khan Development Network (AKDN). Since its establishment, Roshan has experienced fast growth in providing easy communication access to the Afghan population all over the country. Currently over 226 cities and 3 million subscribers are directly benefiting from the Roshan telecommunication system. Roshan provides services to almost all provinces in Afghanistan, and to 159 countries worldwide with international roaming. The company also facilitates international communication with an immediate SMS reach to more than 645 networks worldwide, with an inexpensive price of 10 Af. only. Besides inexpensive national and international telecommunication access, Roshan expanded its activities in Afghanistan by providing high quality internet between 64 kilo bits per second and 4096 kilo bits per second. Roshan has been successful in providing wireless internet for the Afghan population to access their emails, read online news, and have chats via cell phones at the very affordable rate of 50 Af per hour, equivalent to 1 USD. It also established several internet cafes under the name of Ertebat Internet Cafes in more than six provinces of Afghanistan.[15]

The benefits and growth of Roshan Company is not limited to the provision of easy telecommunication and internet access. In recent years, Roshan introduced "Non-Voice Service for M-Paisa," which was a new innovation in the history of Afghanistan, and one of the most beneficial systems of money transfer through mobile phones. This new addition to the technology provides easy access to financial services for Afghans all over the country, which not only facilitates money transfer, but also aids Afghans in paying their microfinance loans, purchasing of mobile credit cards, and salary disbursement through their cell-phones. In general, this new system provided access to financial services for more than three million subscribers of Roshan Telecommunication, nationwide.

The rapid growth of Roshan helps the government of Afghanistan by decreasing unemployment and adding to the job opportunities in the country. As of 2010 more than 1,100 Afghans are directly employed by Roshan company, 20% of whom are female employees. Over 30,000 Afghans are indirect employees, such as dealers of prepaid Roshan credit cards in the market. As a whole, by investing over US$450 million and being the "largest tax payer" in the country, Roshan vastly contributed to the reconstruction of Afghanistan, providing 5% of the overall domestic revenue of the Afghan government.[16]

Another telecommunications firm, Areeba Telecommunication Company arrived in Afghanistan during 2006. Originally, it is an Arabic based company owned by Investcom, which is an international provider of telecommunication services listed on the stock exchanges of Dubai and London. Investcom is majority–owned and controlled by a Lebanese family, the Mikati, and it provides GSM mobile systems with eight stations, in Africa, the Middle East and Europe, offering global services. Areeba began with its initial project in Ghana in 1990. In 1999 it spread to Benin, and then to Syria in 2001, Liberia in 2002, Yemen in 2003, Cyprus and Guinea Bissau in year 2004, and to Guinea Conakry and Afghanistan in 2006. In September 2005, Areeba was awarded the "third nationwide GSM license" in Afghanistan, with a license fee of US$40.1 million. Areeba had to enter a competitive auction process, in order to win the license award in Afghanistan, and it was one of the two bidders selected out of five bidders.[17] The company was also issued a license allowing it to keep with its global operations. Areeba became one of the leading telecommunication operators in Afghanistan, covering 13 provinces by the end of 2006. Later in 2008, the company was renamed Mobile Telephone Network (MTN) Group of companies.[18]

MTN Groups of telecommunication companies provide several different mobile phone packages with different facilities, for all users in the country. Currently the network covers 21 provinces in Afghanistan with 400,000 subscribers, and continues to grow. MTN is looking into expanding its coverage further, in all provinces of the country, in order to better facilitate telecommunication system in Afghanistan. The plus side of MTN's operation is that MTN meets the main priority of the World Bank's MIGA[19] group, such as investment in conflict-affected nations. MTN supports growth of the competitive private sectors in most rural and out of reach areas of Afghanistan, functioning as the most active telecommunication network. Hence, the project helps develop infrastructure of the country and increase fiscal revenues, by real means. Today, MTN, also provides internet and satellite services; installation, operation, and maintenance of 100% digital GSM technology network; and manages public pay phones. The two last services, installation and maintenance of digital GSM, and public pay phones, are the innovations that MTN pioneered as the first telecommunication company to offer these services in Afghanistan.[20]

Etisalat Afghanistan is the third leading telecommunication operator with three million subscribers. According to the MoCIT's reports, Etisalat was first launched commercially in the country, in August 2007. It is a U.A.E. based telecommunication corporation, that signed a contract in May 2006 with Afghan authorities in order to open the fourth GSM network across the country. It first began its operation in major provinces of Afghanistan, including Kabul, Herat, Mazar-i-Sherif, Kunduz, Kandahar and Jalalabad. Later, towards the end of 2007, Etisalat expanded its coverage areas to other cities and provinces in the north, such as Ghazni, Poli Khumri, Baghlan and Paghman. The company was established in Afghanistan with the sole aim of providing the lowest calling rates with quality services. Offering the lowest international calling rates to all the international zones, within its prepaid and postpaid plans, Etisalat Afghanistan has experienced rapid growth[21].

Etisalat, with its innovative services such as GPRS mobile internet service, MMS service, credit transfer from Etisalat to Etisalat, and call conference service, further facilitated networking and telecommunication in Afghanistan. The GPRS mobile internet besides allowing subscribers to surf on the internet also allows download of videos, pictures, graphics, and animations to mobiles. Through the MMS service subscribers can share pictures, clips, and graphics to any local or international number.

Credit transfer is one of the successful innovations of Etisalat, providing easy access for all users to recharge their accounts regardless of time and place. Etisalat's call conference service allows five people to talk at the same time. The company also pioneered a new feature called "Job Alert." This new innovation of Etisalat helps provide its subscribers with easy access to job searches, sending them SMS alerts for every new national and international job that enters the market, without requiring an internet connection.[22]

Besides the privately owned telecommunication companies, Afghanistan's government has a telecommunication corporation, Afghan Telecom. Afghan Telecom brought a rapid improvement to the use of modern technology in Afghanistan, and for the first time the company introduced Digital Subscriber Line (DSL) services in the country. Afghan Telecom not only provided wireless telephone system services, but it also installed 165,000 digital land lines, applied to 24 provinces of Afghanistan. The implementation of digital land line services, using the "Code Division Multiple Access wireless local loop (CDMA WLL)," helped connect all provincial capitals and districts through internet, video conferencing and satellite network providing voice.[23] In addition, it facilitated 74 government offices and several nongovernment organizations with communication services, including "call conferencing", which is designed to connect 50 people at a time.[24]

Multi Office Solutions (MOS) was another new system in Afghanistan introduced by Afghan Telecom. The system was aimed to interconnect organizations with their branch offices, located in the same area. Before MOS was launched, communication between branch offices of an organization was both costly and time consuming. However, Afghan Telecom eased the burden by offering free intercom calling between main offices and their branches in the same area of coverage. Furthermore, Afghan Telecom offered several schemes with affordable fee for wireless and landline phones with internet connectivity which resulted in attracting most Afghans to join Afghan Telecom and have internet access at homes. With its innovative networking systems of Digifone and Mobifone, Afghan Telecom also helped facilitate international calls at the most reasonable price of Af 5/min, connecting the Afghan population with 50 countries around the world[25].

Generally, telecommunication services in Afghanistan greatly contributed to the overall revenue of the country, as it entered an open competitive market. Providing thousands of job opportunities, they helped boost the household economy of the Afghan population as well as opened the gates to education in modern technology and language literacy, for the younger generation of the country.

The telecommunications companies had tremendous success in a very short period of time, providing a better global communication system in Afghanistan and helping in the reconstruction of the infrastructure of the country. They were able to expand their services vastly and very rapidly throughout the country, which was made possible though their huge investments and introduction of globalized modern technology. In only a decade these companies were able to operate not only inside Afghanistan, but also in many countries all over the world. Many of them were pioneers in providing internet facilities, M-Paisas (a kind of e-banking system), public phones, call conferencing, and credit transfer services, in order to better facilitate the country's population and the government with an upgraded cyberspace. The table below shows the success of the companies' efforts during the years 2009 and 2010 as illustrated in the "executive summary" report on Afghanistan.[26]

Fixed-line services:	2009	2010 (e)
Total number of subscribers	129,300	175,000
Annual growth	30%	35%
Fixed-line penetration (population)	0.5%	0.6%
Fixed-line penetration (household)	3.4%	4.2%
Mobile services:		
Total number of subscribers	12.7 million	16.0 million
Annual growth	38%	26%
Mobile penetration (population)	43%	54%

According to the table above, the mobile market in Afghanistan followed a positive annual growth rate of 26% in 2010, with a mobile penetration of 50%. This demonstrates the successful operation of the five main mobile companies in Afghanistan, with their healthy competition in the wireless telecommunication market.

Internet Services

The Internet, as another information and communication system has changed global business ethics, assisting international communities to stay connected and share business online. The Internet also has a great impact on the revenue of a country, as it facilitates trades and business exchanges all over the globe. As Choongok Lee and Sylvia M. Chan-Olmsted state in their article, "Competitive Advantage of Broadband Internet":[27]

> As telecommunications and computing technologies continue to evolve and shape the global business environment, the broadband Internet readiness of a country becomes an increasingly significant aspect in affecting a country's global competitiveness.

Arrival of the internet in Afghanistan provides a common platform from which local and foreign investors can communicate and share information. As a result, apart from telecommunication companies in Afghanistan, there are several other internet providers actively engaged in filling up the communication gap in Afghanistan. In the year 2002, internet providing companies such as Afghanistan Faiz Satellite Communication, Neda Communication, CeReTechs, Insta Telecom, Io Global Services, RANA Technology and LiwalNet entered the market in Afghanistan to provide internet services for the government and nongovernmental sectors.

AFSat, formerly known as Faiz, was the first internet provider established in Afghanistan in early 2002. AFSat started its activities when a huge number of international organizations moved to Afghanistan for development and reconstruction purposes. The "installation" of VSAT systems in most provinces of Afghanistan by AFSat greatly enhanced the international organizations in implementing their projects by having easy internet access to communicate nationwide and internationally. Besides having an active role in facilitating government ministries and private sectors with high quality internet, AFSat by employing Afghans opened the gate for Afghan people to improve their skills in cyberspace[28].

A second internet compnay, Neda Telecommunications, started its operation in Afghanistan as the same year as AFSat. However, Neda advanced its operations very quickly and was able to provide high speed internet to Kabul, Mazar-e-Sharif and Jalalabad. The company initially offered dial–up internet system but soon upgraded its services to facilitate government and nongovernmental sectors with wireless, VSAT and CDMA internet services.

Like Neda and AFSat, other internet providers entered the market in Afghanistan, with new innovations and quality services. The rapid growth in number of internet providers made the internet services market very competitive. This resulted in more efficiency in the operations and growth of the companies.[29] These companies were not only functioning as the internet providers to government and nongovernment organizations, but they also extended their services to small enterprises in the country. Furthermore, besides providing employment to hundreds of Afghans, the companies also created on the job training programs in order to develop the expertise of their local staffs within the fields of IT support, network designing and configurations.

Just as in the telecommunication sector, the internet also brought a great change to the social and economic life of people in the country. However, the internet not only connected people with the global world, but it also provided business opportunities for different foreign and local investors online. Many corporations and companies in the country, such as airline companies expanded their services online, in order to attract more customers with provision of easy and quick access to their services, regardless of time and place. Furthermore, internet aided both employers and employees in finding competitive candidates online and suitable job opportunities, through development of new websites such as 'acbar.org.'[30] The Internet also helped different organizations to have their own domain, build their own web pages, and support other business activities in the country. For instance, afghanyellow.com[31] is a business directory that helps provide information about local businesses, increasing demands for its use all over the country. Overall, internet services facilitated online activities of the private sector and the government such as, online advertisements, access to information, connectivity, limited online purchases and free conference calling, throughout the country. These

services helped boost the economy of the country with annual growth of
internet services for the growing number of internet users.

The following table, from the "executive summary" report on
Afghanistan,[32] provides a statistic on the usage of internet during the year
2009 and 2010.

Internet:	2009	2010(e)
Total number of subscribers (e)	75,000	100,000
Annual growth	15%	33%
Internet subscriber penetration (population)	0.3%	0.4%
Internet subscriber penetration (household)	2.1%	2.8%

According to the table, the internet market had an annual growth of
15% in 2009, with 75,000 users. In 2010, there was rapid growth in the
number of internet users which reached 100,000. Apparently, the percent
of home subscribers grew larger, with 2.1% in 2009 and 2.8% in 2010.
This demonstrates that demand for the internet is vastly increasing among
people in Afghanistan, and consequently there is a higher demand also for
internet provider companies and for better quality internet provision. The
positive growth rate of these companies, immensely add to the overall
GDP of Afghanistan. As illustrated in the table bellow, from *Internet
World Status,*[33] GDP of Afghanistan has met a tremendous increase since
year 2000.

Internet Usage and Population Statistics:				
Year	Users	Population	% Pen.	GDP p.c.
2000	N/A	22,853,500	N/A	N/A
2006	300,000	27,089,593	1.1 %	US$ 289
2010	1,000,000	29,121,286	3.4 %	US$ 572

The table illustrates how Afghanistan's GDP per capita has increased
since 2006 from US$ 289 to US$ 572 in 2010. The next section will
discuss how the growing internet services not only helped people with

their networking and communication, but it also facilitated online banking in Afghanistan.

E-banking

For a long time, due to lack of job opportunity and poor household economy, the Afghan population was dependent on remittances. Thus, due to a poor banking system in the country, people had to travel to Pakistan to receive the money sent by their relatives living abroad. On the one hand, the process was very costly to the people, who had to cover their travel expenses to collect the funded money. On the other hand, the Afghanistan National Bank was losing the money-transfer-fee to the banks of Pakistan that could have been a value added to the economy of Afghanistan. Today the improved banking system in Afghanistan helps this process within the country, so that people do not need to travel to the neighboring countries.

The banking system of Afghanistan recovered after the collapse of the Taliban regime in 2001. The national bank of Afghanistan, Da Afghanistan Bank (DAB), once again started its operation in the country, carrying out the government's financial activities. Later in 2004, a number of private banks entered the market, offering modern banking systems with international standards. These banks were granted a license by DAB to operate under the supervision of the Afghanistan national bank. The new private commercial banks began with their operations in the capital city and gradually expanded their services to other provinces. Among the most successful ones are Kabul Bank, Afghanistan International Bank (AIB), and Azizi Bank. Their success has been mainly due to providing quality and secure services, such as electronic banking. These banks not only helped facilitate financial activities in the country, but also improved social life in Afghanistan, bringing easy and quick access to money through e-banking and providing employment opportunities.

Kabul bank was the first commercial bank starting its operation in June 2004, under Da Afghanistan Bank supervision. Within a short period of time Kabul bank was able to expand its services to all provinces of the country, with 68 branches, 28 of which are located only in Kabul. The bank facilitates money deposit and withdrawal for its customers under different types of accounts, such as current accounts, saving accounts and fixed deposits. Moreover, Kabul bank offers money transfer services, accepting international currencies, such as USD and EUR. SWIFT banking is one of the money transaction systems also supported by Kabul bank, which connects the bank globally. Moreover, Kabul bank also houses Western Union Money Transfer, covering 85% of their total remittances business in Afghanistan.[34] After a period of rapid growth, Kabul bank shifted its attention to providing more accessible services to its customer, regardless of time and space. This was made possible through the launch of e-banking. Within the e-banking services, the bank offers internet banking, mobile banking, ATM machines, and e-money or POS banking systems. These innovations help people with easy and more secure money transactions inside the country. Furthermore, Kabul bank provides hundreds of job opportunities all over the country.

The Afghan International Bank was also founded in 2004, with the support of the Asian Development Bank. AIB began its operation in the capital city and gradually expanded its services to different provinces through 16 branches. The bank offers commercial business services, retail banking, treasury services and e-banking, such as internet banking, mobile banking, ATM, and POS system. Under retail banking, AIB offers current accounts, saving accounts, and term deposit banking services. Moreover, through its corporate or commercial banking services, AIB provides trade finance, loans, and foreign exchange and treasury services[35]. With such innovative services with international standards, and its investment in construction of the infrastructure of the country, AIB greatly contributes to the overall revenue of Afghanistan.

Azizi began its operation in the capital city in 2006, offering various modern banking systems. Within four years of its operation, the bank expanded its services, covering different provinces of Afghanistan, through its 37 provincial branches and 26 Kabul base branches. Like AIB and Kabul Bank, Azizi Bank facilitates advanced banking systems including, ATM, internet banking and mobile banking services to the Afghan population. Through these innovative banking systems, Azizi bank provides easy access to its customers to check and remain updated with their bank accounts through their cell phones[36]. This was an effective step forward to remove the physical barriers between the bank and the Afghan population who were living in long distances from the bank. Furthermore, Azizi bank with the assistance of Western Union Money Transfer services, helps thousands of Afghans to make international and domestic money transactions efficiently. Moreover, the Afghan population also enjoys the job opportunities which are offered by Azizi bank and its branches all over the country. Currently Aziz bank has 1350 national employees, consisting of 20% female staff.[37]

E-banking is one of the latest banking features offered by the private banks which facilitates easy access to bank accounts with a secured password system online, as well as through the networks of ATM machines newly installed around the country. To enable customers to withdraw money from an ATM, private banks offer MasterCards, which also facilitates shopping through e-money. This system in particular helps people gain easy access to their money, regardless of time and space. It has also greatly helped governmental and non-governmental organizations with money transactions and other financial activities. Today, employees in almost all organizations functioning in Afghanistan receive their salaries through direct deposit in the banks, and they can easily use e-money for their purchases.

Generally, private banks in Afghanistan, through their different services of money transfer, money deposit and withdrawal, different types of accounts, e-banking, and hosting Western Union, ease the process of money flow in the country. They not only provide a rather efficient banking system, but also contribute immensely to the overall economy of the country, by providing employment opportunities, offering loans, and expanding the e-banking system. Thus, private banks play an important role in improvement of Afghanistan's economy and infrastructure through their services.

Conclusion

The arrival of cyberspace in Afghanistan, after the fall of the Taliban regime, made great contributions in the development of the country's economy and social affairs. Cyberspace introduced new technology features, such as telecommunications, internet, and e-banking, which greatly impacted the economic and social lives of people in the country. It furthermore, positively affected Afghanistan's position in the world. As a result, Afghanistan has been able to regain its status in the region, and once again re-establish its political and economic relations with the global countries.

Historically, Afghanistan followed the economic liberalism and globalization strategies with an agricultural system, but it has always been comparatively at a lower level and had a limited open market system. Invasion by the Soviet Union closed down the limited open market economy of the country, and enforced a centrally planned economy which was controlled by the state. The closed economy model was followed throughout the civil wars in the country, until 2001, when the US invaded Afghanistan. For the first time after the US invasion of Afghanistan, a complete open economy was introduced in the country. The new system of economy welcomed investors from all over the globe to enter the market and create a healthy competitive place for their commercial businesses. Subsequently, numerous companies, non-governmental organizations, banks, open business, and dealers entered Afghanistan market. These private investors and companies brought globalization to the country, while introducing modern technology and cyberspace.

Decades of civil war had destroyed the infrastructure of Afghanistan as a whole. There were no communication systems, roads and highways were destroyed, and there were no money transaction system, which was a necessity for the citizens, since a large number of the population was living on remittances. Hence, emergence of the new private companies helped rebuild the infrastructures of the country, once again connecting it with countries all over the world. For instance, telecommunication companies helped reconstruct the communication systems in Afghanistan, with new technology. These telecommunication companies provided numerous job opportunities in the country. However, lack of education in technology and language literacy prevented Afghans from benefiting from these opportunities. Subsequently, private institutions were opened in the country, offering education in technology and English language literacy. This resulted in an increased number of national employees in these companies, which helped decrease the unemployment rate in the country. As reported by the ministry of telecommunication, 60,000 Afghans were able to benefit from job opportunities offered by telecommunication companies in 2008. Moreover, they immensely contributed to the economy of the country as a whole. A total of US$ 80 million was added to the revenue of the Afghan government in 2007, and a total of US$ 100 million was added to the government's treasury in 2009, as reported by the ministry of communication.[38]

At the same time as the open market system was improving in Afghanistan, cyberspace introduced internet services and e-banking in the country. The new features of cyberspace were also introduced through private sectors. The private internet providers and private banks, not only facilitated Afghan people with modern and easily accessible systems, but they also made a great contribution in creating more employment opportunities. Consequently, they too added in the revenue of the government. Private Banks also introduced new innovative systems of banking following international standards, such as e-banking, ATM system, mobile banking, e-money and POS.

Overall, introduction of the new technology and cyberspace most clearly resulted in acceleration of productivity and growth, and played an integral role in the improvement of the social life of the nation. Today technology is considered as a key component of sustainable development in Afghanistan, with the means of providing a long-term and much needed solution.

FOOTNOTES

1 "[This paper was] Submitted for the Resource Book of a meeting, *Civilizing Cyberspace: Minding the Matrix*, held in Washington, D.C., June 26 - 27, 1991, and sponsored by Computer Professionals for Social Responsibility and the Electronic Frontier Foundation."

2 Sathasivam, Kanishkan. *Uneasy neighbors India, Pakistan, and US foreign policy*. Aldershot, England: Ashgate, 2005 (P. 133)

3 Afghanistan represents at least twenty four ethnics groups, of which four are the dominant groups: Pashtuns, Tajiks, Uzbeks and Hazaras. (Crews, Tarzi, 28)

4 "...a hardline Pakistani-sponsored movement that emerged in 1994 to end the country's civil war and anarchy." (Crews, Tarzi, 30)

5 Crews, Robert D., and Amin Tarzi. The Taliban and the Crisis of Afghanistan. New York: Harvard UP, 2008. Pages 27, 30

6 Afghanistan. *Asian Development Bank*. Web. 11 Oct. 2009. <http://www.adb.org/ Documents/books/ADO/2003/afg.asp>.

7 *"A Nation on the Line: The Story of the Afghan Wireless Communication Company."* AWCC, Telephone System International, Inc. 19 Dec. 2010. (2002), 3-11

8 Peter F. Korsching, Sami El-Ghamrini, and Gregory Peter. *Rural Telephone Companies: Offering Technology Innovations to Enhance the Economic Development of Communities*. Technology in Society 23 (2001) 79-91.

9 An Afghan-American entrepreneur, who envisioned connecting Afghanistan with global countries (AWCC report, copyright 2002)

10 A company of Mr. Bayat (AWCC report, 2002)

11 Statistics taken from: *A Nation on the Line: The Story of the Afghan Wireless Communication Company*. AWCC, Telephone System International, Inc. 19 Dec. 2010 (2002) 3-11

12 Statistics taken from: *A Nation on the Line: The Story of the Afghan Wireless Communication Company*. AWCC, Telephone System International, Inc. 19 Dec. 2010 (2002) 3-11

13 Maximus, By. *Afghan Wireless Communication Company*. Web. 19 Dec. 2010. <http://www.afghan-wireless.com/>.

14 General Counsel and Head of Government Affairs for Roshan; he has written for the "PROPARCO's Magazine - Private Sectors & Development." The article is: *Rebuilding a Shattered Nation: The Impact of Wireless Communication and Mobile Banking in Afghanistan*. 19 Dec. 2010

15 Statistical data taken from the Roshan official website: *Roshan*. Web. 19 Dec. 2010. <http://www.roshan.af/Roshan/Home.aspx>.

16 Statistics are taken from the Roshan official website: *Roshan*. Web. 19 Dec. 2010. <http://www.roshan.af/Roshan/Home.aspx>.

17 Statistics are taken from the official website of International Finance Corporation (IFC), a member of World Bank Group: *Areeba Afghanistan GSM.* IFC Home. Web. 19 Dec. 2010. <http://www.ifc.org/ifcext/spiwebsite1.nsf/1ca07340e47a35cd85256efb 00700cee/2565FA68C2E97B8A852576C10080CCD3>.

18 Statistics are taken from the official website of MIG, a member of the World Bank Group: *MIGA || Multilateral Investment Guarantee Agency - Projects - Advanced Search - Areeba Afghanistan LLC*. MIGA Political Risk Insurance. Web. 19 Dec. 2010. <http://www.miga.org/projects/index_sv.cfm?pid=717>.

19 the Multilateral Investment Guarantee Agency—is part of the World Bank Group

20 Statistics are taken from the official website of MIG, a member of the World Bank Group: *MIGA || Multilateral Investment Guarantee Agency - Projects - Advanced Search - Areeba Afghanistan LLC*. MIGA Political Risk Insurance. Web. 19 Dec. 2010. <http://www.miga.org/projects/index_sv.cfm?pid=717>.

21 *Latest News || Ministry of Communication and Information Technology, Islamic Republic of Afghanistan*. MoCIT, Islamic Republic of Afghanistan. Web. 19 Dec. 2010. <http://www.mcit.gov.af/detail.asp?CatID=1&ContID=129>..

22 *Emirates Telecommunications Corporation - Etisalat*. Our Services. Web. 19 Dec. 2010. <http://www.etisalat.ae/index.jsp>

23 "[Connecting] over 40 ministries and government offices in Kabul with 34 Governor's offices, providing voice call facility, Internet and Data services and Video Conferencing" (MoCIT)

24 "Afghan Telecom Corporation."*Afghan Telecom Corporation*. Web. 19 Dec. 2010. <http://www.afghantelecom.af/vas.htm>.

25 Statistics and information taken from Ministry of Communications and Information Technology (MoCIT): *Afghan Telecom*. MoCIT, Islamic Republic of Afghanistan. Web. 19 Dec. 2010. <http://www.mcit.gov.af/afghantelecom.asp>.

26 *Afghanistan - Telecoms, Mobile, Internet and Forecasts: Executive Summary*. BuddeComm. Web. 18 Dec. 2010. <http://www.budde.com.au/Research/Afghanistan-Telecoms-Mobile-Internet-and-Forecasts.html>.

BuddeComm is "the largest telecommunications research site on the internet."

27 Choongok Lee, Sylvia M. Chan-Olmsted. *Competitive advantage of broadband Internet: a comparative study between South Korea and the United States.* Telecommunications Policy 28:9-10 (2004), 649-677

28 Information taken from the official website of *AFSAT*: Web. 19 Dec. 2010. <http://www.afsat.net/>.

29 *About Us.* NEDA Telecommunications. Web. 19 Dec. 2010. <http://www.neda.af//site/page/about_us/>.

30 The Agency Coordinating Body for Afghan Relief (ACBAR) is a nongovernmental organization that "...serve[s] and facilitate[s] the work of its NGO [and individual] members in order to...serve [them better] and to act in their interest." ACBAR : *Agency Coordinating Body for Afghan Relief.* Web. 18 Dec. 2010. <http://www.acbar.org/>.

31 "AfghanYellow.com is the largest local business directory, connecting businesses to businesses and businesses to consumers. Over 5,000 local businesses & services, important & useful contacts, local classifieds, news headlines, real time weather & currency exchange rates reports are among the services that make AfghanYellow.com a useful portal for its visitors." AfghanYellow.com - *Afghanistan's First & Largest Online Business Directory & Local Search Engine.* Web. 19 Dec. 2010. <http://www.afghanyellow.com/>.

32 *Afghanistan - Telecoms, Mobile, Internet and Forecasts: Executive Summary.* BuddeComm. Web. 18 Dec. 2010. <http://www.budde.com.au/Research/Afghanistan-Telecoms-Mobile-Internet-and-Forecasts.html>.

33 *Afghanistan Internet Usage and Telecommunications Reports.* Internet World Stats - Usage and Population Statistics. Web. 19 Dec. 2010. <http://www.internetworldstats.com/asia/af.htm>.

34 *Kabul Bank.* Web. 19 Dec. 2010. <http://www.kabulbank.com/html/AboutUs.html>.

35 *KHAAMA PRESS.* Afghan Online Newspaper & Magazine » Kabul Bank. Web. 19 Dec. 2010. <http://www.khaama.com/?p=570>.

36 "SMS Mobile Banking Launched." Azizi Bank. Web. 19 Dec. 2010. <http://www.azizibank.com/?p=9&nid=24>.

37 *AZIZI BANK.* Azizi Bank. Web. 19 Dec. 2010. <http://www.azizibank.com/aboutus_profile.html>.

38 *Summary of Achievement in the Year 1386.* Islamic Republic of Afghanistan MoCIT. Web. 22 Nov. 2010. <http://www.mcit.gov.af/Documents/publication/MCIT%20Brochure%20-%20english%202008.pdf>.